THE ROCKY TWINS
NORWAY'S OUTRAGEOUS JAZZ AGE BEAUTIES

GARY CHAPMAN

Edditt Publishing

www.eddittpublishing.com

THE ROCKY TWINS
NORWAY'S OUTRAGEOUS JAZZ AGE BEAUTIES

GARY CHAPMAN

First published in 2018 by Edditt Publishing

© Copyright Gary Chapman, Edditt Publishing, 2018

All rights reserved. No part of this publication may be reproduced, stored in a retrieval system, or transmitted in any form or by any means, electronic, mechanical, photocopying, recording or otherwise, without prior written permission of the publisher/author.

Paperback
ISBN: 978-1-909230-28-6

Other formats available:
ebook (epub/apple) ISBN: 978-1-909230-29-3
ebook (mobi/kindle) ISBN: 978-1-909230-30-9

Visit the websites
www.eddittpublishing.com
www.jazzageclub.com

CONTENTS

	Author's Note
1-4	Introduction
5-12	Chapter One: The Early Years 1909-1927
13-22	Chapter Two: The Heavenlies' or 'The Black Orchids of the North' in London
23-50	Chapter Three: Double Rendezvous, Paris 1927-1928
51-83	Chapter Four: European Tour 1928-1930
84-99	Chapter Five: First trip to New York and back to Europe 1930-1931
100-129	Chapter Six: Hollywood, MGM and the Pansy Craze 1931-1932
130-148	Chapter Seven: Larry Hart and Low and Behold 1932-1933
149-168	Chapter Eight: New York Cabaret 1933-1936
169-187	Chapter Nine: Europe and Separation 1936 - 1941
188-198	Chapter Ten: The War Years and Later Life
199	Acknowlegements
199	Picture Credits
199	About the Author
200-202	Chronology
203- 212	Footnotes

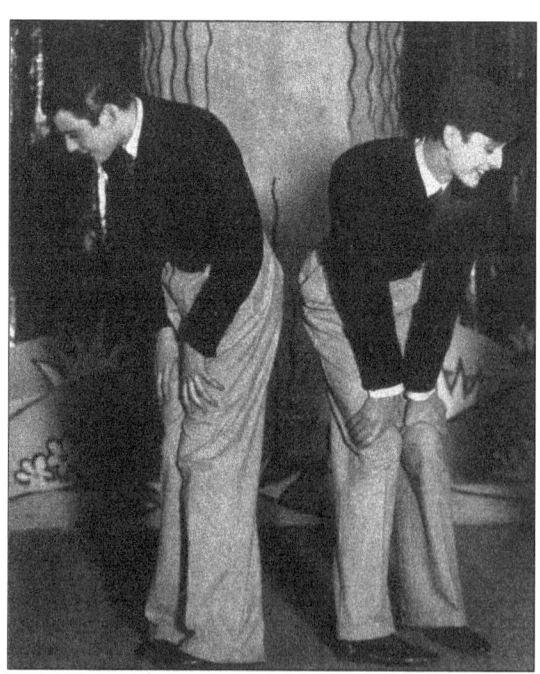

Left: The Rocky Twins in *La Volupte de Paris* at the Concert Mayol, Paris, 1928

AUTHOR'S NOTE

I first became aware of the Rocky Twins (Paal and Leif) when I was doing the research for my biography about the Dolly Sisters, perhaps as much as twenty-five years ago. It was a poignant fact, that, when the Dolly Sisters retired in late 1927, the Rocky Twins attempted to take their place in more ways than one. Naturally, like my attraction to the Dolly Sisters, I became entranced with the magic of the Rocky Twins and began to unearth their story.

Above: A costume design for the Dolly Sisters by Jean Le Seyeux from 1926, Paris

This has not been an entirely easy task, unlike the research on the Dolly Sisters. This is simply because the Dolly Sisters were undoubtedly more famous and because they were the constant source of gossip with worldwide press interest and there are a vast amount of references about them in archives on both sides of the Atlantic.

The Rocky Twins strove for the same fame and recognition but did not generate the same amount of diverse worldwide coverage.

What I did discover was in fact two parallel stories running side by side – the official story of their rise to fame and fortune and their brief career on the stage, in cabaret and in film, covering no more than ten years, and the unofficial story - their secret life navigating the somewhat obscure gay world of London, Paris, New York and Hollywood.

Although the former is a relatively easy task to construct, the latter is hidden and shrouded in silence, and only obliquely mentioned. With careful research and by connecting the jigsaw pieces and connections, there is enough to paint a reasonably vivid picture. But much of the detail will remain elusive and can only be surmised.

In some instances entangling the truth has not been easy. In interviews, both Paal and Leif were prone to forgetfulness and exaggeration. As a result, there are a lot of contradictions in their accounts, which has meant that I have had to form my own objective interpretation.

For example, one such inconsistency was an account regarding Frank Sinatra. Relating his experience in Hollywood in the early 1930s, Leif claimed that Sinatra needed company to go to a dental surgeon one day. Since at the time, Leif was not busy, he went with him and for 12 straight hours they sat and played poker, while Sinatra got his teeth sorted.[1] However, Sinatra was only born in 1915 and grew up in Hoboken, New Jersey and only got his first break as a singer in 1935. He certainly was not in California in the early 1930s. So how and where, did Leif get to know Sinatra?

I was hampered initially by not speaking Norwegian and much of the press coverage was in Norwegian. Thankfully, Google translate came to

Above: The Rocky Twins in their sailor outfits doing an acrobatic routine, Paris, late 1920s

the rescue but I was further aided immensely by Marethe Turner, a Norwegian who lives near me in Stroud. She volunteered to help with all the translations and assisted in various other questions relating to Norway. Her help has been invaluable.

Finally, I make no apology for the detail in this book. I have painted a picture of the life and times of the Rocky Twins and have therefore included much background information about the people they met and engaged with, the places they visited and what night-life they might have enjoyed. For me this gives a clear, more rounded view of their lives and places them in context of time and place.

INTRODUCTION

Admired for being stunningly handsome, the Norwegian Rocky Twins (born Leif and Paal Roschberg) made a name for themselves as dancers in the Paris music hall in the late 1920s at the tender age of eighteen and their unique performance led to a ten-year career in Europe and America appearing on stage and in film between 1927-1937.

Their fame was secured immediately they performed at the Casino de Paris in late 1927 by their parody of the famous Dolly Sisters who had just retired. It was this impersonation that became their enduring swan song and what has defined them at the time and in recent years.

They were once described as 'just a pair of hoofers but they do look gorgeous'[1] and this was largely true. They were just dancers, but they achieved fame not only for their dancing but because of their incredible good looks and the fact that they were reputed to be the snappiest and best-dressed male twins in the world.[2]

The Jazz Age represented great style and if you were stylish and beautiful you epitomised the era and the Rocky Twins did simply that. They were typical Jazz Age Beauties and as 'Bright Young Things' their good looks became highly sought after by connoisseurs of the body beautiful of either sex. Their beauty, their androgynous look and their outrageous antics made them legendary.

They often talked about the Dolly Sisters, who they imitated on the stage and sought to be compared. But although the story of the Dollies was definitely one of rags to riches, the Rocky Twins were born into a comfortable middle-class Oslo family and endured no real hardships.

The Dolly Sisters – Jenny and Rosie - were Hungarian twins who moved to America at an early age and began making their living as entertainers to help make ends meet. From their rather humble origins they swiftly danced their way to fame and fortune on Broadway before conquering London and Paris. Although they were not the first sister act to appear on the stage, they were certainly the most famous and paved the way for so many later duos and trios that proliferated in their wake. Earning incredible salaries and having the benefit of wealthy admirers, the Dollies invested in property and vast collections of jewellry and became recognised as the most extravagant gamblers in Europe.[3]

Both the Rocky Twins and the Dolly Sisters were identical twins but although there were huge differences between the two pairs of twins, there were also many notable comparisons. In an interview with Leif in 1963, a Norwegian journalist said that there were striking similarities between the Rocky Twins and the Dolly Sisters and that their fate would be about the same.[4] Rosie married three times, so did Leif. Paal allegedly married once so did Jenny.

Like the Dolly Sisters, wherever they went the Rocky Twins became the centre of attention and barometers of style. Both sets of twins had wealthy admirers that showered them with gifts of valuable jewellery and more poignantly, tragedy struck Jenny at an early age and she took her own life and Paal died in mysterious circumstances. They both lived close to the rhythm of the time and their lives mirrored the incredibly luxurious existence of 'society' on both sides of the Atlantic and their lives provide a fascinating glimpse of this privileged world that was eventually swept away by the Second World War.

After establishing their fame in Europe, they made two trips to America, the first to New York in 1929-1930 and then Hollywood in late 1931. Given their androgynous looks and predilection for female impersonation their arrival in both places was nothing short of auspicious since the so-called Pansy Craze first flowered in New York while they were there and then after being shut down, re-emerged in Hollywood in the early 1930s. They became part of this extraordinary flirtation with a camp, gay subculture by the smart Hollywood set alongside the flamboyant entertainer and female impersonator Jean Malin. At the same time, they flirted with Hollywood and a contract at MGM and appeared alongside Marion Davis in *Blondie of the Follies* (1932) but never really made the grade. Besides circulating with the elite of Hollywood and staying at William Randolf Hearst's San Simeon retreat, they also embraced the secret gay social circles of tinsel town.

Above: The Dolly Sisters in a pose that was replicated by the Rocky Twins

In 1933 they moved back to New York and for several years became 'prime favourites of the so-called sophisticates'[5] and then returned to Europe and eventually separated as an act in 1937. They tried individual careers but World War 2 intervened and the Rocky Twins disappeared from the world of entertainment. They were out of history but Leif and Paal would live on and would use all their resources and money and live on their memories.

Strangely, they were never feted in their home country in the same way that they had been elsewhere as first-class world artists. Perhaps this was because they made few appearances in Oslo during their career and although their foreign achievements were acknowledged to some extent by the local press, their fame was largely ignored and remains so today. However, when Leif died in 1967, the Oslo newspaper Dagbladet acknowledged that Norway had finally 'lost two brilliant entertainers' and that above their heads had shone the tremendously shining letters - The Rocky Twins - a world-famous act.[6]

In subsequent years their legacy continues to mesmerize. One image of them as the Dolly Sisters from the Schwules Museum in Berlin re-surfaces with regularity in books and blogs. In a recent production of *Red Hot and Cole*, a play about the life and music of Cole Porter staged by the University of Colorado in 2017, the Rocky Twins had cameo appearances.[7] In 1973, the photographer and designer Cecil Beaton wrote in his diary that he overheard Diana Vreeland, the famous fashion editor, trying to convince Andy Warhol's business manager that a movie should be made about the Rocky Twins and that the end should feature a shot of them high-kicking up the stairs of the Élysée Palace in the arms of Adolf Hitler.[8] This was a somewhat disturbing vision but arrived at because of Paal's later flirtation in German movies in the late 1930s and exaggerated press reports of his connection with Hitler. Paal rejected these connections fully by fighting against the Nazis during World War 2 by joining the Free Norwegian Air force.

When I uploaded a blog about the Rocky Twins many years ago,[9] I was bombarded with comments and my images and content was effectively stolen and used by others without my consent or credit. Clearly, something about them resonated with people. Perhaps, because of the images of them as the Dolly Sisters in drag, it would appear that they have achieved some form of cult status and have become something of gay icons. I hope this book will enlighten everyone to the reality of their lives and their world.

The Rocky Twins in their sailor outfits, late 1920s

CHAPTER ONE
THE EARLY YEARS 1909-1927

The Rocky Twins were born Leif and Paal Roschberg on 27th February 1909 in Kristiania (Oslo), Norway and they had an elder brother called Gunnar (born 1905). They arrived into the world with silver spoons in their mouths as their family lived a somewhat privileged and affluent life in a smart part of Oslo.

Their mother was Gudrun Holst (born 1882, and the daughter of a district governor) and their father was Adolf Roscher Roschberg (born 1872 in Akerhus, Christiania) and they were married 8th November 1902. Their first child Peter Holst Roschberg was born in 1903 but died a year later. The twins were born several minutes apart – Paal being first, Leif second, but their mother could not distinguish between the two until they were about five months old, so who knows in reality which was which.[1]

Adolf's father was Christian August Henriksen, described as a timber merchant. Adolf had two siblings – Gulbrand and Paul Berg, both with the surname Henriksen – and yet Adolf's surname was initially Henriksen Roscher, but later he was re-named Roscher Roschberg. What this means is elusive, but it is perplexing. Could it be that Adolf had a different mother to Gulbrand and Paul and that his mother had the surname Roscher and he was taken in and adopted by the family?

Adolf forged a successful career in the military, and by 1895 he was an officer, then captain of the cavalry in 1909 and Major by 1930. But he was referred to as being a Lieutenant Colonel. He was a teacher and inspector of military schools from 1900-1930 and then involved in land protection from 1932-1940.[2] According to a later interview, Adolf came from a family with a long military background, although if this is true, it is odd that his father was listed as a timber merchant.

Apparently, the extended family chose various other professional occupations but, their elder brother, graduated from the Norwegian War school in 1926 and became a Lieutenant in the Second Infantry Division and made a career like his father in the armed forces, but later became a director for the insurance company Hussopp Forsikring.

It was admitted that Leif and Paal could have done well in the traditional professions that had attracted other family members if they had only been ordinary, handsome and just slightly gifted. 'But average and ordinary, Leif and Paal were not at all.'[3]

Above left: The Rocky Twins when very young with their mother
Above right: Gudrun Roschberg, the mother of the Rocky Twins, when young

The family lived at 7 Incognito Terrace for a long period, in a large apartment with two servants.[4] This home was located in the upper part of the district of Frognar, an exclusive residential and retail area in the West End of the city of Oslo and not far from the Royal Palace and gardens. It was a rather salubrious location likened to Knightsbridge in London with some of the highest property prices attracting the most affluent.

The twins looked so much like each other that you could tell them apart. They were also so handsome that kind old ladies stopped on the street to adore them and make a fuss. At five years old they started at primary school and attended the exclusive Frognar school, established at 52 Niels Juels Gade in 1900, that was situated not far from their home.

One of their teachers was Kaare Fostervoll who was later a cabinet minister and vice-president. He applauded Leif as being so charming that he could get whatever he wanted. But Paal was sometimes uncontrollable and could be wilful and cheeky. For example, one day he was eating in class, when he should not be, and reciting poetry. Fostervoll caught him red-handed and asked 'What are you chewing on?' Paal replied 'at least it is not tobacco' referring to the well-known secret that Fostervoll chewed tobacco in class.

Paal's classmates were shocked, and Fostervoll was not amused. But he was one of the first people to notice their artistic abilities and skills.[5]

In the summer of 1920, when they were about 10 years of age, they made their theatrical debut in the gardens of where they lived and called their performance 'Amor Sommer Theatre' (Theatre in the Summertime). The garden was secluded and tucked away, and even though they were young, they were shrewd, thinking that it was wise to choose somewhere off-the-beaten-track and not too public to avoid any undue scrutiny and possible luxury and amusement tax. Margrethe Munthes wrote the play as a children's comedy, and Paal was the stage manager and Leif, the director.

They had organised everything well with benches around a stage and the Norwegian flag as the curtain backdrop. The front row seats cost 10 cents and the back row 5 cents. They had dressing rooms, a garbage box and had dug a hole in the garden and placed a box inside for Lillemor Planck (later to become a notable actress and songwriter in Sweden). Planck acted as the prompt because she was too young (5 years old) and too small to be an actress. Of course, because she was so young, she couldn't remember everything, and so they were forced to improvise most of the time.

During rehearsals, they met another young boy who was sobbing and saying he did not want to go to school as all the boys called him names and teased him for being a red-head. He was, in fact, Sven Soot von During (born 1915 and later to become a prominent Norwegian actor) and the son of the red-haired entertainer Botten Soot. They invited him to join their theatre group and decided to donate most of the profits to Sven's grandmother, the famous Inga Bjornson. She was a renowned philanthropist and theatre leader and instrumental in the foundation of her own Children's theatre. Affectionately called 'the Gray Angels Guardian Angel' she was also well-known for providing funds to look after unfortunate people particularly the elderly organised trips to the country for them.

The first two weeks of the Summer Theatre generated 41 kroner. Forty went to Bjornson, and one went toward administrative expenses. These management expenses were merely ice cream for all the cast and supporters – with the thought that 'Kids get drunk with ice cream'.

The twins decided to invite Bjornson for a final, gala performance and created a special box for her. The twins had learned such expressions from the posters of the Cirkus Norbeck at Bestfarstomten, which they apparently attended and admired. She was impressed and told them she would arrange to transfer the show for a performance in a downtown theatre. But she then went on vacation. They wrote to her and affirmed their interest and told her that they had ideas for a proper show, which they called *Cinderella*.

Left: Leif Roschberg at an early age

Bjornson wrote to Nobel Roede, a multi-talented businessman, musician, composer and owner of theatres and cinemas in Oslo to enlist his help. She asked if she could have the Palace Theatre (Paladstheatret), but in response, he offered her the Circus World Theatre in the Circus Building on the corner of Klingenberggata and Bakkegata in Tivoli.

On her return, Inga Bjorson took the twins to meet the legendary Karlone Bjornson at the Grand Hotel and then to see a performance at the National Theatre. She was organising everything for the show at the Circus World Theatre and had engaged Oliver Neerland to make the sets, Per Abel to arrange the dances and Signe Heide Steen as stage director.

The twins were dizzy with excitement and were becoming even more crazy about the theatre describing themselves as 'the most ardent theatre rats in the world.' They practised every day for two hours in the theatre, had dance-lessons, singing lessons and endured the pins of a seamstress who made their costumes.

At the premiere of *Cinderella*, many people were turned away, but the result was marvellous and proved to be the start of Inga Bjorson's Children's Theatre, the first theatre in Scandinavia where children played for children and gave regular annual performances after that.[6]

In the summer months, the family retreated north of Oslo to a farm they owned in an area called Sjoa. Named after the Sjoa river that provided an outlet from lake Gjende at Gjendesheim in the Jotunheimen mountains it was part of Norway's Jotunheim National Park.

When the twins were 12 or 13 years old, in the summer of 1921 or 1922, the famous Norwegian composer and pianist Signe Lund (1868-1950), who was a cousin of their mother Gudrun, visited from Vienna where she lived. Signe described Leif and Paal as strange or weird boys because they were obsessed with performing, playing comedy, dressing up, dancing bizarre things, making costumes and drawing and painting stage sets.[7]

They begged her to write a piece of theatre for them and said they could act in a children's or adult play. Their powers of persuasion were overwhelming, and she finally relented and indulged them. It took her a week to write something that was a story set in China. Her play gave the twins a rich opportunity to create costumes, sets, self-made fans and a lot of other things. There were in all six actors, and they all enjoyed the rehearsals. One day, the chairman of the Sjoa youth association came to visit and was so enthralled he wanted to give the show a public performance. Signe was incredulous as she didn't believe it was that good, but the chairman kept asking, and in the end, she agreed on the basis that any profit would be shared 50/50 with Signe's share going to a charity for the poor in Vienna. The audiences were full, and people came from far and wide. Signe thought that it was fun and the profit surprisingly good.

Their teacher Fostervoll had recognised their good use of the Norwegian language and had advised them to try writing for newspapers. Thus, Paal and Leif became regular contributors of little adventures for the children's slot in the Oslo newspaper *Tidens Tegn* and were paid 10 kroner a week.[8] But they did not care much about it, and it wasn't enough. So when the twins were 15 (in 1924) Leif wrote, and Paal illustrated, a small book entitled '*Til eventyrland*' (To Fairytale Land) and it was published by Somes Forlag.[9]

It was clear that as they grew up, their good looks and persuasive personalities meant that they were spoiled thoroughly by family, friends and passers-by. They had a gift that made them able to twist anyone around their fingers to get precisely what they wanted. But differences existed between them and this was illustrated by their temperament. 'Leif was the down-to-earth of the two. Early on he learned how to treat people well, he had a cultivated manner and had some practical facilities.' Paal, on the other hand, was always a dreamer. 'He had the distinguished nature of an artist, and he could say and do the most incredible things, often to the greatest despair of those around him.' He was so frivolous at times that he would bring Leif to desperation, such as the time driving in a car, Paal lit a cigarette and threw the cigarette lighter out of the window. Paal was merely mischievous and rather full of himself.[10]

Even at an early age, it was clear that they were gifted and had talent. The twins were very young when somehow the dancing bug got into their system, and they decided they wanted to become dancers. But it could not have been until after their theatrical debut at Incognito Terrace that their parents were persuaded to indulge them and send them for dancing lessons at a ballet school in Oslo. It was here that they received their first dancing lessons under Per Aabel who was eight years older and was later to become a key cultural personality in Oslo and prominent in the Oslo theatre. He was the son of actors educated in Paris and London where he was taught drawing and ballet and also took dancing lessons from the legendary German theatre director Max Reinhardt. He made his stage debut in 1921 before becoming a dance instructor. The twins also took dancing lessons from Love Krohn, another well-known Norwegian dance instructor. At the time their parents were calm about this development thinking that some dance lessons now and then could not hurt. But for the boys, it was deadly serious.[11]

At this time jazz music captured them, they played vinyl records, went to the cinema, sneaked in to see theatrical shows and cabarets and used every opportunity to learn dancing techniques and ideas. They were highly motivated and created a training schedule for themselves in acrobatic dancing. They even had lots of gymnastic equipment installed in their bedroom and did many crazy routines. But they worked hard to master all the techniques and frequently wore themselves out.

Their father, clearly misguided, was happy and pleased because all he saw was his son's exercising, building muscles and improving their physical appearance which was all a perfect base to eventually make them the ideal soldiers. He could have saved his sons from a theatrical life by stopping them, but he didn't because he was naïve enough to think they would grow out of what he thought was a childish obsession. This was a strategic mistake that he would later regret. Their mother was not so naive and must have concluded that if she tried to dissuade them or stop them dancing it would be without result.

Interestingly, when they were very young, they did dream of joining the navy, and they did say that they had done some training in the navy in their late teens.[12] Surprisingly, their excellence at physical exercise and keenness for gymnastics made them well suited to some military training, which must have pleased their father immensely. In 1928, a journalist from the magazine Oslo Illustrate met them for an interview after their performance at the Concert Mayol in Paris and reminded them of meeting them in about 1923 at Fredriksvern, a Norwegian naval base, just south of Larvik in Vestfold and south of Oslo.[13]

Finally, in 1927, as Leif and Paal had their exams, there were discussions about a visit to London. The pretext was for the twins to study English and other languages. This was the 'official' version, which even now is still acknowledged by members of the Roschberg family. However, Paal and Leif most definitely had other ideas. It was clear that their actual objective was to try and secure dancing engagements, and their mother, Gudrun, must have been a co-conspirator from the outset. The true aim of their London trip was to try and secure dancing engagements.

They realised that if they were to have any chance of family approval at least, they had to get useful exam results. For Leif in particular, it became quite a test. He was smart enough but when did he have time to revise maths? He realised he needed help and one of the girls in his class was a mathematics genius and so she helped him. During an exam, she went outside wrote out the answers and placed them in Leif's packed lunch in his jacket in the hall. When he went to get his lunch, he got the answers. He cheated but was saved.

When their father realised the truth about their ambitions, he did not want them to tarnish the family by going on the stage dancing and earning money like dancing girls. However, he did realise that the boys had learned to dance well and with hard work they had built up an original repertoire that even he understood could make a success. From their perspective, it was not a youthful obsession that drove them. They just had to dance at any price! Once again their persuasiveness prevailed, and their father finally agreed for them to go to London.

If nothing else, it was hoped that the boys would have a great adventure. Although they sought fame and fortune, they had no idea that they would hit fame's highest peaks in Paris and would be regarded as two of the world's most handsome men and almost exalted as gods, before experiencing a staggering fall back to earth.

A sketch of the Rocky Twins dressed as sailors, late 1920s or early 1930s. Courtesy of the Shubert Archive, New York

CHAPTER TWO
THE 'HEAVENLIES' OR 'THE BLACK ORCHIDS OF THE NORTH' IN LONDON

The twins and their mother Gudrun left Oslo using the Fred Olsen Norway line aboard either the Blenheim or Braemar, arriving in Newcastle-Upon-Tyne bound for London sometime at the end of August 1927.[1] For their trip, they had already assumed a stage name – the Roschy Brothers – and this was emblazoned in red on their suitcases. Perhaps hastily done before their departure to avoid their father's disproval.

Arriving in London, they booked into what was described as a 'dirty' guest-house in South Kensington and presumably, they began their language lessons. But their true purpose was to audition for agents and theatrical producers. Amongst all the necessary clothing such as underwear and galoshes, Gudrun, their mother, had packed a range of dance costumes. These included an American style military uniform, oriental suits and white trousers and golf jackets all intended to be worn in their acrobatic dancing routines. She had created these costumes herself. Although she felt uncomfortable and out of place in London, she had reached the inevitable conclusion that all she could do was to accept the consequences and try to help her dance mad sons realise their dream.[2]

Within a short space of time, they were visiting all the relevant agents and producers, which indicates that they had done their research beforehand and knew just who to see. The London entertainment scene in late 1927 was extensive and not just confined to the legitimate stage but also the hugely popular and vibrant cabaret scene. There were also numerous venues for dinner and dancing in hotels, nightclubs and restaurants. Since dancing and the stage was one of the twins significant interests, it must be a foregone conclusion that the twins and their mother went to see some key London shows where dancing was an important feature and perhaps even visited some of the ballrooms.

The most likely West End show they went to see was Charles Cochran's lavish revue *One Damn Thing After Another* at the London Pavilion featuring Edythe Baker, Mimi Crawford, Jessie Matthews and Sonnie Hale. There were numerous dancing tableaux such as the Grannies and their Gigolos, the top hat number and the Charleston finale in the scene Progress. There was also the comic acrobatic antics and dancing of Max Wall and Greta Fayne.[3] For obvious reasons, the Rocky Twins may also have felt drawn to see the American Dodge Twins in the musical comedy *Oh Kay*, starring Gertrude Lawrence, that was launched at His Majesty's Theatre on 21st September.[4]

The cabaret craze had blossomed in London in the early 1920s with several venues catering to a wealthy clientele offering night-time frolics of dinner, dancing and a mini-revue. The original venues at the Hotel Metropole, Grafton Galleries, Queens Hall Roof and Murray's club had declined or closed, and their place was taken in 1924 by the Piccadilly Hotel, the New Princes Restaurant and the Trocadero. It was these three key venues that were still popular in 1927.

The Piccadilly Revels shows in the ballroom of the Piccadilly Hotel had made London brighter but the chorus girls and revue-style shows that reigned supreme for several years had been dispensed with and replaced by just a range of different acts by mid-1927. At the New Princes Restaurant on Piccadilly, the 8th edition of Percy Athos' *New Princes Frivolities* was launched on at the beginning of September, with dancing a key feature.[5] *Champagne Time* was the name of the cabaret staged by Charles Cochran in the Grill Room of the Trocadero in Piccadilly Circus, where originality abounded with the dancing of William Cavanagh and others.

A portrait of the Rocky Twins most likely at the time of their trip to London

Champagne Time had opened in June 1927, but was still going strong in late 1927 but although the productions numbers stayed the same the acts were regularly changed to maintain interest.[6]

London was also awash with a host of other fashionable dance places in nightclubs such as Ciro's, the Embassy and the Silver Slipper, restaurants such as Verrey's, Tricity and The Devonshire House and the ballrooms of all the major hotels including the Mayfair, Park Lane, The Savoy, Hotel Cecil and the Empress Rooms. There were also the popular dance palaces like the Hammersmith Palais and the Astoria. Many held tea dances in the afternoon besides night-time revelries.[7] Perhaps the most salubrious of all was the newly created chain called the Hotels de Paris run by Major Robin Humphreys with the Café De Paris and the Café Anglais along with the Kit-Cat restaurant in the Haymarket that re-opened in early October 1927.[8]

One of the most important auditions the twins had was with the great London producer Charles B. Cochran who staged regular revues and musicals in London, particularly at his Pavilion Theatre. But he was also responsible for the cabaret show at the Trocadero in Piccadilly Circus. For Cochran, the twins choose to impress him with their Oriental number. Included in this dance, they swirled a bowl of burning incense around, and by mistake, Leif dropped it on the stage floor causing some consternation from Cochran who shrieked 'oh my god what are doing? Are you trying to burn my theatre down?' and pointed disdainfully to the exit door.[9]

At another audition, they claimed only to know three words of English and four words of French, which was probably a somewhat flippant comment. They were asked to dance with a group, and when they went to the left, the twins moved to the right and got muddled up resulting in everyone laughing at them.[10] Despite the rejections they carried on undeterred since they were so convinced of their skill and originality.

Earlier in the spring of 1927, many of the cabarets had seen a reduction in audiences, which was thought to be the result of a lack of originality on behalf of the producers. Punters were bored with the same old thing and needed something new, which was thought to be a 'novelty.'[11] For the autumn 1927 season, this was clearly on the agenda, so it is strange that the twins were not snapped up since they did present 'novelty'. One thing they constantly stressed was that they strove for 'originality'.[12] Perhaps it was the fact that their dance routines were not mainstream and were too 'original' or that they were deemed too amateurish and not polished was the reason they did not secure any bookings.

London was teeming with dance teachers and dancing schools, all of which must have been hugely alluring. So it is no surprise that there are indications that the twins also took some dancing lessons during this period and they did claim that they received acrobatic lessons of some kind.[13] Mostly, the schools taught the various ballroom dances (specifically the Foxtrot, Waltz, Quick Step, Charleston, Tango and the Black bottom) but some, such as Italia Conti, the Espinosa school, Ruth French and Purcell also taught musical comedy, operatic, character and acrobatic dancing.

With further rejections and money running low their mother wanted to return home. She was homesick but also her silver wedding anniversary was coming up on the 8th November. The twins were distraught at the thought of leaving. They knew about the fame and fortune of the famous twin Dolly Sisters, who at the time were the stars of the big revue at the Casino de Paris in Paris, and they wanted the same kind of recognition, opportunity and adoration.

While visiting the producer of the cabaret show at the Piccadilly Hotel, the boys distracted him, and Leif stole a blank contract form. They secretly filled it in confirming a month-long engagement at the Piccadilly Hotel with a salary of £35 a week. They showed the contract to their mother who naively must have been delighted and thrilled that they had finally achieved their objective and happiness was assured. As a result, she felt confident in leaving them to their own devices in London and returned to Oslo.

The boys were alone in the world and allegedly, without any money, support, friends or family. But naive and guileless they were most definitely not.[14] It was observed that ever since they were young, Leif and Paal had a strange influence on their surroundings and the people around them. This was definitely due to their striking similarity and their allure as twins. But of greater significance was the fact that they had a childish innocence characterised as charming, cute and sweet. They exuded an air of being helpless boys in need of care. It was a natural trait, but they exaggerated this behaviour and made the most if it, almost like a game. Whatever, it was a trick that worked, attracted attention and appealed explicitly to those with a maternal instinct.[15]

It was at this juncture, at a somewhat critical time in their lives, that Charlotte King Palmer, an American divorcee and millionaire, stumbled across them and became their friend and benefactor. It was thanks to her that they got their big break and a flying start on their road to fame and fortune.[16]

One night, at a time when good kids really should have been in bed a long time ago, the twins were seated outside the restaurant of the Alhambra Theatre in Leicester Square watching the people go by and presumably somewhat despondent.

Chapter Two: The 'Heavenlies' or 'The Black Orchids of the North' in London

They suddenly heard a scream and the words 'Help. I have to go home. I'm drunk. I'm seeing double!' Charlotte King Palmer, with an extensive entourage, stared at the boys with an incredulous look and their fate was sealed.[17] Charlotte was at the time, aged 37 and certainly not over 50 as the twins later claimed. She was born in Boston in 1890 and had made a career on the stage in New York, London and Paris before marrying the wealthy James C. Parrish, Jr, a relative of the Vanderbilt family in 1910. The marriage was ill-fated and ended in divorce in 1916, but she did retain a rather splendid house at 57-61 East 90th street in New York. She was a well-connected globetrotter and a social butterfly with some fascinating friends such as Queen Marie of Rumania.

In 1920, however, Charlotte became the centre of lurid press interest when she returned to her home from a dinner party about one o'clock in the morning to find it in possession of five armed thugs and her butler and maid locked in closets. The gang stole a large selection of her jewellery valued at $500,000. After that, she abandoned her New York home and visited Europe more frequently to seek rest for her shattered nerves and clear the nightmare memories of that night by flooding it with new experiences. She also became more actively involved in various business activities, especially real estate and continued her diversions of social and charitable affairs.[18]

In her entourage at that time in London were several titled British nobles and the millionaire Charles Templeton Crocker from San Francisco, who was the third generation of one of the prominent four railroad millionaires and was at the time, aged 43. A philanthropist, he had dipped his toes into stage production writing the lyrics for an opera in 1917, and an operetta staged in Monte Carlo and San Francisco in 1930 and later became an avid yachtsman and sailed around the world.

Charlotte bundled the boys in a taxi and took off for the very short journey around the corner to the Café de Paris. They said that they were hardly dressed for the occasion and were perhaps too young to gain entry but she exclaimed 'My darlings! You guys are my children - and I can't believe the security will refuse to let in my children into the nightclub!' Leif said she was happy and charming but like a firework, because she was lively and animated and could talk beyond anything he had experienced before. But she had a kind and generous heart and grasped enthusiastically every new interesting opportunity that came her way.

The Café de Paris was one of the most fashionable dining haunts in London in 1920s. Intimate and elegant it was described as 'the smartest dance restaurant in London'[19] and had opened in 1924 taking over the premises of the Elysee Restaurant, at 3 Coventry Street in the basement of the West End Cinema (Rialto) and opposite the Prince of Wales Theatre.

Catering for 400 people, one descended a flight of stairs into a little lounge that led onto the balcony, and the famous double staircase reached the dance floor. The whole place, except the dance floor, was carpeted in blue-green and the decor was meant to be a replica of the Palm Court of the Lusitania.[20]

The management had a cabaret of sorts with a series of acts and in September 1927 proceedings were administered by the American, Barrie Oliver as Master of Ceremonies. He talked, danced and fooled about with the Lyricals, the dance band at the Café, and was once described as the Charleston King.[21] The twins would have been entranced by Oliver's act and the dancing of the two dance teams appearing at the time: Ernest and Yvonne (German) and Miller and Farrell (American).

Above: A sketch of the interior of the Cafe de Paris, London, late 1920s

Leif remembered that first night of champagne and caviar and was alarmed that the caviar cost the same as a pair of shoes that he needed. He said that it annoyed him to sit there and eat shoes. The boys played their defenceless, penniless, lost act. In the course of conversation (where by now they had miraculously learned enough English) they told Charlotte and her friends the entire story of their failed auditions, their misunderstood talent, the empty stomachs and being left on their own by their parents.

Charlotte decided to call them her 'Heavenlies' and made it clear to her entourage that something had to be done to help out these poor dear boys and that they had to have new shoes and anything else they needed. Templeton Crocker got out his chequebook and gave them £100, and presumably, the others in her party also offered financial gifts. Part of the money they invested in tuxedo's from Pleydell and Smith, a tailor that would become one of their favourite outfitters.[22]

What happened next is anyone's guess – but I suspect Charlotte must have moved them into her hotel or London residence and proceeded to mother them and take them out and about in London at her expense. Of course, the twins were obsessed with performing in public, and so Charlotte took them to see Victor Peresino, the owner of another of London's exclusive nightclubs called Chez Victor at 9 Grafton Street. Victor had started at the Savoy, became maitre d'hotel at the Carlton, then the Grafton Galleries and the Mayfair club before establishing his place in 1924.

Chez Victor was described as a luxurious rendezvous with a membership of over 1,000 and was a favourite haunt with the gilded youth and flapperdom.[23] A lovely spiral staircase took you downstairs to the ballroom decorated in dove grey and sky blue with chandeliers of beaten copper and Gloire de Difon tinted shades. On walls were beautiful oil paintings of Italian scenes. Here was a moderately sized oval ebony dance floor with surrounding seating. Upstairs was the small Chinese room where the black singer and pianist Leslie Hutchinson, known as 'Hutch' presided.[24] Interestingly, in November 1927, Chez Victor was raided by the police and Victor himself was fined and deported for customs and excise fraud.[25]

Charlotte told Victor that he had to hire the boys. No doubt they did gave him a dancing audition, and unsurprisingly he hired them on the spot. But there was a legal problem that the twins did not know about – they didn't have an artist contract, and Victor explained to them that under British law they had to apply for such a contract from abroad. Charlotte quickly came to the rescue and immediately sent them off to Paris for a few days with a friend, who was a titled gentleman, as escort and minder. After the twins had applied for the contract, they had a good time exploring Paris.

Above: A sketch of the entrance to Chez Victor
Below: A sketch of the interior of Chez Victor's showing the small, intimate nature of the dance floor

In one of the Parisian nightclubs or bars, they were taken for 14-year-olds and were refused either entry or service. They created such a scene that they must have been reported to the police, and as a result, they were summoned to the Norwegian foreign diplomat in Paris - Fritz Wedel Jarlsberg. He said he was going to return them back home to Oslo. At which Leif and Paal got on their knees and begged for mercy and showed him their return tickets to London and told him about their contract at Chez Victor.

Eventually, Jarlsberg calmed down and, like so many others before him, succumbed to their charms, but he was not happy. He told them that he had spoken to the great Swedish actor Frans Gösta Viktor Ekman, who explained to him that they were called 'the black orchids of the north'. This term was described as 'gloomy' so one can only assume that it was different in tone to being called the black sheep of the family and might refer to the fact that they were beautiful like orchids but black, in other words naughty. How Ekman came to believe that this was an apt description given that the twins had not done much with their young lives to date will remain a mystery, but clearly there were already rumours about them in circulation. As they parted company, Jarlsberg said that he hoped they did not wilt too quickly.

Back in London Victor gave them a two-week engagement and they made their debut at Chez Victor hoping to impress with a concoction of their eccentric dances. On the first night, Leif made a giant leap and ended up under one of the tables. Victor was horrified since at the table sat David, Prince of Wales (later King Edward V111), who had recently returned to London from his Canadian trip. Despite Victor's dismay, the Prince invited them to sit with him and enjoy the rest of the evening. Leif and Paal gave each other a solid handshake; now their happiness was secured. Sadly, their debut was a bit of disappointment as they finished after a week, but they had earned enough money to get them back to Paris.[26]

The Rocky Twins in Paris, 1928, probably from Les Ailes de Paris at the Casino de Paris

CHAPTER THREE
DOUBLE RENDEZVOUS,
PARIS 1927-1928

Following their debut at Chez Victor's in London, they decided to return to Paris. They must have felt that they had drawn a blank in the London theatrical scene and needed to try pastures new. Paris at the time was a huge magnetic draw since it was the undisputed international capital of pleasure and extravagance, and the cultural and artistic centre of Europe. During the 1920s it was the most fashionable and desirable place to be, with its diverse attractions of fashion, art, café society, jazz, nightclubs, the French music hall and the wide availability of sex, drugs and alcohol. It was further attractive because it was a place of tolerance, where diversity was allowed free expression regarding sexual orientation, colour of skin and background. It was also the home of the big spectacular revue, which had reached a pinnacle of extravagance in the 1920s with sumptuous international super-productions designed to attract tourists and not just the local Parisians. These showcased the leading talents of the day, including performers, costumiers, designers, choreographers, lyricists and composers.

The Rocky Twins must have made the rounds of all the major theatrical producers and were quite surprised that they did not immediately make a fuss of them and sign them up to a contract. At the same time, they also visited many of the Parisian night-spots and in the course of these excursions met a new benefactor, called Monsieur von Neuman. But who was this person and what was his real name?[1]

Entranced by them, Von Neuman claimed he had good social connections and said he would be able to help them further their career. He moved them into his house and told them that if he was to help them, they had to listen to his advice. First of all, he grounded them, insisting that there was to be no more late night excursions visiting the bars and night-clubs. He convinced them that this was because they had to be prepared for their big entrance into the arena of life.

Finally, the day arrived, and Von Neuman planned to introduce them at a cocktail party. He gave them what he claimed to be Norwegian national costumes. But the twins thought they were an odd mix of Naples and Tyrol. There had to be some boundaries, so they refused to wear the outfits and locked themselves in the bathroom and went on strike. Von Neuman conceded and gave them two sky blue silk jerseys and two red, white-tipped dressing gowns so that the national colours of Norway should at least be worn.[2]

When his guests had arrived at the appointed hour, he opened the door and shouted: 'Children! Just come in as you are – its all right!' Allegedly it took Leif and Paal a very short time to realise that there was not much dancing expected of them and that Von Neuman's ambitions were perhaps more sinister. They perceived that he intended to use them as gigolos and the implication was therefore quite alarming. Later that night, they must have been in a forthright mood for they gave Von Neuman an ultimatum, either secure a dancing engagement for them, as promised, or they would leave.

Von Neuman made good his promise and a few days later, via connections with a particular high-level society hostess called Madame Hamlin, he took the twins to dance in her house in the presence of the Belgian Royal family and several of the royal princesses. Leif explained 'It was at midnight we made our entrance in the Hamlin house down the wide stairs into the ballroom.' They danced and danced and ended with a leap with splits from the stairs. Their performance was excellent, and they received a rapturous reception, but they had made a mistake by dancing with their backs to the Belgian monarchy, and so were asked to perform again.

When they were changing out of their costumes in one of the bedrooms, a man ran in and waved his arms around and talked as if he was angry. But it turned out he was very excited instead and offered them an engagement to appear at the new show scheduled at the Casino de Paris. The man was, in fact, Jean Le Seyeux, a multi-talented French painter, illustrator, costumer and librettist born in 1894. He had started out his career as an illustrator but by 1920 was designing costumes for the Paris music Hall including for the Bataclan, Concert Mayol and the Folies Bergère, before he became aligned to the Casino de Paris. Although he was not the actual producer for the Casino de Paris – he held great influence. Leif and Paal looked at each other with complete surprise followed no doubt by delight, and they said that they almost died or fainted on the spot. Leif observed 'It seems that we came easily to this result, but the fact is that we had worked quite hard. Our technique was as perfect as possible. It was as though our thoughts and thus our legs followed as a rope on a swing.'

Le Seyeux summoned them to see him the next day and dance for him privately as an assessment. He expressed some disappointment, and for the next 14 days they were given the opportunity to prove themselves. To their relief they improved each day under his scrutiny and when the premiere took place Le Seyeux was more than happy.[3] It was an interesting point that they maintained an obsession with creating all their steps and dances themselves everything had to be original.[4]

However, problems continued as Leif and Paal were not authoritative and when the contract was signed Von Neuman intervened on their behalf. For his assistance, Von Neuman had stipulated that he would receive 60% and the twins 40%. They would receive 15,000 francs a month plus 250 Francs extra per matinee. Leif was not perfect at reading French, but he could read figures very well (no doubt due to the excellence of his maths exam), and at the law firm, where he reviewed the contract, he was aghast. Defending his actions, Von Neuman explained that it would cost him a fortune to make them 'stars'. Both Leif and Paal had difficulty in understanding what would cost such a fortune and were far from happy.

That same night there was a knock at the front door of the Von Neuman residence and there outside was the animated Charlotte Palmer. She gave them both a massive hug and they disappeared into her fur coat as she announced 'Angels! I have some good friends outside, they own half South America, and now they want to buy half of Europe too. Throw on your tuxedo's and join us.'

She declared they were going on an excursion to visit the Russian cabarets in Paris including the Troika, Kazbek, Casanova and others. Since the Russian revolution, Paris had become home to over 60,000 white Russians, and many became involved in the thriving cabaret scene. The smart Chateau Caveau with the cabaret Caucasien in Pigalle was one of the first and most prestigious of the Russian nightspots that opened in October 1922 and was owned, ironically, by the Greek businessman Georges Varounis. It was on three floors with two orchestras and became one of the hottest spots in Montmartre. Here the waiters were dressed as Cossacks, and the cabaret featured the dances and songs of Russia. The Male dancers were fine handsome men, many ex-officers of the Imperial guard. The Tsar's chef made borscht at L'Ermitage Moscovite and the one time admiral of the Imperial fleet was the maître d'hotel.

Charlotte had come to their rescue, and they escaped the clutches of Von Neuman. He may have disappeared into the background but their idyll with Von Neuman was significant as it was the first of many dalliances with rich, older, male benefactors. What became of their original contract is anyone's guess. Le Seyeux would have introduced them to Leon Volterra, the producer of the show (part of a prominent family who owned and ran many famous Parisian entertainment venues) to discuss roles and the routines they would introduce. They would have also endured endless costume fittings and rehearsals. But more importantly, with Charlotte, they would have explored the Parisian music hall and the extensive night-life and cabaret scene that made Paris the envy of the world.

The Russian nightclubs were only the tip of the iceberg, but when it came to the nocturnal adventures that Paris had to offer it was wise to remember that there was the Paris of the Parisians and the fake Paris of the tourists. And, in the 1920s, the vast majority of these tourists were American who flocked to Paris primarily due to an extremely favourable foreign exchange rate, not to mention the fact that prohibition was left behind as soon as they arrived. The French called the seeker of the night romance of Paris 'une belle poire' which roughly translated to 'sucker', and many resorts were 'especially contrived for the benefit of Americans.'[5]

However, new smart 'dancings' emerged each season with hubs in Montmartre, Place Pigalle and the Rue Caumartin. Firm favourites included Le Rat Mort, the Abbaye de Theleme, Zelli's Royal Box, Le Capitole, Canari, Imperial, LaJunie, Pigall's, Le Garron, Le Palermo and Le Perroquet (within the Casino de Paris). Significant places and acts that the twins may have been drawn to in late 1927 would have been The Florida Club that featured the incredible acrobatic, if not somewhat salacious, dancing antics of Roseray and Capella and the Blue Room, which was the re-christened Jardin de Ma Soeur at 17 Rue Caumartin. Decorated in a symphony of silver and blue it looked like a private ballroom with a deep blue ceiling covered in stars made of little tubes of blue light giving out violet rays. It was run by the American socialite and dancer Billy Reardon, who had been a partner at one time to the ballroom dancer Irene Castle, and usually got on the floor and strutted his stuff with a cane singing 'My Hair is Curly.'[6]

Most of the big Paris shows were coming to the end of their run having started in the spring of 1927. Given the fact that the twins were confirmed 'theatre rats' it is highly likely that they would have been taken to the Folies Bergere to see the spectacular revue *Un Vent de Folie* with the sensational black star Josephine Baker and the incredible dancing of the American dance team Fowler and Tamara. They also must have gone to the Casino de Paris itself to see the glamorous Dolly Sisters, in what would be their last show *Paris-New York*, that finally finished its run in early December to make way for the new Casino show.

Many of the winter Paris revues had already been launched. *Palace Aux Nues* at the Palace Theatre had opened in September with Jenny Golder and Harry Pilcer, and *Paris Etoiles* at the Moulin Rouge had opened in November with the black American dancer Johnny Hudgins, Dollie and Billie, the Albertina Rasch girls and Jane Aubert. The new Casino de Paris show *Les Ailes de Paris* was delayed because of the enormous success of the Dolly Sisters show and had a late opening on 15th December 1927.

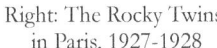

Left: The Exterior of the Casino de Paris, Paris.

Right: The Rocky Twins in Paris, 1927-1928

The Rocky Twins: Norway's Outrageous Jazz Age Beauties

Above and below: The Rocky Twins dressed in drag as the Dolly Sisters in the scene 'Les Petites Sportives' from *Les Ailes de Paris* at the Casino de Paris, Paris, 1927-1928

Chapter Three: Double Rendezvous, Paris 1927-1928

Right: The Rocky Twins in *Les Ailes de Paris*, 1927

Presented by the impresario Leon Volterra, *Les Ailes de Paris* was written by A. Willemetz, Saint Granier and Jean Le Seyeaux. Le Seyeaux was also responsible for designing the costumes along with Jean Aumont and Zig that were all executed by Antoinette. There were some staggeringly beautiful, spectacular scenes namely 'Silks' (with representations of different types of silks), 'The Serpent Forest', 'Mysteries of the Night' and the final scene 'the Fountains of Versailles' with its ravishing light effects on water. Humour, dance and music complemented these significant tableaux and the star of the show Maurice Chevalier, as usual, never failed to amuse and delight his audience.

Other featured players included the comedienne, singer and dancer Therese Dorny, the beautiful American dancer Miss Florence formerly from the Hoffman dance troupe, the clever acrobatic dancers of Horam and Myrtill, the American dancer Jack Forester, the Welly Sisters, the Woods Sisters, Endja Mogoul, Helle Nice and the Lawrence Tiller girls.[7]

The newly christened Rocky Twins were given prominent treatment in the programme and appeared in aviation gear in the first scene 'Sous Les Alle' (Under the Wings), and in the tableaux Les Chansons en Marches in la Marche Americaine with Suzette O'Nil and Wood Sisters. Their biggest number was in 'Les Petites Sportives' where they gave their first sensational imitation of the Dolly Sisters, alongside the Wood and Welly Sisters. One wonders how this idea to dress up in drag as the Dolly Sisters came to be. The twins already had an avid interest in the Dolly Sisters, but Le Seyeaux had also created many costumes for the Dolly Sisters and must have known them reasonably well.

Did they suggest doing this number or was it Le Seyeaux's idea to get them to do an imitation? Whatever the origin, it was more than a novelty and quite an audacious thing for two male twins of only 18 to attempt. When they took off their black bobbed wigs at the end of the number to reveal themselves, the audience may have gasped, perhaps echoing the delight that Paris had found with the American drag artist Barbette, who had stunned Paris with his stylish trapeze act a few years earlier.

Female impersonation on the Parisian Music Hall in the 1920s had been relatively limited as it was on the London stage with only the peculiarity of pantomime in the latter to enable such visible displays of drag. Bizarrely, in America, female impersonation was not frowned upon too much as in Europe, and several big names had established themselves as major legitimate stars particularly Julian Eltinge, Bothwell Brown, Bert Savoy and later Frederick Kovert, Karyl Norman and Francis Renault. For a Parisian audience, the Rocky Twins dressed in drag was nothing short of sensational. It indeed created considerable interest in them and helped define an androgynous image, which they continued to cultivate for many years after that. But most importantly for the twins to be finally performing in a big spectacular show was happiness fulfilled.

During the run of *Les Ailes de Paris*, the Rocky Twins became good friends with one of their co-stars Hélène Nice who was about the same age. Helene or Hellé had arrived in Paris in 1916 and found work as a model and a dancer before partnering with Robert Lizet. She accepted a solo spot in the Dolly Sisters show *Paris-New York* at the Casino de Paris in 1927 and went into *Les Ailes de Paris*. The big draw was Maurice Chevalier, but the other attraction was most definitely the Rocky Twins wo were described as 'ravishingly beautiful.'

Above: The sensational Barbette, the acrobatic female impersonator who took Paris by storm in the mid-1920s

For a time Hélène, the Rocky Twins and a pretty, sports-loving singer called Diana became a devoted foursome. Hélène lived a fast life in more ways that one and her love of fast motorcars meant that later she became known as the Bugatti Queen as she developed her racing career.[8]

Above: A classic Rocky Twins pose in tuxedo's, top-hats and canes looking extremely young, Paris, 1927-1928

It was also common practice for entertainers in the Paris music hall to double in cabaret, after the completion of their numbers. The Rocky Twins began this pattern in earnest shortly after their debut in *Les Ailes de Paris* by appearing in cabaret at Au Chiquito at 34 Rue de Colisee, a Basque bar, described as 'Biarritz in Paris' on Christmas Eve 1927. They performed with the beautiful Alanova, a glamorous Russian-American ballet dancer and actress.

This was the start of another pattern, as the twins began to forge arrangements as a trio with a third female dancer.[9] At the end of December, they were still dancing at Au Chiquito, but now with the additional support of the Russian dancers Niko-Romoff and Alexis from the Concert Mayol.[10]

Les Ailes de Paris continued through the first half of 1928. On 23rd February the twins took part in a high profile, one-off event, entitled Le Bal de la Fourrure, staged at the Opera. Here the Parisian fur Federation organised an evening with sumptuous presentations of fur creations from all the leading fur houses. Following the mannequin parade was a cabaret featuring the dancing of June Roberts, Emma Magliani and Kennedy, the Rocky Twins and Alexis and Nico-Romoff. The finale was a replica of one of the scenes from the Casino de Paris show *Les Ailes de Paris* entitled 'Une Femme dans Une Fourrure' with the showgirls and fifty of the Lawrence Tiller girls all dressed in gorgeous furs from Maison Weil, the latter in ermine.[11]

At some point in early 1928, they met Charles Gesmar, who was the principal costume designer for Mistinguett, the famed Queen of the Paris Music Hall. Gesmar sketched two outfits for the Rocky Twins, one in white and one in blue for an unknown performance labelled merely on the design 'Le Presentation' along with the American dancer Earl Leslie, who had been Mistinguett's dancing partner for several years. She described Leslie as 'a very handsome man' who had great success with men and women.[12] Since Gesmar died in late February 1928,[13] this 'presentation' must have occurred in the early part of 1928 and perhaps the sketch was for their appearance at Le Bal de la Fourrure, at the Opera.

In early 1928, the Rocky Twins met the Swedish writer and artist Thora Dardel, who was at the time wife of the Swedish artist Nils Dardel. She had studied sculpture and art in Stockholm, Copenhagen and Paris and by 1919 had become part of Dardel's artistic set in Paris. They lived a bohemian lifestyle and mixed with many of the artistic and fashionable elite in Paris with a modest residence on the Rue Lepic in Montmartre. Thora spent a lot of time with her two friends Marta Cedercrantz (Bunny) and Elsa de Castro Feijo (Frida). Both were Swedish. The six-foot Bunny was a former model and fashion editor whose father was a lawyer for the King of Sweden spoke six languages and resembled Marlene Dietrich. Frida was married to António de Castro Feijó, the son of a Portuguese poet and diplomat.

Charles Gesmar's sketch for the Rocky Twins in blue suits, 1928

One night both friends lured Thora to visit a costume ball arranged by some of Bunny's 'mysterious' French gentlemen. They rented costumes at the last minute that did not specifically appeal to their imagination or taste, but ended up having a jolly time with a mass of 'pretty quirky individuals'.

One can only deduce from these descriptions that the party was predominately gay and that many of the men were dressed in drag. Halfway through the festivities, a large man dressed in Chinese garb addressed Thora in a commanding Norwegian voice. Having heard her talk Swedish, he knew she was a Nordic comrade. He introduced himself as 'Calle' and said that he was the secretary or business manager to the Rocky Twins, explaining that they were Norwegian and currently appearing at the Casino de Paris. He pointed to two, dark, incredibly beautiful men in white sweaters with an embroidered R. on their chest.[14]

Clearly, after the fiasco with Von Neuman, the twins had swiftly secured a new agent or manager and how perfect it must have been to have a fellow Norwegian looking after their business interests.

The identity of 'Calle' – short for Carl - is not clear, but he does appear to have worked for the Rocky Twins for most of their stay in Paris and Europe from 1927 until their departure for Hollywood in 1931. In a later press story there was a reference to a Kalle Carlsen as a theatrical impresario who represented the Rocky Twins and the Ibsen family.[15] When they were in Budapest in 1929, they were accompanied by their manager who was thought to be about ten years older and was undoubtedly Calle.[16]

Intriguingly, Carsten Carlsen, a Norwegian pianist and composer was head of the orchestra at the Chat Noir cabaret in Oslo and in 1926 was named as Calle Carlsen. Married to the singer and actress Lalla Carlsen, he was born in 1892 and so was 17 years older than the twins.[17]

Thora suddenly realised who the twins were since Frida had gone to see *Les Ailes de Paris* at the Casino de Paris a few days before and told her about the fantastic twins who had given 'a radiant imitation of the Dolly Sisters' and then at the end tore of their wigs to reveal themselves as men. 'Calle' called the twins over and introduced them to Thora and her friends. Before long they had all bonded and left the party as they had all agreed to visit the Grand Ecart in Montmartre since Thora was a friend of the owner Louis Moyses, who also ran Le Boeuf Sur Le Toit.[18]

At the time the Grand Ecart, 7 Rue Fromentin (just off the Boulevard Clichy and not far from Place Blanche and the Moulin Rouge), was still the real treat of the evening. It was the chicest little place to go in Paris with the smallest dance floor in the world. The walls were alternately covered with mirrors and surfaces covered with shiny black oil cloth which reflected colours, lights and people.

The ceiling was made of squares of corrugated paper, and the cornices and angles of the room were outlined in strings of the smallest coloured electric lights like those hanging from a Christmas tree. The place sparkled. The bar was in the little room that formed the entrance from the street with chairs and banquettes made of straw coloured wicker. Vogue described the place as 'the spot where we find familiar young men, habitues of the Ritz bar, gathered in groups on high stools. These young men are the barometers of Paris, because where they are is the place where we should also be, as they follow the chic world of the nightlife, and indeed they may have even given such a place as this it's reputation.'[19]

Right: An artists impression of the interior of Le Boeuf Sur Le Toit

Below: An advert for Le Boeuf Sur Le Toit and Le Grand Ecart

LE BŒUF SUR LE TOIT
28, Rue Boissy-d'Anglas - Elysées 25-84
AU BAR DANCING "C. Doucet - Vance Loury"
LE GRAND ECART
7, Rue Fromentin
OUVERT A MINUIT   Trudaine 13-34

Since the twins were apparently mixing with a very exotic and alternative crowd, it is highly likely that they also explored the secret gay world of Paris. Like Berlin, Paris had gained a reputation for its free and easy attitude toward sexuality and a gay sub-culture thrived in the 1920s with several same-sex venues, especially for men. One of most popular was the Claire de Lune in the Café Biard near Place Pigalle. This modest little space was usually full of dozens of men all in close proximity to each other. There was always a large sprinkling of military and naval types and a sprinkling of 'fairies' or men dressed as women. Chez Ma Cousine, at the top of Rue Lepic (behind the Moulin Rouge) was another favourite spot always full of a wide range of different people including a large contingent of men dressed as women.

Another nightclub was called La Petite Chaumiere situated on the slopes of Montmartre. It was a picturesque small cottage-like-building with a rustic front and windows covered in turkey red cotton. Inside the walls were decorated with cubist paintings and a pianist played. Because of the large number of men in drag it became well-known to tourists seeking a thrilling view of the Parisian underworld. The larger and more salubrious La Petit Moulin Rouge also called La Feuillee Montmartre was a very smart nightclub and dancehall with a large capacity and a very mixed and sophisticated crowd.

There were also numerous drag balls that mostly took place during the high season for fun and frivolity between Mardi Gras and mid-Lent in mid-February and on Bastille Day. The cream of the Parisian gay world met to party without distinction of class, race or age dressed up in every conceivable type of gown complete with hats, lingerie, wigs, jewellery, perfumes, makeup and a smile. One of the more famous dance halls was the Montagne Sainte-Jeanvieve located on the summit of the hill behind the Pantheon. There was no ban on homosexuality in France, and the police were tolerant toward particular nightclubs providing that customers maintained decorum. Although women were allowed to dance together, men dancing together was not usually encouraged. The owner, who was an ex-movie starlet, deliberately created a mixed atmosphere of lesbians and gay men so that if the police arrived, lookouts would tip everyone off and the men would dance with the women.

The other famous venue was the ballroom at the Magic City on the left bank near Pont Alma. This outdoor pleasure palace was opened in 1911 and hosted drag balls at Mardi Gras that became famous until it was banned in 1934. A similar ambience prevailed at the Salle Wagram ball (near the Etoile) also held during Lent. Other high profile balls engulfed Paris each year – those organised for medical students and another for art students. Although these were private affairs, the streets of Paris thronged with revellers in a range of bizarre costumes and some wearing little at all. The medical ball took place in September or

October and started out around the medical schools before descending on the Salle Wagram for a wild party night. The more famous Bal Des Quat'z Arts was organised by the students of the four arts at the end of June and started off on the left bank with the revellers making their way across the river and up to the Moulin Rouge. Both confirmed the view that Paris and the French were 'dangerous and mad' and full of 'debauchery, vice and perversion.'[20] The Rocky Twins would have been fascinated.

There was also a more salubrious haunt, the fashionable Le Boeuf Sur Le Toit, owned by Louis Moyses that had opened in 1921 at 28 Rue Boissy Anglais, but by 1928, had moved to 26 rue de Penthièvre. It was not an out and out queer place, but very bohemian and open and attracted a mixed crowd of arty types headed by the famous Jean Cocteau and his entourage.

Le Boeuf Sur Le Toit was also known to be a picking up place for gigolos by wealthy society ladies and where men could pick up other men. It became one of the smartest rendezvous in Paris society with an atmosphere all of its own and a perfect little dance orchestra and always crowded. The bar had photographs by Man Ray on the walls that featured some of the celebrities that inhabited the place. Next door there was a restaurant with a gipsy band, and talented cabaret performers rivalled the mouth-watering cuisine.[21]

The Rocky Twins swiftly became the barometers of Paris and firmly part of the Parisian smart set. A new elegant ranking scheme came into being almost by itself. At the top, there were the happy ones who could claim Leif and Paal Rocky as their friends, followed by those who just knew them casually, or who had talked to them or at least had been drinking cocktails under the same roof with them. Those who did not claim any of these were merely nothing.[22]

Thora Dardal herself explained why everyone was entranced with them 'Leif had a magnetic attraction towards all people, both men and women. They were crazy about him, and I have never been so popular as when people flocked to me because they thought that they could get to know him through me. He was Leif Rocky, one half of the Rocky Twins. An idolised dancer, a celebrated millionaire and - as a French writer expressed it - one of the most beautiful men in the world.'[23]

In early 1928, Thora met the Swedish movie director Mauritz Stiller, through her friend the Swedish actress and sculptor Mårta Halldén, who had started her acting career in Stiller's film *Madame de Thèbes* (1915). Mårta was staying in Paris with her friend, another Swedish sculptor, Lena Börjeson who owned the Maison Watteau art gallery, which had a reputation as a meeting place not just for the Scandinavian community, but the entire Paris art scene.

Stiller was a pioneer of the Swedish film industry, and when MGM invited him to Hollywood as a director in 1925, he arrived with his new discovery Greta Gustafsson, who became Greta Garbo. But Stiller did not settle and had frequent disagreements with studio executives at MGM and then Paramount. He returned home in December 1927 before arriving in Paris.[24]

Thora and Frida had become good friends with the Rocky Twins and met them quite often, especially since they moved to a hotel near where Thora lived on the Rue Lepic in Montmartre. So one night Thora decided to arrange a lunch party at the restaurant Manière, 65 Rue Caulaincourt, with Stiller, her husband, Nils Dardel and Mårta.

Thora related that at first, the conversation was a challenge to get started after all the twins were beautiful like angels and a delight for the eye, but what did you talk to them about? After a while, the twins discussed friends they knew and then concentrated on the fact that animals were better than humans. In the end, the ice was broken and the age gap removed.

One must assume that the twins were fascinated by Stiller and his Hollywood adventures and the fact that he had discovered Greta Garbo. He explained that he believed the sound film would triumph and that in a short space of time English would become the world language. He also described his abortive attempt to make the Swedish film actress Mona Mårtenson into a Hollywood star thus highlight the fickle nature of Hollywood and the star system.[25] Sadly in late 1928, Stiller was admitted to hospital in Stockholm and after a month died of pleurisy on 8th November.

The twins became regular and welcome guests at the Dardel home in Montmartre and became models for Nils. He made a pencil sketch of both of them and then a larger watercolour, a drawing of Paal on his own and later used an image of both of them in his composition entitled 'Oxogat'. This portrait featured a small group of models each of which he had drawn earlier in his studio. It was designed to fill a sizeable ornate round frame and featured the twins along with Elsa de Casto (Frida), Simone Luce, Claudia Loiseaux and Sonia Jablonska. It was exhibited at the Swedish summer exhibition at the Musee Jeu de Paume.[26]

The months rolled by as the Rocky Twins enjoyed their daily routine at the Casino de Paris, but eventually after mid-April 1928, they did leave the cast. The show carried on for several months before a new edition entitled *Paris Sans Voiles* was launched in August 1928. Presumably, they took a break and a period of rest, and, possibly accompanied by Charlotte King Palmer, made a short trip to the Riviera.

The Paris summer season opened with the first big private dance given by the Henri Van Heukelom's in their beautiful house at 52 Rue de Bassano at the end of May 1928. Their drawing room was huge and well adapted to dancing, and the Rocky Twins gave their famous imitation of the Dolly Sisters.[27]

Above: The Rocky Twins and Gina Palerme excercising at Palerme's -country estate.
Courtesy of the Mary Evans Picture Library

Then on 9th June 1928, the twins made their debut in the summer Concert Mayol revue called *La Volupte de Paris*. Presented by Oscar Dufrenne and produced by Henri Varna, the show starred Gina Palerme, along with Mismarguett (doing her impersonation of Mistinguett), the famous comic Poulot, the Sisters Ree Bertin, the acrobatic dancers Nico-Romoff (with whom they had danced in the cabaret at Au Chiquito in late 1927) and the dancers Youla and Rene Thano.

The Rocky Twins bonded firmly with the star of the show the French actress, model and dancer Gina Palerme. She had made her debut in Paris in 1909 and after that became a favourite performer in Paris and London and had made a great success as the star of the Moulin Rouge show *Montmartre aux Nues* in 1926. From 1920 she also became a celebrated French film star.

Mistinguett was friends with Palerme and claimed she was a society woman 'very rich and ravishing to look at, who went in for revue as a sideline.'[28] Palerme was a gifted athlete, and a firm believer in physical exercise and her enthusiasm for gymnastics chimed with the Rocky Twins as was seen in a photograph from the time where they were practising together at Palerme's out-of-town estate on the banks of the Marne at La Varenne-Saint-Hilaire.[29]

Above: One of the scenes from *La Volupte de Paris*, Concert Mayol, Paris, 1928 with the Rocky Twins and Gina Palerme (centre) and the Sisters Ree Bertin

LE DOUBLE RENDEZ-VOUS

Les Rée Bertin — Les Rocky Twins

René Thano — Rocky Twins — Gina PALERME — Rocky Twins — Rée Bertin — Youla
Rée Bertin — "LA VOLUPTÉ DE PARIS" — Nico Romoff

The Rocky twins appeared in eight numbers. The first was La Mode au Bain (Fashions at the Baths) where they appeared as Narcissus, who was a figure in Greek mythology who was so handsome that he fell in love with his own image reflected in a pool of water. It was a very apt and appropriate use of their talent and looks.

With the dark-haired exotic beauties, the Sisters Ree Bertin, as the young ladies, the Rocky Twins were the collegians in the charming Le Double Rendezvous where they deployed 'their soft and ironic, caustic and graceful talent.'[30] This was a clever hide and seek act behind a tree that proved to be a sensation[31]

In Mousselines they danced with Gina Palerme, and on an American boat they were American sailors (Le Marins Americains) and their sailors' dance was seen as a brisk 'sweepingly fresh and lovely feat'[32] In Impressions d'Orient they gave their Hindu dance with Claude Avery, which was viewed as a serious and beautiful number.[33] They were also Les Gentlemens with the Ree Bertin girls in Mayol's Cocktail with Gina Palerme as the cocktail and appeared in 'Aint She Sweet a Mayol' with the Mayol Beauties, Ree Bertin and Rene Thano and also in the Grand Finale.

The twins were described as ravishing, ingenious, and elegant[34] and as 'two boys of ambiguous grace whose gestures, steps, pirouettes, and large double splits are all done with mechanical precision.'[35] Another journal thought that they were remarkable artists, 'who should be, if there were justice, the stars of the Concert Mayol.'[36]

The prestigious theatrical paper Comoedia thought that they possessed a 'charming vivacity' and added that a good part of the success of the show was due to the two dancing couples of Ree-Bertin and the Rocky Twins.[37] Even an observer from Oslo said that they had something rarely seen on the stage: 'they unite astonishing acrobatic skill with taste and real culture' and added that they also possessed humour, an astute ability for mimicry and noticeable facial expressions.[38]

Shortly after the launch of *La Volupte de Paris*, when they were the talk of the town, the great French film director Marcel L'Herbier signed them along with the Ree-Bertin girls for his hugely ambitious film *L'Argent*. Filmed during August - September 1928 in the Francouer studios at Joinville, it was a modernisation of an Emile Zola novel and Herbier's most ambitious work to date, and was released on 10th January 1929. With a budget of 5 million francs and with 2,000 extras, it was the biggest French film of the season and starred Mary Glory, Henry Victor, Brigitte Helm, Yvette Guibert and Marcelle Pradot.

Opposite page: Two scenes with the Rocky Twins in *La Volupte de Paris*
at the Concert Mayol, Paris, 1928

The art directors Andre Barsacq and Lazare Meerson constructed several monumental sets for the key scenes: the grand interiors of the respective banks of Saccard and Gunderman, the Hamelins' apartment with its view over the skyline of Paris and the baroness Sandorf's mansion with its split-level gaming room. Saccard's party was staged in a massive room in his house with one wall consisting of organ-pipes and a central pool and fountains with a bridge providing a stage for the entertainers. It was in this latter scene that the Rocky Twins, dressed in smart tuxedo's were seen dancing. The sisters Ree Bertin also appeared wearing identical costumes to those they wore in *La Volupte de Paris*. L'Argent must have been the first film in which the Rocky Twins appeared.

According to Mistinguett, it was during their run in *La Volupte de Paris* at the Concert Mayol that she 'discovered them'. An amusing term since they had already been discovered and made into big Parisian stars. Given that she was headlining in her own revue *Paris Qui Tourne* at the Moulin Rouge from April 1928 it must have been virtually impossible for her to see the twins perform. She may well have been aware of them via Gesmar or Earl Leslie, her dancing partner, who had also danced with them at an event in the first half of 1928. A more likely account of their first meeting appears in her autobiography when she describes Gina Palerme coming to see her in her dressing room with the Rocky Twins after a performance of *Paris Qui Tourne*.[39]

The timing may have been before August 1928 when Palerme and the Rocky Twins were rehearsing for the Concert Mayol show, and it was thus Palerme who introduced the twins to Mistinguett. Eventually, Mistinguett became entranced by the twins and came to recognise their worth as dancing partners, and a novelty that would embellish her own act. But in the first instance, she quietly slipped into the same mothering role that Charlotte King Palmer provided.

Mistinguett was one of the enduring mega-stars of the Paris music hall, who had made her debut at the Casino de Paris in 1895. Her risqué routines captivated Paris, and she became the highest paid female entertainer in the world, known for her flamboyance, vitality, conviction, overwhelming personality and stunning star quality.[40] She was allegedly born in 1875, and so in 1928 she was about 53, but Miss (as she was affectionately called) was notoriously guarded about her age and was reputed to be considerably older than she claimed.

Despite her age, she was incredibly agile, and her youthfulness was attributed in part to her amazing smile and her marvellous legs (usually covered with three pairs of stockings) that were insured for a million dollars. According to Billy Milton, she was 'vivid, vibrant and had unflagging energy' and could still perform an adagio dance which made the audience hold its breath in admiration.[41]

Above: Mistinguett in a classic pose from *Paris Qui Tourne*, Moulin Rouge, Paris, 1928

Regarding personality, she was a conundrum because although she possessed considerable professionalism and discipline, she could be equally generous and incredibly mean. According to Lynn Haney, she was also 'a first-rate bitch and the more she aged, the more impossible she became'[42] Although she had perfected the many nuances of her act with flair and style, including her star entrance down a staircase, she relied heavily on excellent male dancing partners. These had included the legendary Maurice Chevalier and the American dancer Harry Pilcer, once partner to the famous Gaby Deslys, but from 1921 she had been associated with the American dancer Earl Leslie.

Throughout the summer of 1928, and in following years, the twins were frequently seen with Mistinguett and her extensive entourage that included Earl Leslie, out and about in Paris at dinners and nightclubs and at some point on holiday by the sea, either the Riviera or Biarritz.[43]

One of Mistinguett's close companions in the late 1920s was Arturo Lopez, the Chilean millionaire. Born in 1900 and so aged 28 in 1928, Lopez was the son of Arturo Lopez Perez, a Chilean industrialist who made his fortune in the trade of guano (a fertiliser derived from bird excrement), and his first wife, Sara Willshaw. Nicknamed Arturito, and openly homosexual, he moved to Paris after the First World War and was an attaché to the embassy of Chile.

Lopez became a leading figure in Parisian society and in 1928, he bought the magnificent mansion of the Rodocanachi hotel in Neuilly-sur-Seine and proceeded to refurbish it with panache with his collection of Louis XIV furniture.[44] He would later marry his cousin Patricia López Huici but from 1941 had a male lover and companion - Alexis von Rosenberg (Baron de Rédé). He was described as being short and a tad pretentious, and a man who loved pomp, excelled at organising parties and balls and wanted to model himself into a miniature edition of Louis XIV.[45]

Mistinguett and Lopez would often go out at night in search of the best oysters, accompanied by Jean Desses, the dressmaker (born 1904 and worked for the couture house called Maison Jane in Paris from about 1924). They would also frequent the Grand Ecart and the Boeuf Sur le Toit where Jean Cocteau, who went there virtually every night, would always welcome them.

They were visiting the same night-spots favoured by the Rocky Twins, and so it is no surprise that sooner or later they would have all met and became part of the same crowd of night-time revellers. Indeed, Lopez became very much associated with one of the Rocky Twins in the next few years, raising speculation about their relationship. Lopez figured in the lives of both twins during this period and undoubtedly became one of their wealthy, older male benefactors.

As Mistinguett said 'speeding along the boulevards in big American cars at all hours of the night, dancing until dawn – that was my idea of living.'[46] This could have equally been a quote from the Rocky Twins themselves.

According to Bricktop, the legendary black entertainer and night-club hostess in Paris, there were numerous private parties in Paris all the time - everything from garden affairs to lavish costume balls and formal dinners. Bricktop organised the entertainment for a lot of parties for the charming and vivacious Lady Mendl (the former Elsie de Wolfe), an American who married Sir Charles Mendl in early 1926, who was noted for treating her entertainers like guests. The Mendl's lived in a beautiful villa in Versailles, and Lady Mendl entertained the cream of Paris society and all the most notable members of American and British society. Another avid party giver was Arturo Lopez. Entertainers, particularly new and exciting dancers, were in great demand to appear at such functions. The Rocky Twins must have performed at such events and perhaps this is how they met Lopez and significantly, in later interviews they did mention that they did know Lady Mendl.[47]

With *La Volupte de Paris*, the Rocky Twins had finally established themselves not just as celebrated dancers but as a vital ingredient in Paris social life. They swiftly became idols of Paris and adored by everyone and as the years rolled by their images appeared everywhere on posters, postcards, adverts and magazine editorials.[48]

Although they cultivated an androgynous look on the stage, physically they were so fit they were stunningly masculine and were always stylishly dressed. They had become Jazz Age beauties. Mistinguett described them as 'two tall disturbingly attractive youths' and they were imposing figures at 5ft 11" tall, well built, muscular, with brown hair and brown eyes.[49] On stage and off it was impossible to tell them apart – you simply could not tell which was which - as they were alike as two peas in a pod.

However, one was slightly taller than the other and Mistinguett said the only way to tell them apart was to set them up side by side in profile and view their noses. The older twin was a millimetre longer in the nose![50]

They were regarded as 'two of the most handsome young men you'll ever see'[51] and 'beauties that set hearts on fire.' People were crazy about them[52], and they were so strikingly attractive that they were mobbed each night at the stage door by connoisseurs of the body beautiful of either sex.[53] The gossipy entertainer Billy Milton, who knew them said 'as one hostess remarked, you could never be sure which one you were talking to or had gone to bed with.'[54]

Regarding their sexuality, many later observers have wanted them to be gay. In Paris and later in America, they indeed mixed in circles that could be defined as 'gay'.

Above: The Rocky Twins dressed as sailors, late 1920s or early 1930s.
Courtesy of the Shubert Archive, New York

Their androgynous look on the stage was seen as a key to the identity of their true natures and the fact they dressed up in drag as the Dolly Sisters another. But perhaps they were on the other hand pioneers of sexual ambiguity, a concept so prevalent today with words such as pansexual. At this early stage in their lives, they were most likely experimental and swayed by the attractiveness of both men and women.

The twins were also earning vast sums of money, and according to later reports, for the next ten years, they were among the top ten best-paid artists in the world, which is most likely a slight over-exaggeration. However, they did earn a minimum of 1000 Norwegian Kroner per night or $267 or £55 or 6800 French Francs. In modern terms that would equate to 22,000 euros per week or nearly 89,000 euros a month – a vast sum in those days. ($267 in 1930 was worth $3477 in 2015, and 6800 FF in 1930 was worth 3137 Euro in 2015). This was a first-rate fee and even taking into account expenses like agents, tax and living expenses, there was also a lot of money left, and they each became millionaires.[55]

There were many reasons for their success, but they claimed, somewhat tongue in cheek I suspect, that the most important thing was that they showed up on time.[56] Leif did elaborate by saying 'I do not know how to explain it, but we were in a way in the air, the audience had been waiting for us.'[57]

Actually, they were fresh, new and different and in a Paris newspaper, Jean Cocteau, the famous French writer and artist (who must have also known them from their visits to Le Boeuf Sur le Toit) said they did not do anything new, but they made everything else look old fashioned. They did not consider themselves to be lucky either, saying that they had to train for hours every day and struggled like crazy all the time with acrobatic exercises to keep themselves in shape.[58] So their success was in part due to their good looks, originality, charisma, physical prowess and sheer determination.

How did they manage the intoxication of fame as they became idolised like gods?[59] A reporter they knew from Oslo claimed that fame had not gone to their heads and that in mid-1928 they were just as childish as when he had met them years ago in Norway. They were aware that it was the time to take advantage of their youth and one of them said 'now we must take the time and make money…. soon we become too old.'[60]

The Rocky Twins dressed in drag imitating the Dolly Sisters, late 1920s

CHAPTER FOUR
EUROPEAN TOUR 1928-1930

In the summer of 1928, while they were performing at the Concert Mayol in Paris, the Rocky Twins announced that they had received 'an excellent offer from America' and to take it they must go to the USA in September.[1] The offer, for whatever reason, did not materialise, and instead, they accepted another offer to appear in Vienna for about 5 months.

They starred in the Emil Schwarz revue *You Will Laugh!* (*Sie Werden Lachen*) at the Stadt Theatre from 9th October 1928 through to 22nd February 1929. Schwarz was Viennese and had established himself as a successful producer of cabaret and revues in both Vienna and Berlin including the Femina cabaret and Ronacher theatre in Vienna and the Theatre des Westens in Berlin before he leased the Stadt theatre for the period 1927-1928.[2]

You Will Laugh! was a thoroughly Parisian revue with an undoubted Viennese twist. Most of the costumes were designed by Jose de Zamora and Gesmar in Paris and executed by the pre-eminent costume houses of Max Weldy and Gaston Zanel, so they would have had that certain Parisian air. Additional costuming was by a local Viennese designer Stella Weissenberg-Junker and Ladislas Czettel from Hungary, who also had a foothold in Paris.[3]

The revue was written by the team of Karl Farkas (one of Austria's leading cabaret performers), Emil Schwarz and Fritz Lehner and starred a host of performers with Karl Farkas, Christl Mardayn (film actress), Trude Brionne, Olly Gehauer, Lisl Sweet, Maly Podszuk (dancer), Max Brod, Hugo Fischer-Koppe (German film actor), Mimi Sharp (singer and dancer), Betty Werner, Marga Bernard (the fashion queen of Vienna), Zammit and Grube (acrobatic dancers), the Alfred Jackson Girls and the Sisters G.

By far the most praise was heaped on The Rocky Twins, doing their impersonation of the Dolly Sisters. They were described as 'outstanding,'[4] 'beautiful'[5] and 'enchanting.'[6] Although their similarity was thought to be incredible, they were also thought to look like girls.

With their dark bobbed hair, the Sisters G looked identical to the Dolly Sisters (a look that perhaps they had intentionally perfected). Even today images of them are frequently mistaken for the Dolly Sisters. They were twins born Karla and Eleanor Gutchrlcin (or Gutchklcin or Gutöhrlein), and they were German from Berlin.

Right:
A portrait of
the Sisters G

Under the sharp eye of their mother, they had made their debut in *Ca C'est Paris* at the Moulin Rouge in December 1926 but performed as a threesome with Mlle Floryane. The show ran through two editions into late 1927 after that the sisters returned to Berlin and presumably performed locally until their departure for Vienna.[7]

Beside appearing nightly at the Stadt theatre, the Rocky Twins were also secured by Sacha Films to appear in one or more of their silent films. The business was established in 1910 by Alexander Joseph 'Sascha', Count Kolowrat-Krakowsky and was the most significant Austrian film production company of the silent film and early sound film period with a studio in Vienna. Sadly, no details of any of these films can be found.[8]

To many, Vienna was quite a different place to Paris. In comparison, Vienna was regarded as more vibrant, authentic, genuine, refined and sophisticated whereas Paris was cosmetic and superficial. And yet, in 1933, Mistinguett said Vienna was a 'mysterious, wild, disturbing, unexpected Paris.'[9]

Above: The Rocky Twins dressed in drag imitating the Dolly Sisters, late 1920s

However, overall, nightlife in Vienna was regarded as 'elaborate and genuine and woven into the fabric of Viennese life.'[10] It was thought that as a place of amusement Vienna rivalled Paris. It most certainly did regarding operas and concerts but was outdone in the matter of revues and general after dark attractions.[11] Vienna laid claim to a bright constellation of great musical composers: Gluck, Haydn, Mozart, Beethoven and Schubert, and had become the undisputed capital of the music world.[12]

The Rocky Twins would have revelled in the diverse attractions that Vienna offered from the café's, theatres, nightclubs and cabarets, operetta's, the dancing and the masked balls of carnival.

Despite the frivolity there was a darker side to life as Austria was struggling with economic and political turmoil following World War I. There was a national conflict between the Marxist Social Democrats, who had instigated numerous social reforms, and a powerful alliance of wealthy industrialists with fascist tendencies. In the summer of 1927 things had come to a head with riots leaving dozens dead. Ferment continued for years to come.

Where the Rocky Twins stayed in Vienna is not known but the Stadt theatre was outside of the main city centre and most of the hotels were within the boundary of the central area. The three most prestigious hotels were The Imperial, The Grand and The Bristol and it was here where you would find the really smart people. They were undoubtedly places that the Rocky Twins would have gravitated toward. Sacher's Hotel was a landmark but upheld a restrictive upper-class reputation although the cuisine in the restaurant was world famous. It was also the home of the world-famous Sachertorte – a chocolate cake with apricot filling[13]

Since Vienna was the birthplace of the famous Johann Strauss waltz it was not surprising that dancing was a prominent and universal entertainment especially in the winter-time.[14] Dancing in the afternoon from 5-7pm was a favourite pastime at the various hotels and cafes. One of the most fashionable places was the Yellow Hall (situated in the basement of Kaiser-Bar in Krugerstrasse) or at the Grand Hotel, the Kursalon and Hopfner's. But the Grill Room of the Bristol Hotel was particularly smart and fashionable.[15]

Of the 15 first class playhouses in Vienna, all but four were devoted to musical productions and opera and operetta triumphed in the ratings. The most famous was Theatre An Der Wein – which had seen the premieres of Beethoven and Mozart and the home of Franz Lehar, the Waltz King and was regarded as Vienna's leading playhouse devoted to operetta.[16] 7.30pm was the latest for a play to begin in Vienna and an opera at 7pm. Afterwards was supper in one of the smart gilt and marble dining rooms of the three best hotels – the Bristol, Grand or Imperial.

One of the great restaurants was the old, picturesque and mammoth Rathaus Keller in the basement of the city hall, with its magnificent vaulted ceiling. It was here you could see the real Viennese – not the wealthy cosmopolitan but the well-to-do. At 11 pm the day was over for most people – but there were numerous popular bars, coffee houses and cabarets to visit.[17]

The café or coffee house was the most important institution in Vienna unlike anywhere else in the world and in 1927 there were at least 1,154 cafes in

Three of the night-time attractions in Vienna

Top: The Konzert-Saal of the Restaurant St Annahof on Annagasse (also the home of the famous Tabarin)

Middle: The interior of Maxim's

Below: One of the Kellers in the Rathaus

operation all neat, snug and luxurious.[18] Some of the more prominent venues were the Café Museum (a general meeting place for artists), Herr Ludwig Reidl's Café de l'Europe (for the worldly set and the bright young things with artistic leanings), Café Payr and Café Socher (popular with the stars of musical comedy like the Rocky Twins), Café Lebmann and Café Ritz (favoured by foreigners with music from 4-7pm) and the Café Heinrichshof (favoured by leading actors and musicians).[19]

There were also many popular late night cabaret venues that were headed by the salubrious Tabarin (part of the restaurant St Annahof on the Annagasse), which was by far the poshest place in Vienna, with two bands and dancing acts. There was also Le Chapeau Rouge bar, Maxim's (brazenly called the Montmartre of Vienna), the Palais de Danse, the Trocadero (a typical Parisian style rendezvous), the Pavillon and the Femina.[20] Night-time excursions for supper, dancing and cabaret, after their performance at the Stadt theatre, must have been part of the Rocky Twins itinerary. Since Emil Schwarz and Karl Farkas were major theatrical personalities in Vienna and had participated in the Viennese cabaret scene, they would have showed them the sights.

The Rocky Twins were clearly in Vienna during the right season, in the winter, because from New Year to Lent there was the fabulous Fasching or Carnival season with the famous mask balls (Redouten). Representing the genuine gaiety of Vienna, there were dozens of public balls in the largest concert halls and ballrooms every night that started at 10 pm but became popular after 1 am. Gentlemen wore costume or dinner suits, and ladies wore wigs and evening gowns. It was a luxurious and exhilarating experience marked by splendour, spontaneity and youth 'and the stranger was likely to have many spicy encounters.'[21]

One of the most prestigious locations was the Grosses Konzerthaus, perhaps the most beautiful concert hall in Vienna. Here, on 2nd February 1929, the theatrical magazine Die Buhne staged one of the biggest masked balls of the season. The directors and people who staged the ball were derived from all the main theatrical producers in Vienna and included Emil Schwarz. Many of the cast from *Sie Werden Lachen* were in attendance including the Rocky Twins.[22] The Opera Redoute was another highlight of the Viennese carnival season and was a gay and brilliant fete staged in the Vienna State Opera on the 7th February 1929.[23]

During their stay in Vienna, it would appear that the mother of the Rocky Twins arrived to see them since a photograph of all three of them together appeared in an Austrian newspaper taken by the photographer Laszlo Willinger, who in 1929 opened studios in Paris, Berlin and Vienna and later became famous in Hollywood.[24]

The Rocky Twins may have also spent time with their aunt, the composer and pianist Signe Lund who lived part of the time in Vienna. The twins also met the silent film star and dancer Julanne Johnston, who had arrived in Europe on an extended trip in July 1928 before returning to Hollywood later in the year. They became firm friends, and as avid dancers, they must have enjoyed the nocturnal fun of Vienna together. Subsequently, they met again and danced together in Hollywood a few years later.[25]

On completion of their contract in Vienna, the Rocky Twins moved to Budapest and appeared for a month in a show headlined by the incredible black performer Josephine Baker, but their sojourn in Budapest culminated in a rather bizarre series of events revolving around the Paris music hall star Mistinguett.

Josephine Baker had made her mark with her beauty and comic dancing appearing in cabaret and two shows on Broadway – *Shuffle Along* and *Chocolate Dandies*. In October 1925, at the age of 19, she crossed the Atlantic and appeared in the *Revue Negre* in Paris at the Theatre des Champs-Elysees. Parisians had not seen anything like this show or Josephine, and it created an open fascination with black culture, and black became beautiful and fashionable.

The scantily dressed young black singer and dancer was an instant hit and swiftly became the toast of Paris. As the years rolled by she became Mistinguett's chief rival in the popularity stakes. Interestingly, Edmund Sayag also imported the Lew Leslie show *Blackbirds* with another black troupe and the equally glamorous black singer and dancer Florence Mills at the Ambassadeurs Theatre-Restaurant in mid-1926.

Josephine was described as 'a highly polished animal,' who had an exquisite lithe body, which you could not take your eyes off. She was beautiful, elegant and charming with a unique and individual personality.[26] According to Bricktop, another black cabaret performer who made Paris her home in the 1920s, 'she had a live, wonderful, natural talent.'[27]

When Mistinguett went to see *Revue Negre*, she thought that it was vulgar since Josephine and her dancing partner were virtually naked.[28] As Josephine's fame developed so Mistinguett's jealousy grew, and she became increasingly disparaging about her. The rivalry between the two continued for decades, and Mistinguett called Josephine 'banana tits,' in reference to a costume she wore, and Josephine called her 'La Vieille' (the old one). They were both, of course, similar in the sense they were both perfectionists and would never allow anyone to compete with them onstage.[29]

Following Josephine's debut in Paris, she went Berlin with the Revue Negre in early 1926 before being cast as the star of the Folies Bergere show *La Folie du Jour* from Spring 1926.[30]

Above: Josephine Baker wearing her famous banana costume from *La Folie du Jour* at the Folies Bergere, Paris, 1926-1927
Above left inset: Josephine Baker in her revealing costume from *Un Vent De Folie* at the Folies Bergere, Paris, 1927

During this period she met the so-called Italian count named Pepito Abatino and began a personal and professional relationship. He was no count and in fact, had started out as a gigolo at Joe Zelli's nightclub in Montmartre. Despite his dubious background, he became her manager and lover.[31] She was also the star of the next Folies Bergere show *Un Vent de Folie* in 1927.

In addition to appearing at the Folies Bergere, she also opened her own club, Chez Josephine, on the Rue Fontaine in late 1926. It swiftly became a favourite late-night haunt, and Vogue described her as the 'most extravagant thing in the most extravagant revue that Paris has yet produced.'[32]

In March 1928 Josephine began an extensive European tour, but there were protests at first in Vienna and Budapest. Priests denounced her from pulpits and anti-racists handed out leaflets urging a boycott, and she acquired the title of the Black Devil.[33] Despite the protests, she did perform and went on to visit various major cities including Leipzig, Prague, Zagreb, Oslo, Stockholm, Volendam (Holland), Copenhagen Bucharest and Madrid. Her appearance in Berlin at Theatre des Westens in late 1928 did not go down well, and critics said she had lost much for her zip and naivety.[34] She returned to Paris at the end of 1928 and was about to visit Poland in early 1929 when she was banned, followed by another ban from Munich.[35] These events precipitated her return to Budapest in March 1929 and once again, as before in 1928, she must have stayed at the salubrious Grand Hotel Royal (now the Corinthia Hotel).

In January 1929, before Josephine's arrival in Budapest, it was revealed that she had been preparing for more speaking roles and that at some point in late 1928, in either Berlin or Vienna she had studied under the theatrical impresario Max Reinhardt.[36] Reinhardt had seen her perform in New York prior to her debut in Paris and was entranced and offered to help at that time, but it was not until the end of 1928 that he had been able to train her. The results of his efforts would be seen in the Budapest show – even though she would speak in French. Baker also announced that she would join Reinhardt at his Festspiele in Salzburg.[37]

The Josephine Baker show that was staged at the Royal Orfeum, Budapest in late February 1929 gave the Rocky Twins star billing along with a variety of other acts. These included the five Poncherry's (a German variety act), Globe Leyghtons (acrobatic act), Severus and Severus (dancers), Bill Amac (a British illusionist) Stetson and the British juggler Bert Elliot (famous for his dancing hats technique).[38]

Whether the Rocky Twins had already met Josephine Baker before this time in Paris is not known. But if they did meet, there was only a short window between late 1927 and early 1928 before Baker went on her European tour. So it would appear unlikely.

Above: The Rocky Twins emerging from the Royal Orfeum Theatre door, Budapest, 1929

The Rocky Twins were apparently in the right place at the right time so that when their contract in Vienna ended they could accept an offer from the Royal Orfeum to join the Josephine Baker ensemble.

In addition to Baker's performance it was thought that modern dancing was the most popular aspect of the show and in this respect, the Rocky Twin had the premier feature and 'their personal charm, their excellent shape, their unmissable humour' proved to be a tremendous asset.[39]

Paal Rocky later said their time in Budapest was 'unforgettable' and the days were rich because the theatre was sold out and the bonus percentage was excellent. He regarded Josephine as being in top form despite various antagonisms.

The Pope had issued a proclamation from the Vatican that banned both Josephine and the Rocky Twins from performing in Italy, as well as encouraging all good Catholics worldwide to stay away from establishments that depicted both of them. Initially, there were demonstrations from straight-minded Catholics and women's clubs, but the commotion only created sensational publicity.[40]

Before their debut, they had to give a private view of the show to the police censor, and Josephine complained about the cold in the room, and so did her numbers in a fur coat. The censors insisted on seeing her stage costumes because they knew that she had a liking for wearing very little. Accordingly, her wardrobe, which had been hastily camouflaged, was brought in for viewing and passed their test. The papers were stamped OK and the clear signal given for the premiere, which took place the following day. In the first song, Josephine was dressed as a kind of fantastic tropical bird. Attached to her arms, she had a pair of impressive wings around her, but when she opened these wings there was only the slightest blemish of fabric concealing her bosom. The authorities issued warnings that nudity was not allowed and that if the mischief recurred, she would be arrested. So an elaborate brassiere was hastily created. However, Josephine had a significant weakness with animals. She slipped out in the garden behind the theatre and discovered a little, frozen puppy that she picked up and brought to her changing room. That evening when she went to put on the brassiere the puppy had chewed it to bits. Bela Zerkowitz, the manager, had a fit but the show went on, and thankfully there were no arrests.[41]

As in Vienna, after the nightly performance, the twins must have explored the varied night-life of Budapest. There was a vibrant cabaret scene with such places as the Moulin Rouge club (where Josephine Baker had performed in 1928), Papagaj Kabare (Parrot Cabaret), Apollo Kabare and the Parisien Grill.

After over a month with Josephine Baker at the Orfeum Theatre, there was tremendous commotion when Mistinguett arrived from Paris onboard the Orient Express for a short stay on the evening of Sunday 27th March 1929. Only a small number of people knew about her arrival. There to meet her was the Rocky Twins, their manager Calle Carlsen, Josephine Baker in a long fur coat, Pepito, some musicians and Bela Zerkowitz, the Hungarian composer and theatre director who at the time was in charge of the Orfeum Theatre. As the train pulled up to the station, Josephine shouted 'There she is!' pointing to one of the windows. Paal Rocky ran up as the train stopped and as Mistinguett disembarked he shook her hand, but she then embraced him, kissed him and sobbed 'how are you, Paul.' Of course, there was a photographer to record her arrival, and Mistinguett was given bouquets of red roses and white lilacs.[42]

The press in Budapest were agog with excitement and speculation about the purpose of her visit although in Paris it was merely described as being a simple trip for pleasure and rest – this was apparently just the official pronouncement.[43] Mistinguett checked into the plush Dunapalota Ritz Hotel (Danube Palace) situated on the Danube Riverside, with 12 suitcases containing 40 dresses, 24 pairs of shoes, along with a maid and the Chilean millionaire Arturo Lopez, who had been a regular companion to the Rocky Twins in Paris.[44]

The Rocky Twins: Norway's Outrageous Jazz Age Beauties

Above: The Rocky Twins and Mistinguett in Budapest, 1929

Above: Mistinguett arriving at Budapest railway station, March 1929. Bela Zerkowitzi s in the centre, the Rocky Twins either side, Josephine Baker to the left and Pepito to far left

To have the two most celebrated Parisian music hall stars in the same place at the same time, given that they did not like each other and were huge rivals, was representative of something rather significant.

Over the next few days Mistinguett was continuously seen with the Rocky Twins and Arturo Lopez, and they were interviewed and photographed, as the mystery of her visit unravelled. According to Paal many years later, the rumours of their success with Josephine Baker in Budapest, had reached Mistinguett in Paris and she realised that she had to do something. She had evidently taken them under her wing in Paris and had been planning to introduce them into her next Parisian stage project and was far from happy that Josephine intended to steal them from under her nose. So she planned the trip to Budapest with the sole intent of securing the boys and defeating Josephine.

As Paal said '…in Budapest, a veritable battle will be fought' as Josephine and Mistinguett each try to convince the celestial Rocky Twins to dance with them. Mistinguett's tactics were uncompromising, and she was determined to win no matter what the cost.[45]

Two of the night-spots in Budapest
Above: The Royal Bar in the Grand Hotel Royal
Below: The Parisian Grill

The day after her arrival in Budapest, Mistinguett went for lunch with the Rocky Twins and Arturo Lopez and journalists. They sat and posed for photographs on the Danube Corso (Duna-korzón), a pedestrian street along the River Danube on the Pest side of Budapest, that was lined with restaurants, hotels and cafés. Tourists much loved the area because of its location and the view to the river, bridges, castle district and Buda mountains. 'What a divine town' said Mistinguett.

The Rocky Twins in the late 1920s - a similar pose and likeness to the image of them in The Illustrated Graphic from 1928.
Courtesy of the Shubert Archive, New York

One journalist asked 'And what brought you here?' Ah 'the secret!' she replied and then exclaimed 'Paul?' Who laughed.[46] Gossip and rumour abounded and more than one journalist put two and two together. At first, they hit the nail on the head and suggested that Mistinguett – the divine diva - wanted the Rocky Twins as dancing partners but then qualified the thought by saying that it would result in a 'comedic complication' since Mistinguett always fell in love with her dancing partners and what would happen with twins?[47] There were several close-up pictures of Paal and Mistinguett, including one with Mistinguett in a lounging robe looking adoringly up at Paal as they snuggled together on a sofa. The implication was that there was some romantic liaison between the two[48] suggesting that Mistinguett tried to lure Paal away from Leif and thus causing the Rocky Twins as an act to end.

The Norwegian paper *Dagbladet* reported that Mistinguett was thinking of taking one of the twins as her new dancing partner.[49] Various press reports later revealed that to be on the safe side Mistinguett had even proposed to Paal so that she could most definitely win the battle with Josephine Baker. This was most likely a publicity stunt, but although she did not get Paal, she did win and got both of the twins and promptly whisked them off back to Paris.[50]

In March 1929, as the Rocky Twins were enjoying their time in Budapest, a rather remarkable photograph, showing them heavily made-up and androgynously styled, appeared in the London magazine The Illustrated Graphic in a feature representing 'Today's Athletic Young Women and Men.'[51] The caption described them as 'well known on the continent' and added 'the young girl of the period shares in even the most strenuous of her brother's sports and the consequent modifications in physique sometimes make it difficult to distinguish from their appearance in athletic kit, which is youth and which is girl.'

The feature caused enormous publicity and much disquiet as many believed the story that one of the Rocky Twins was, in fact, a girl, not a boy. The implication was that they were not male twins at all and so audiences had been duped. There was considerable outrage in Vienna and Budapest where they had both just appeared.[52] In Vienna, the major papers were inundated with indignant letters and telephone calls until their aunt Singe Lund, who lived in Vienna, asserted that she had known the twins since they were young and had seen them in the bath and could confirm they were both indeed male![53]

On the departure from Budapest, the station was crowded and the composer, and manager of the Orfeum theatre Bela Zerkowitz gave the Rocky Twins his latest song that the crowds sang. In translation, it meant something like 'It's a shame that you do not love me.' But Leif and Paal loved everyone, and despite trotting off with Mistinguett, they managed somehow to stay on friendly terms with Josephine Baker,[54] who subsequently visited South America before returning to Paris in late 1929.

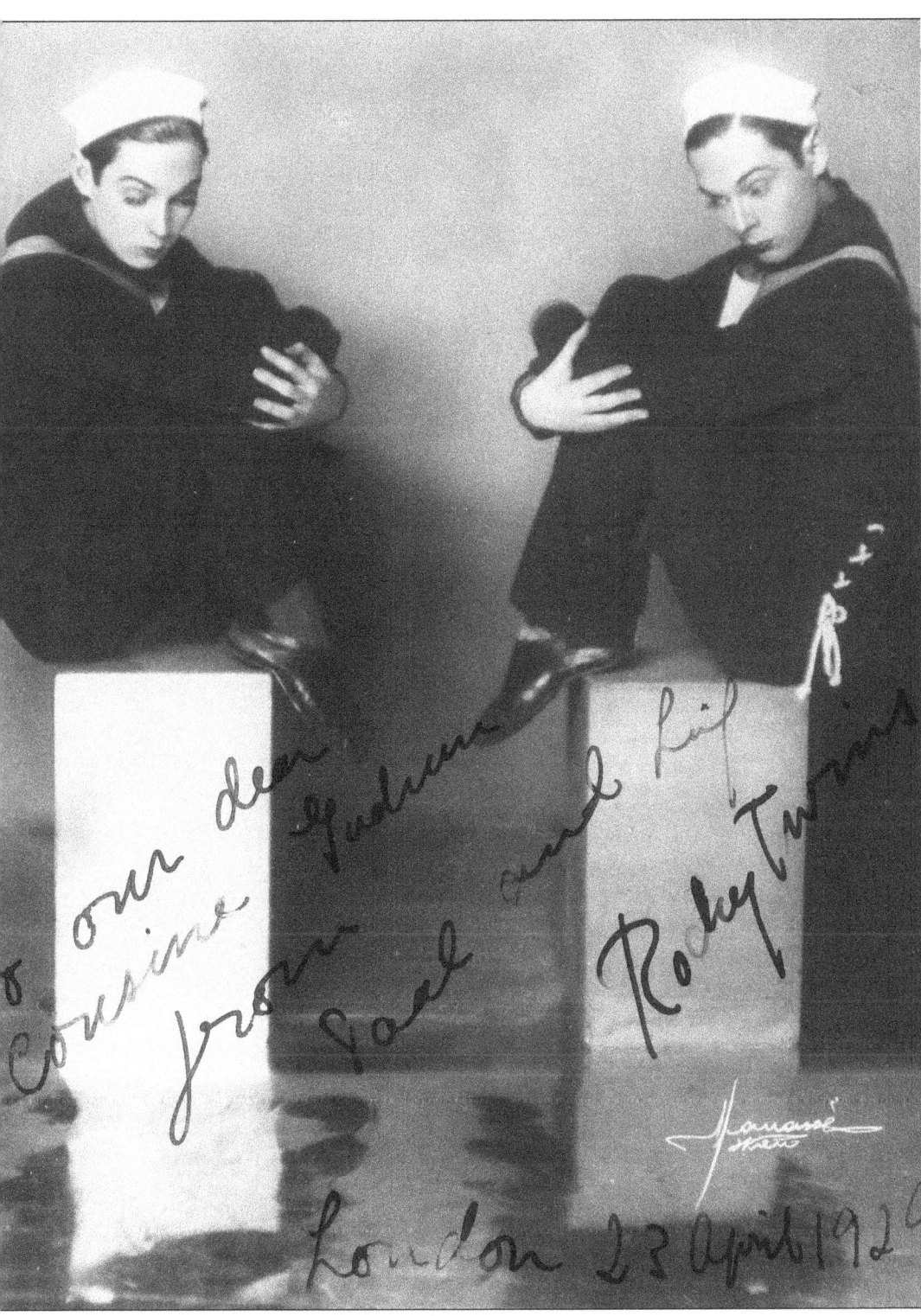

Above: The Rocky Twins in their sailor outfits,
signed and dated London, 23rd April 1928

Above left: The cover of a programme from the Kit-Cat Restaurant, London, late 1920s.
Above right: A sketch of the interior of the Kit-Cat Restaurant

The Rocky Twins along with Mistinguett and Arturo Lopez boarded the Orient Express and made their way back to Paris, arriving at the beginning of April.[55] After a short stopover in Paris, they all boarded the Golden Arrow train from Paris to London via Calais and checked into the Piccadilly Hotel staying for a few weeks. Reporters and photographers assaulted Mistinguett on her arrival in London, and it was revealed that the purpose of her visit was to negotiate with a Franco-British-American group to try and buy the Moulin Rouge in Paris for £120,000 and for her to become both artistic director and manager. Amusingly The Daily Express called her 'Mussolini de Montmartre' because of her so called 'autocratic methods.' She replied that she was no Mussolini, but decreed that one must have order in one's affairs to succeed in the theatre. She added that many things had been said about her that were not true and cited the example that in one press report her age was given as 60 when she said she was only 40. As usual, she was the one telling lies as at the time she was at least 54.

On Charles Cochran's invitation, they all went to see his 1929 revue, *Wake Up Dream* at the London Pavilion with the graceful singing and dancing of Jessie Matthews and Sonnie Hale, the elegant ballet of Tillie Losch, the light comedy of Douglas Byng and a speciality waltz by June Roper and Jack Kinney. The show was described as continually showing 'sheer beauty' and was punctuated by Cole Porter's songs, including the classic Let's Do It.[56] The twins would have also renewed their acquaintance with the beautiful dancer Alanova, who was also in the cast of *Wake Up Dream*, with whom they had danced in late 1927 in Paris at Au Chiquito.[57]

It was also announced that Mistinguett would appear in a Cochran revue in London in the summer of 1930, no doubt with the Rocky Twins. Miss also said that she would be embarking on a world tour, presumably in an attempt not to be outdone by Josephine Baker's endeavours.[58] Mistinguett with the Rocky Twins would have seen Cochran on several occasions for social events, and it must have been amusing for the twins to be in his professional company after the fiasco of him showing them the door in 1927. No doubt it was the subject of much joviality in their conversations.[59] One meeting was noted at the home of Charles Cochran, in the company of the Duff-Coopers and Arturo Lopez.[60]

Besides socialising and exploring London once more, the Rocky Twins spent at least two weeks, performing at the world famous Kit-Cat Restaurant. Whether this engagement was pre-arranged by their manager Calle Carlsen, or booked on arrival in London is not known. The fashionable Kit-Cat Restaurant in the Haymarket had opened in the summer of 1925 as the Kit-Cat Club with the headlining act of the Dolly Sisters and became one of the most famous nocturnal haunts in London. It was an ultra-chic members-only club described as 'luxurious, but wonderfully comfy… a vastly patronised and fashionable resort' and such was its popularity that within a short space of time membership exceeded 6,000 including Princes, cabinet ministers, dukes and peers.

A glass-fronted entrance, suggestive of a hotel, led into a large lobby with showcases and a cloakroom and then through to a lounge. Two floors below the street level was the ballroom, restaurant, grill room and American bar, accessed by a wide staircase that went down to the balcony and then down to the dance floor. The ballroom itself was high and spacious 80 x 60 feet rectangle, that was twice as big as the ballroom at the Piccadilly hotel.

There was a wide balcony all the way around and opposite the stairs was a recessed space for the orchestra. At the sides of the room were two parallel rows of supper tables. The décor was in ivory, gold and turquoise on Italian Renaissance lines. Tall royal blue and gold pillars rose right up to the roof, and the balcony had painted heraldic shields on the balustrade and a floral edging. Interestingly, the colour scheme continually changed caused by kaleidoscopic shafts of light -purple, blue and orange projected onto the dance floor from above. This large, comfortable and handsomely furnished club opened for drinks and dinner and at 10 pm and midnight when entertainment was given that often featured American and continental acts.

However, in December 1926, the Kit-Cat Club was raided by the police and was de-registered for three months as a result of liquor been served after hours to non-members. It was not until May 1927 that the Kit-Cat Club re-opened as a restaurant under a new syndicate who did not make it work and another took over.

This new group was called the Hotels de Paris and controlled three of the major nightspots in London – the Kit-Cat Restaurant, the Café de Paris and the Café Anglais. The new Kit-Cat Restaurant opened on 10th October 1927 with a sparkling new show, and within a short time the magic spell of the venue began to work again, and it was being described as a high-class dance restaurant with a smart little entertainment given every night after dinner and supper.

At the end of March and beginning of April, the star attraction was the American dance band of Abe Lyman who caused a massive stir as they attracted the regular interest of Prince George and the Prince of Wales. The Rocky Twins also performed but there are no descriptions of what dance routines they gave, although in likelihood it may have included their sailor dance, since a photograph of them in these outfits is signed and dated London, April 1929.[61] As before The Kit-Cat was called the HQ of Americans and no doubt the Rocky twins met many people who told them to try and visit America.

It was strange that staying at the Piccadilly Hotel the Rocky Twins were not given a spot in the Piccadilly Revels cabaret that was staged there in the ballroom. They must have seen the acrobatic dancing act of Balliol and Merton in cabaret and in mid-April they were spotted with Mistinguett at a midnight mannequin parade in the Piccadilly Hotel ballroom. The show mainly featured furs and was an attraction for the wealthy overseas visitors, and one American bought a sable coat for his wife for £2,500.[62]

The cabaret scene in London had gone through a bit of a blip in the late 1920s but was just re-establishing itself again in 1929. The Rocky Twins must have gone to see the new Cochran cabaret show at the Trocadero entitled *Down With Dora* that had started a full year run in January 1929. It was viewed primarily as a dancing show headed by William Cavanagh, and contained several first-rate acts that were changed regularly. The main act was the three singing and dancing American Adams Sisters. There were two dance troupes - the Trocadero Girls and the John Tiller girls – and the first ensemble featured the chorus as waiters who appeared to be carrying pretty girls around the room on dishes. In fact, the waiter's trousers contained the girl's real legs and the crossed legs on the trays were dummies.

Since they were signed by Andre Charlot to appear later in the year in cabaret, the twins would have gone to see Charlot's new show at the Hotel Splendide, which was along the lines of what was produced about two years before, with a full chorus and a range of dancing acts. The main feature of the show was the American dancers, Joan Barry and Dave Fitzgibbon.[63] They would have also visited the Cafe de Paris where the glamorous American dancing act of Fowler and Tamara were performing.[64]

In their spare time, they also went with Mistinguett to the Max Rivers school of dancing where they were described as 'dancing Stars with International Reputations' and presumably had some dance instruction. Rivers had staged the dances for Cochran's *Wake Up and Dream* and was a celebrated choreographer for stage shows and cabaret.[65]

Allegedly, at the end of their London stay, the Rocky Twins got a little carried away and seemingly went out in public in drag and were arrested for public indecency. We are told that Mistinguett, of course, rescued them from prison, ticking off the judge in the process[66] and they all returned to Paris arriving at the end of April 1929.[67]

It was now time for a rest and a break for a few weeks, and it is likely that the twins may have gone on a vacation to the Riviera[68] enjoying the salubrious surroundings of such places as the Carlton Hotel, the municipal Casino and the new Palm Beach Casino at Cannes, the Negresco Hotel in Nice and the Ambassadeurs, Ciro's, the Carlton restaurant and the Café de Paris in Monte Carlo.

The Riviera had been solely a winter resort, but since the mid-1920s it had become fashionable to sunbathe and so had opened up for the summer months. Indeed, so popular had it become that in July 1929, *Variety* published a feature entitled 'Nude on Riviera' and described that the beach resorts allowed boys to run round in shorts and no shirts and girls dropping shoulder straps and giving their backs and chests 'plenty of sun-kissed exposure.'[69] It was during this holiday that they were observed to be something unique and alluring to onlookers. We are told that people looked at them through a haze of champagne with 'delightful horror' since they looked too young and yet they were fit, handsome and desirable and so they decided to seduce them. And, they simply let themselves be seduced.

As we have seen they were both clever at manipulating people and getting what they wanted by playing up with an innocent and naïve air. They had an uncanny knack of being able to play the innocent and beguile both rich society ladies and men of means. But it was also thought that this was a 'role' they were 'forced into with their circle of people as guests of Counts and Barons.'[70]

From the Riviera they went onto the Venice Lido with their old friend Charlotte King Palmer. A photograph of them all together wearing pyjamas and long smoking jackets with Charlotte, in an equally splendid creation, was taken outside the luxurious Excelsior Hotel on the Lido.[71] They were back in Paris in late May 1929 to help celebrate the 30th birthday of their friend the Swedish writer and artist Thora Dardel, which, given they had been away from Paris for nearly 8 months, must have been a very happy reunion.

At the dinner held in what is now called La Bonne Franquette at 18 Rue Saint-Rustique, a restaurant frequented by many artistic types near the Place Tertre in Montmartre. Thora decided, for some reason to invite many of her single male friends. So along with Leif and Paal were Jean Börlin, a Swedish ballet dancer and choreographer, the French artist Etienne Drian, Swedish film actor Eric Barclay, who had appeared in French and German silent films, the French film actor Marcel Herrand, American author and artist Walter Shaw, who had studied photography with Man Ray and the Finish diplomat Goddy Wrede (Sten Goddert Wrede).

To add colour Thora also had her two Swedish friends Marta Cedercrantz (Bunny) and Elsa de Castro Feijo (Frida) at each end of the table. The Rocky Twins would have relished telling all their stories about their recent trip to the Riviera and the Lido, their antics in London, the debacle between Mistinguett and Josephine Baker in Budapest and their stay in Vienna.

During their time in the sunshine on the Riviera and the Lido it was announced back home in Oslo that they were going to appear in a revue in the New Theatre (Det Nye Theatre)[72] that had opened in February 1929 with Victor Bernau as the artistic director, previously director of the famous Chat Noir in Oslo from 1917-1928. The twins must have returned home to Norway at the end of June for the opening at the beginning of July and stayed for the summer. It must have been wonderful to be back home with family for the first time in over two years.[73]

The new Bernau revue opened at the beginning of July and was staged and decorated by Pal Abel. Besides the Rocky Twins, there was Bernau himself, Conrad Arnesen (the Norwegian actor and opera singer who sang one of the French successes called Paname), Booten Soot (an old friend of the Rocky Twins from their younger days in Oslo), Rich Hayes (the incredible goofy juggler and clown), Irmelin Grahm (the Swedish singer) Ingalil Söderman (Swedish singer), Jens Holstad (actor), Myron Pearl (dancer), Lillebil Ibsen (singer, dancer and actress), Mally Haaland (comedian) and Snoja Mjoen.[74]

It was admitted that the Rocky Twins were world-famous and Norway was honoured to have fostered them. They were described as beautiful, really nice to eat, like 'little chocolate princes, cheeky and weird.' But their dance numbers and costumes were thought to be too mundane and nothing out of the ordinary and that a little change would have been more acceptable.[75]

Once again there must have been plans to visit America because the twins were booked to leave Oslo on the 16th August travelling to New York via France perhaps on the Ile de France that left Cherbourg 20th August. For whatever reason they did not cross the Atlantic, so once again whatever American booking was being considered evaporated.[76]

They were however back in Paris and one night were spotted with Mistinguett, who was hung with diamonds, and Arturo Lopez at the Ritz bar that was described by the writer and journalist Basil Woon as 'the bar for men about town, the smart set and sycophants, millionaires and actors.'[77]

They were soon back in London, once again with Mistinguett and Arturo Lopez. Mistinguett's plans to purchase the Moulin Rouge had not worked out, and she was back in London for discussions about the possibility of her having a starring role in American talkies.[78] She was also in the process of organising a new show for the Casino de Paris that would also feature the Rocky Twins. As a result, she spent several mornings at the dance studio of J.W. Jackson watching the boys and girls in training in readiness for two troupes to be selected to go to Paris.[79]

The London night-club scene was now abuzz with a police clampdown to eradicate lawlessness. In the past, there had been raids, prosecutions and fines but now the new police chief was being more strident and imprisoning severe offenders like the infamous Mrs Merrick who ran the 43 club and was involved in the Silver Slipper club. The older more established clubs and cabarets that adhered to the law continued unabated like the Trocadero, the Kit-Cat, Ciro's and the Café de Paris and newer venues, mostly in the hotels began to flourish.[80] For example, the Rocky Twins joined Andre Charlot's new cabaret revue at the Grosvenor House Hotel from the beginning of September 1929. This luxury hotel had recently opened in Park Lane, and Charlot had migrated his cabaret show there from the Hotel Splendide.

Charlot's entertainment was regarded as being of 'excellent quality somewhat along the lines of the Cochran shows at the Trocadero'[81] and had a chorus of thirteen attractive girls.[82] The acts were changed regularly and at first, along with the twins, there was the comedian Clay Keyes, and next the juggler and comedian Eddie Gray (later part of the Crazy Gang).

The twins did a number called 'guess which is which' a version of what they did at the Concert Mayol in 1928 with the sisters Ree Bertin. This time it was just the two of them, and they played a hide-and-seek game that took place behind a tree. One twin as a gallant young man went behind the tree and immediately the second twin would appear as a gorgeous woman. The audience were astonished and believed some sort of magic trick was in play, or they were witnessing a quick change until the truth was revealed.[83]

In London, they met the handsome Frankie Leveson, who was called the 'dapper little Dane.' Leveson was part of the smart society set in Jazz Age London with the likes of Noel Coward, designer Gladys Calthrop, Gladys Cooper and Ivor Novello. He had made a name for himself as an exhibition dancer in the 1920s but had another career as an interior designer eventually becoming the manager for Syrie Maugham's business in the late 1920s.

Above left: Advert for the Grosvenor House Hotel
Above right: A programme for Andre Charlot's cabaret show at the Grosvenor House Hotel

One night Frankie introduced them to the singer and dancer Billy Milton with whom he was having an affair. It was as Frankie had said they were indeed 'two of the most handsome young men you'll ever see.' Billy added that they were unbelievably handsome and so alike you couldn't tell which was which. In fact, he related that 'as one hostess remarked, you could never be sure which one you were talking to or had gone to bed with.' He also had the chance to catch their impersonation of the Dolly Sisters and remarked that 'you could hardly tell the Dolly's from the Rocky's', so perhaps this was one of their dancing numbers at the Grosvenor House.[84]

Finally, there was some confirmed news about an American booking and in mid-October 1929 it was revealed that a deal had been made via an international agent called Irvin Marks, who had a foothold in Paris, New York and Hollywood, with the Shubert Brothers in New York and that they would leave in the Spring of 1930 after their conclusion in the new Mistinguett show that was due to open at the Casino de Paris.[85]

One month later it was again stated that the Shubert's had indeed signed the Rocky Twins.[86] And yet oddly in January 1930, E.R. Simmons, the European representative of the Shuberts' wrote to J. J. Shubert saying 'I know about the Rocky Twins. I understand they make a very good appearance and are very smart socially and were rather popular in London. I understand at the time, the Prince of Wales took rather an interest in the boys, but I believe I remember that their ideas of salary were rather exaggerated.'

Above: Front cover of the souvenir brochure for *Paris Miss* at the Casino de Paris, 1929

J.J. Shubert replied 'keep attached on your desk in case we need them.' So was there a deal on the table or was the talk of a deal just purely speculative[87]

Eventually, after many weeks of rehearsals and postponements the new Mistinquett show entitled *Paris-Miss* was staged at the Casino de Paris in mid-November 1929, with the Rocky Twins prominently featured. The Oscar Dufrenne and Henri Varna production cost 3 million Francs to produce and was funded by a syndicate of 14 Frenchman including the gambling Casino potentate Francois Andree. It was thought to be a beautiful production but second rate and dull and only saved by a few American and English imports such as the American Charles Ahearn and his millionaire band and the British Jackson dancing troupe of girls and boys.

Above: The Rocky Twins on either side of Mistinguett
Below: The Rocky Twins in their Hindou dance in Paris-Miss at the Casino de Paris, 1929

Above: The Rocky Twins on either side of Mistinguett in one of their dance numbers in Paris-Miss at the Casino de Paris, 1929
Below: The Rocky Twins with Mistinguett, Paris, 1929

Right: The Rocky Twins wearing smart tuxedos from the time of *Paris-Miss* at the Casino de Paris, 1929

The entire show revolved around Mistinguett who despite being over 50 looked 35 in her costumes and deportment. It was a typical Mistinguett show with staircases, feathers, and more feathers and it was made clear that she was not 'prone to permit any individual to overshadow her'. Variety thought she offered a 'poor entertainment' with nothing new or novel that usually characterised the Casino de Paris or Folies Bergere revues, although there were the obligatory staircase sequences.

However, the entrance build up for Mistinguett was phenomenal and the entire cast paraded and manoeuvred on the staircase set, with a series of drops and curtains raised and receded and all the famous Mistinguett song hits from My Man and Paree to Valencia were reprised.

Even Mistinguett admitted that the show was 'was not revolutionary as revues go' and said that the critics thought the show lacked originality. But in the end, the gross receipts at the end of the first week were remarkable[88] and broke all existing box office records in Paris.[89]

There was a lovely scene called The Streets of Europe with magnificent decors representing Regent Street in the time of Dickens, Rome's Via Veneto, the Rue de Lappe and finally the Champs Elysees. Another exciting scene featured a roof-top panorama of Broadway showing the chorus walking from roof to roof in the Broadway Melody number.

The Rocky Twins were presented well in seven numbers and were seen as Arlequins, military officers and as other decorous dandies including wearing top hats and tails with Mistinguett as Les Elegants in Les Champs Elysees and as water lilies wearing Hindu costumes in Fleur de Lotus.

They were described as being 'gorgeous to behold' and 'stunning' but 'just a pair of hoofers.' It was thought that with showmanly handling they would probably 'click in New York'[90] and they 'might show up better if properly presented.'[91]

However, other critics thought that they combined American step dancing with an original and artistic manner of execution that distinguished them from other dancing teams.[92] The rest of the cast were thought to be 'so-so.' Earl Leslie, long Mistinguett's partner, did little in an ordinary manner, and there was also Mona Lee, a dance specialist and Ladd and Olive an Adagio acrobatic dancing team.[93]

By January 1930 there was some salary cutting, and general pruning of costs in *Paris-Miss* and Charles Ahearn's Millionaire band was forced out with other acts expecting to quit.[94] In February, it was announced that Mistinguett was preparing a new spring-summer edition of *Paris-Miss* designed to compete with the new Folies Bergere show that was due. However, little appeared to change, and the Rocky Twins remained in the cast.[95]

Mistinguett said of them 'on stage it was impossible to tell one from t'other….they were alike as two peas and so strikingly attractive that they were mobbed each night at the stage door by connoisseurs of the Body Beautiful of either sex.'[96] Allegedly she also said 'they were so ravishing… that they would allow themselves to be kidnapped by beauty enthusiasts of both sexes. I suppose it was to be expected because they were Norwegian, but I disapproved.'[97]

Thanks to Mistinguett and *Paris-Miss* they were attracting even more attention and in January 1930, Erik Charell, one of the leading German revue producers, who was often called the German Mr Ziegfeld, signed them to appear in Berlin later in the year in a revue-opera at the Grosses Schauspielhaus with a salary of 15,000 marks per month (this was equivalent to $3,750 or £750 and in terms of 2017 equates to $52,000 or £44,000).

This production was most likely *White Horse Inn* (*Im weißen Rößl*) that finally premiered on 8th November 1930 and became one of Charell's most successful productions. But sadly, it would appear that the booking was not taken up.[98]

While still appearing in *Paris-Miss*, in the Spring of 1930, the Rocky Twins were in demand for various one-off performances and danced at a party for the French president and another for Baron Rothschild.[99] They also appeared at the annual ball of the pharmacy students of the University of Paris (Le Bal de la Pharmacie) at the Hotel Continental in early March. Proceedings started at 10 pm with dancing to five orchestras and then at midnight the main attractions began with the Rocky Twins, Mona Lee and Miss Yolande Ray and there was a dance contest.[100]

In late 1929, at the time of their debut in *Paris-Miss*, and in early 1930, they also began appearing once again in moving pictures – but this time in some early talkies and shorts –for the Jacques Haik film company. It was later noted that in these French films they played the roles of 'innocent boys' aged about 14 years old even though they were 20.[101]

Jacques Haïk (1893–1950) was a French film producer born in French-controlled Tunisia who became successful in the French film industry and built up a chain of cinemas and established his own production company Les Établissements Jacques Haïk. In Mid 1929, it was announced that Haik had engaged the leading lights in the French stage - Yvonne Printemps and Sacha Guitry - to make talking pictures and that work would start soon as Haik got his new studio ready,[102] but it was not until late 1929 that the studio at Joinville was up and running working on features and shorts.[103] The shorts were to supplement his features that he intended to show at his remodelled and rewired Olympia Theatre when it opened in December 1929.[104]

Some of these shorts included stage personalities. Georgia Graves from the Folies Bergere was seen dancing,[105] and there was a comedy song skit with 'Albert' behind a bar explaining that a song cocktail can be made by mixing styles of singing.[106] The Rocky Twins must have made several of these shorts on this basis, and one that was documented was entitled *Dix Minutes au Music-Hall* and was directed by Alexandre Ryder (a Polish-born French film director). Made up of several acts from the Paris music hall it featured the Hochney's dancing to 'Bakerinata', a tap dance number by Faraboni and two numbers by the Irvin sisters. The first was a dance of roses with the girls wearing swimsuits in rhinestones and a long white cape, and in the second, they were dressed as sailors in 'our boat' and undressed to finish in swimwear and danced in a seabed setting. The Rocky Twins, dressed as sailors, danced in a scene representing the deck of a ship. Then they were arguing as kids with pigtails in a classroom and then performed a freestyle dance synchronised to a song with a sofa somewhere in proceedings! The film was finally screened in early 1931.[107]

The Rocky Twins had a short break from the *Paris-Miss* show in late March and early April as it was announced that they were leaving for a quick tour of the Riviera on 1st April to appear in selected venues in Cannes, Nice and Monte Carlo.[108] During this trip, the Rocky Twins, perhaps via the introduction of Charlotte Palmer, were guests at a private party by the American millionaire Frank Jay Gould in his villa.

At the party, they met the Norwegian artist Ferdinand Finne who was about the same age. Finne had been spending some time in Paris where he was working as an assistant in a fashion establishment and was mixing with the bohemian and arty Parisian set. He had been asked by a wealthy American to visit Cap d'Antibes and for the celebration of his 30th birthday, this friend had rented the salubrious and exclusive Hotel Cap the Roc, a great classic building in an elegant park on the narrow promontory that stuck out in the bay with views of the Gulf of Juan de Pins. The 100 guests at the party were all in white, and a simple buffet with only fish and seafood was served with champagne. After dinner Finne was presented to Frank Jay Gould, who asked 'do you know the Rocky Twins?' He replied that he didn't know them since he avoided Norwegian expatriates in Paris, but added he had seen them on stage with Mistinguett. Gould said he was having a dinner party the following evening and invited Finne, saying that the twins were coming with some friends from Paris and he could meet them.[109]

Frank Jay Gould, was heir to the great American Railway fortune but had moved to France in 1913 and had made the Riviera his home in the 1920s. He had become one of the great developers of Juan Le Pin as a year-round destination and had renovated the local casino, established the Hotel Le Provencal and had purchased the villa de Vigie in 1928 as his home. He was also at the time riding high following the opening of the grand Palais de la Mediterranee in Nice, Europe's most sumptuous casino at the cost of $5 million the previous year.[110]

According to Finne, Gould was well- known for being somewhat bold in his choice of friends, mistresses and lovers. His circle included members of the English royalty, European aristocracy, American's with money, celebrities, film stars, writers like F. Scott Fitzgerald and Ernest Hemingway and he was attracted to the body beautiful of both sexes. No doubt the Rocky Twins fitted into the latter category. Finne said that they had 'set Paris on their heads through their beauty and elegance' and because they were 'just as two drops of water.'[111]

The author Thore Elton explained that Finne 'was clear in implying that the twins primarily 'financed' their lives through relationships with older rich men. They were the talk of the town, and it was 'trés chic' to be able to present them as entertainment in private contexts. Finne was also clear 'that he found the twins not particularly intelligent and that they were easily exploited' and had little empathy for them.[112]

The twins were most definitely back in Paris by 23rd April since they were spotted with Mistinguett and Earl Leslie at the opening of a new night haunt called Les Champs Elysees, run by Albert, late of the Le Perroquet cabaret fame. All of Paris went to the opening, and it was amusing to note that Miss was now universally known as Grandmere – and had accepted her sobriquet philosophically. The Rocky Twins were referred to as her grandchildren, and Earl Leslie was accompanied by many of his little boyfriends![113] The twins were still regular night-owls, and their favourite haunts of Le Boeuf Sur le Toit and the Grand Ecart were still going strong, but Louis Moyses had now opened a new venue called L'Enfant Terrible underneath the Theatre Pigalle.[114] This became the smartest club in Paris favoured both by Parisiens, visiting Americans and high society generally.[115]

They perceived that at the time they were having good luck and happiness and even rented or bought, what was described as a 'villa' or a large country house, by the Boulogne forest in the Bois de Boulogne, giving a hint of the country, but not far from central Paris and a very luxurious and salubrious district.[116]

Paris-Miss continued through 1930, but in July 1930 it was reported by *Variety* that Mistinguett's star was slipping, that her name was worth more on paper now than on the stage and that she had quietly faded from the show and had taken her partner Earl Leslie to Switzerland for a vacation.[117]

The comments from *Variety* were unfair and inaccurate. Miss clearly needed a break after over 9 months on the stage and she, in fact, left the show in August at the same time as the Rocky Twins and was scheduled to play a few performances in September with Earl Leslie and another new dancer called Ladd in Biarritz and Juan le Pins. It is not inconceivable that the Rocky Twins tagged along for a break.[118]

A portrait of the Rocky Twins at the time of their arrival in New York
Courtesy of the Theatre Collection, Lincoln Center, New York

CHAPTER FIVE
FIRST TRIP TO NEW YORK & BACK TO EUROPE 1930-1931

The Rocky Twins were undoubtedly obsessed with getting to America, and once again the offer from the Shubert's surfaced and in August 1930, it was announced that 'the Rocky Twins speak good enough English to insist on a good Shubert contract.'[1] As a result, the twins left Cherbourg on 30th August travelling first class on the German-built SS Bremen and arrived in New York City on 4th September 1930 and stayed there for at least 5-6 months.[2]

They checked into the Elysee Hotel, situated at 60 East 54th Street between Madison and Park Avenues, just south of Central Park. Founded in 1926 as a European-style hotel by Swiss-born by Max Haering, it was regarded as the most Parisian hotel that Manhattan offered. When Maurice Chevalier and his wife Yvonne Valle passed through New York in 1930 on their way to Hollywood, and back they stayed at the Elysee, and another famous guest was the actress Tallulah Bankhead, who would later become a friend of the Rocky Twins.[3]

Despite the accounts of there being an American offer and a specific contract to appear in a Shubert production in New York, there were no confirmed credits for any appearances at the end of 1930, and so it is not clear as to what the Rocky Twins were, in fact, doing in New York. One thing is for sure, it is unlikely that they left Paris for no reason. The Shuberts' did stage a big musical called *Nina Rosa* on 20th September 1930 at the Majestic Theatre, but there is no listing for the Rocky Twins. Also, at the end of August 1930, the Shuberts' had begun rehearsals for another show called *Hello Paris* starring the hilarious mimic Chic Sale. This was subsequently opened at Newark on 15th September for an out of town run, before being launched at the Shubert Theatre in New York on 15th November. It was a loosely plotted musical based on Homar Croy's novel *They Had to See Paris*, with scenes set on an oil field, in a New York speakeasy, on a pier, in the salon of a liner, and in the Cafe Lapin Agile in Paris. It was filled with specialities and thus a more appropriate setting for the Rocky Twins, although they were not listed in the programme. But if they did have a Shubert contract and were brought to New York to appear in a Shubert show, this must be the likely candidate. The show was not a success and only ran for 33 performances.

On arrival in New York, they claimed to have received an overwhelming reception and new admirers clamoured to be with them, but instead of champagne it was the cocktails that flowed, and it felt like a Spring break.

The Rocky Twins decided to rent the banqueting hall of the Ritz-Carlton hotel in New York and presumably with the help of their New York agent Irvin Marks and personal contacts like Elsie De Wolfe, invited over 100 guests to a special 'cocktail' party to introduce themselves to New York. The Ritz was situated at Madison Avenue and West 46th Street and was considered one of the smartest hotels in the city with two famous function rooms the Persian Gardens and the Crystal Room. The party 'became a bit of a giddy event' with, in fact, over 400 guests who consumed over 200 bottles of champagne and the Rocky Twins gave several turns to show-off their dancing skills.[4]

We are told that for some reason the Maitre d' thought that something untoward might happen and so had removed valuable carpets, furniture and object d'art. Sure enough, there was an accident with the trolleys carrying glasses and several hundred were smashed, and Paal did his best to set the hotel on fire when he lit up four stoves that were only installed as decoration. The restrooms had sofas and first relief aids kits, all of which were used. They said that everyone who was everyone attended including the Astors, Vanderbilts and Rockefellers and even their old friend Charlotte King Palmer, but this time she was without her diamond rings, as a result of the Wall Street crash. She must have been a little worried about money because in the spring of 1930 she had taken her ex-husband, who was a broker, to court in a suit for $50,000 claiming that he had persuaded her to invest heavily in Wall Street on his tips and guaranteed to make good any losses she might suffer.[5]

Somewhat erroneously the Rocky Twins claimed that many Hollywood stars attended their party including Bette Davies, Joan Crawford, Myrna Loy and William Powell and yet all were most definitely in Hollywood and not New York at the time.[6]

The twins were overjoyed with their reception, but despite the fact that they considered their party a huge success it would appear that the lavish spending achieved little in terms of actual theatrical bookings, but perhaps they did get requests to dance privately at various social events.

Since they stayed in New York for between 5-6 months, one cannot but wonder how their accommodation at the Elysee Hotel and living expenses were funded? No doubt they had arrived prepared with a healthy bank account due to their successes in Paris, but at the end of the day they must have somehow earned some money doing something, and they may well have danced and entertained at private functions.

According to later reports, Lady Mendl (Elsie de Wolfe) introduced them to New York society, and they were paid large sums to dance and present their clever impersonations.[7]

Above: The Rocky Twins wearing smart tuxedos and clutching a fashionable accessory in the form of a boudoir doll, Paris, Late 1920s.
Courtesy of the Shubert Archive, New York

De Wolfe is regarded as single-handedly inventing the profession of interior decorating. She was also one of the most widely known hostesses in New York and Paris society. Her parties were famous because she mixed people like a cocktail and the result was sheer genius. She surprised everyone in 1926, at the age of sixty, when she married Sir Charles Mendl, the press attaché for the British Embassy in Paris. He was charming, and she was rich, and they shared the same enthusiasm for people, parties, and the fine art of luxurious living.[8]

One playboy, Wall Street broker, Harold Russell Ryder, paid the twins $5,000 for entertaining his guests.[9] But was this during their first trip to New York in late 1930, or was it earlier when Ryder visited Paris with his wife in mid-1928?

Ryder got caught up in a high profile fraud case and was arrested and charged with grand larceny in June 1930 but released on bail. He claimed the failure of his company, with losses of $2-3 million, was due to the stock market crash. Before this, he was considered a genius of the financial world and was one of the $100 tippers on the Broadway nightclub route. He may have still had sufficient funds after his arrest to fund parties prior to his internment in Sing Sing in May 1931.[10]

With time on their hands, the twins must have networked, socialised, taken in the sights of New York, went to see some Broadway shows and explored the cabaret scene. However, 1929-1930 had been bleak years for the theatre industry partly due to the growth of the movies, and there was a lack of activity amongst the producers of large musical shows.[11]

But there were still a few top shows in late 1930 that would have been appealing for the twins to see including *Fine and Dandy*, with the principal attraction of the clowning of Joe Cook and the vivacious tap dancing of Eleanor Powell, *Girl Crazy* with Ethel Merman, soon to be Broadway's leading musical comedy star, *Three's a Crowd* with the dancer Clifton Webb, Lew Leslie's *Blackbirds* with Ethel Waters and Ziegfeld's *Smiles* with the dancing stars Marilyn Miller and Fred and Adele Astaire.

Even the once buoyant cabaret scene was in a bit of slump but not quite dead. Prohibition must have been a shock to the Rocky Twins, and the nightclubs must have also been an education being so different to Europe. Enacted in January 1920, prohibition had decimated the once buoyant and thriving cabaret scene in New York and many of the salubrious cabarets, dancing venues and restaurants, like the earlier grand lobster palaces of Murray's, Sherry's and Rector's, had been forced out of business.

The new venues – speakeasies - were smaller and more intimate, primarily run by gangsters and changed hands regularly due to police raids or eventual indifference on the part of punters who sought novelty.

The effect of prohibition and the banning of liquor did not have the effect campaigners wanted, and instead, it criminalised nightlife, undermined policing and led to the flouting of public morality. It did break down class barriers and enabled the upper and middle classes to visit the speakeasies that were considered part of this demimonde sub-culture by 'slumming it'.[12]

By 1928-1929 New Yorkers were getting bored with the usual razzmatazz and were opting instead for simple more sophisticated bars,[13] and as a result, cabaret bills in nightclubs shrank from thirty-six in late 1927 to only eight in September 1929. By late 1930 only five class night-spots opened with the Lido, Montmartre, Club Richman (with the legendary performer Harry Richman) and the equal famous nightclub host Texas Guinan at the old 300 Club. Top of the list was the swanky El Patio (formerly the Casanova Roof at West 52nd Street) with the stunning dancing of Rosita and Roman and Emil Coleman and his orchestra.[14] In addition, the grill rooms of some of the smart hotels such as The Paramount Grill, The New Yorker, the Central Park Casino and Roosevelt, offered dancing to well-known orchestras and sometimes provided a floor-show.[15]

Of course, the negro vogue of the 1920s or Harlem Rennaissance was still prevalent, and Harlem was always a favourite after-dark playground for whites from all walks of life. There were eleven class white trade nightclubs - Cotton club, Connie's Inn, the Nest, Small's Paradise (where the waiters did the Charleston while carrying fully loaded trays), Barons, Spider Webb, Saratoga, Ward's Swanee and Catagona, along with fifteen major bands including that of Duke Ellington. By the late 1920s, it was thought to have surpassed even that of Broadway, but new clubs opened such as the Everglades, Club Alabam and the Plantation, with black floor-shows in central Manhattan catering for those who preferred the security of a white environment without going to Harlem.[16]

One interesting development that invigorated the cabaret scene in late 1930 was, what has been now termed the Pansy Craze, a phenomenon that had been brewing for many years and became the latest novelty. A gay sub-culture, made more viable by prohibition, had been thriving in Harlem and Greenwich Village. Also, a series of salacious 'sex' plays on Broadway in the mid-1920s such as *The Shanghai Gesture*, *Lulu Belle*, *The Captive* and Mae West's *Sex* (1926), *The Drag* (1927) and *The Pleasure Man* (1928) paved the way.

A sophisticated look at lesbianism, *The Captive*, did great business and Mae West decided to create *The Drag*, her homosexual play described as 'the male Captive.' It was a lurid glimpse of New York's shadowy gay underworld and had a series of out-of-town previews and a midnight premiere at Daly's Theatre on 8th February 1927. But the vice squad raided both *Sex* and *The Captive* and Mae West was arrested on charges of public obscenity and went to jail.

The production of *The Drag* was halted, and New York State banned the open depiction of homosexuality on the stage thereafter. During Mae West's success with *Diamond Lil* (1928), she decided to stage *The Pleasure Man*, a comedy-drama set in a third-rate vaudeville house featuring a troupe of female impersonators, which was largely a re-working of *The Drag*. Once again the police stepped in and raided the show, provoking West's second arrest.

Of course, we must mention here that female impersonation had been seen on Broadway by the likes of Julian Eltinge, Bert Errol and Bert Savoy, but they had all created a sophisticated illusion and a unique high art form. Their performance was also not vulgar or associated with any remotely gay references. This was different to what was presented in the late 1920s and during the Pansy Craze since female impersonation and drag acknowledged a gay context and the performance was often bawdy and lewd.

Both *The Drag* and *The Pleasure Man* featured drag balls that had become a unique facet of New York nightlife. Masquerade balls had a long tradition in the city and were common at the turn of the century. Hugely popular, they intermingled race, class and gender but as the 1920s progressed, the gay element became more prominent and by 1926 it was reported that half the audience were fairies.[17] There were often several thousand attendees both spectators and those in drag, and there were prizes for the best costume.

By the late 1920s, there were between 6-10 enormous affairs staged every year. The Harlem drag balls were staged at the Savoy Ballroom on Lenox Avenue, the New Star Casino in Italian Harlem or later the Elks Lodge. But, by far the biggest was the Hamilton Lodge ball held annually in February in the Manhattan Casino (Rockland Palace). The spectators often arranged in boxes overlooking proceedings ranged from the leading lights of black society and the Harlem Renaissance, downtown celebrities and gay favourites Tallulah Bankhead, Beatrice Lillie, and Clifton Webb and pillars of old New York respectability such as the Astors and Vanderbilts. In Manhattan itself, drag balls were also regularly held at Madison Square Gardens, Webster Hall, Central Opera House and the Astor Hotel in midtown.[18]

The balls were described as a meeting place 'where the shadow world might gather, and men might dance with each other.' Thousands of observers came to look at the men in drag. There were 'slim figures almost nude and often to all appearances as sexless as angels. There were feathers trailing in brilliant clouds back from early naked bodies, while monstrous plumed headdresses waved like the undulating fronds of palms trees in the wind. Necklaces, earrings and bracelets glittered. Faces were powdered and rouged with the curved development of young girls and figures with the rounded swinging hips and the soft flesh characteristic of women.'[19]

As the 1920s progressed, gay visibility became more pronounced and began to extend into Times Square, the city's cultural centre. As George Chauncey said 'gay men became a highly visible part of New York's prohibition culture' and to accompany the drag balls, speakeasies and nightclubs opened that catered for the 'horticultural set' and those eager to be thrilled by the thought of seeing part of the gay shadowlands.[20] There was a marked division between the obvious pansies or fairies – those who were outrageous, wore women's clothes or were simply effeminate – and the 'normal' straight acting gay men, often the professionals and businessmen, who wanted to keep their secret a secret and not lose their social standing. These well-dressed and mannered men congregated and cruised graciously in the more refined locations of the Oak Room in the resplendent Plaza Hotel, at the southeast corner of Central Park, the King Cole Room in St. Regis Hotel, on Fifth Avenue at 55th Street and the men's bar of the Knickerbocker Hotel on 42nd Street.[21]

Like many of the legitimate New York clubs who had a personality front person like Texas Guinan, Harry Richman and Helen Morgan, the new gay nightspots often featured someone as master of ceremonies. In Harlem Gloria Swanson (Walter Winston) became the most famous gay club host in a cellar club. He was plump, jolly, bawdy and very feminine and is thought to have begun the vogue for impersonating Broadway and Hollywood starlets.[22]

In Manhattan, Jean Malin took the limelight and became the leading light of the Pansy Craze that reached its height in New York in late 1930. Young and smart, he was a striking figure at 6 foot tall and 200 pounds and knew how to handle himself and hecklers. Malin, from Brooklyn, had started out as a female impersonator called Imogen Wilson and had attracted sophisticated throngs to the Rubaiyat in Greenwich Village until it was raided.[23] He then re-invented himself without the drag and became the tuxedoed Master of Ceremonies and featured entertainer of the small and plain Club Abbey located on the site where Texas Guinan once held forth at 46th and 8th Avenue. Throughout 1930 Malin became the toast of New York with his high-camp, waspish wit.[24]

Club Abbey with its all-night policy, became the rendezvous of all the Broadway wise-crackers, columnists and most of the racketeers. Malin's personality dominated the dance floor, and he capitalised 'on a supposed effeminacy' which he accentuated and deliberately heightened, while the floor-show itself was 'daring, fast and full of double entendre.'[25] Malin's success was emulated by numerous other entertainers and club owners who climbed on the bandwagon, so much so that in September 1930, Variety's front page described the pansy places on Broadway saying that the season's newest thing was the nite places with pansies as the prime draw.

Above: A sketch of the interior of Club Abbey with Jean Malin and the female impersonator Helen Morgan giving their performance
Courtesy of J.D. Doyle Archives

New York clamoured for a glimpse of pansy nightlife, and it was reported that Greenwich Village 'had a number of funny spots.'26 These included The new Club Calais that opened at 125 West 51st street with Arthur Budd as MOC (he had also won prizes at drag balls) and Jackie Maye and Francis Fay as entertainers and the Two Thirty Club in Wooster Street, run by Frank E. Carroll, the promoter of the pansy balls at the Central Opera House with Jean Robbins, female impersonator, heading the show.27

A few weeks later in December, it was announced that the 'Pansy Club racket (was) getting bolder' when the Pansy Club (formerly the Picardy) opened on 48th Street at Broadway with a cabaret called Pansies on Parade,

Above: Sheet music depicting the female impersonator Karyl Norman

headed by female impersonator Karyl Norman 'the Creole Fashion Plate.' Opposite, the Everglades, previously a black and tan nightclub, also staged a floor-show headed by Francis Renault, another female impersonator.[28]

The Rocky Twins had become de rigueur in smart Parisian society and inhabited both the exclusive night resorts and must have also visited the more risqué gay resorts. They were chameleons that could fit in anywhere – one minute they could be as camp as Christmas, androgynous and dressed in drag – and the next, totally respectful in their smart dress suits and ties. They would have moved from one environment to the other with complete ease.

When the Rocky Twins arrived in New York in September 1930, the Pansy Craze blossomed into full swing and to think that they did not enjoy the pleasures of drag balls and the pansy nightclubs is quite unlikely. They would have also met some of the leading gay performers like Jean Malin, with whom they would work in Hollywood the following year in 1932.

Interestingly, in October 1930, two vaudeville producers, Irving Tishman and Jimmy O'Neal proposed the idea of a legitimate musical to be called *Pansy* on the basis that they thought the public was sufficiently 'Pansy' conscious to accept the concept. They were casting all available female impersonators in New York and were issuing contracts to, 'all boys that wear girls clothes on the stage' including Karyl Norman, Francis Renault, Jackie May and Cecil Mason. The list included the 'Lynch Twins', but no record can be found of them – perhaps the Rocky Twins were under consideration and the name was merely spelt wrong.[29]

The Pansy Craze was short-lived. Following mounting public and media objections and police harassment, things came to a head when gunfire broke out at Malin's Abbey Club on 25th January 1931 and the place closed. The police then clamped down and closed all the main pansy places and raided the Pansy Club and Club Calais and charged the owners with liquor violations. Once again the gay presence reverted to the shadowy underworld, but it was not extinguished.

The Rocky Twins were back in Paris in February 1931. They were so impressed with America and had enjoyed themselves so much that it was reported that they were 'yearning for the statue' – a reference to the Statue of Liberty.[30] It was also made clear that they were waiting until their quota date arrived and then they were returning to America. The mention of the quota confirms that they had indeed performed in a show in New York[31] since the Council of the Actors Equity Association stipulated that as aliens they must await the expiration of a 6 month period before entering another production.

Their first known re-appearance in Paris was at the end of March 1931 when they performed in a musical gala along with Serge Lifar, Georgia Graves and Mlle Edmonde Guy in a conference by Andre Rivollet entitled 'The Poets of the Dance' at L'Université des Annales (Rue la Boette).[32]

One of the first things they did on arrival in Paris was to move out of their Bois de Boulogne villa and buy what they called 'a fun apartment on the top of an apartment block in Montmartre.' It is likely that it was located near their friend Thora Dardel's apartment on the Rue Lepic – an area where they had lived before. There was a bar in the apartment and most of the time it was a 'free' bar where friends usually met from 6-8 in the early evening. Among their many friends that came to join the fun was Josephine Baker, who was at the time riding high with a big success in her revue *Paris Qui Remue* (Paris Which Stirs) at the Casino de Paris, that had been launched at the end of September 1930 when the boys were in New York.[33]

With Mistinguett on tour in Europe and no big stage offer, the Twins decided to form a partnership with the American dancer Mona Lee who they had performed with them in *Paris Miss*, during the previous season. From California, Lee was four years older than the twins (born in 1905) and was trim, athletic with short dark hair and a very delicate appearance. Reviewing *Paris-Miss*, one critic called her 'delicious' and after that Mistinguett 'was a royal pain to her' – a clear indication of how Miss hated anyone to compete with her onstage. Lee said of Mistinguett 'she was already in her sixties, she could barely kick her leg up past her knee, but the public was always on her side.' Undoubtedly the Rocky Twins protected her.[34] Mona Lee was also lesbian since in the USA 1940 census she was living in Manhattan with Mirian Kornmann, who was described as the head of the household with Lee as partner.

Her first credits appeared in Kansas City when she headed the chorus in a revue at the Hotel Biltmore in late 1923.[35] In 1925 she was still in Kansas City working in Frank Newman's revue[36] but then joined a Newman picture house presentation called *Rose Marie* at the Metropolitan in Los Angeles.[37] After appearing in cabaret in New York in 1926,[38] Lee returned to the West Coast and was in cabaret at Westlake in Los Angeles in 1927.[39] She then joined Fanchon and Marco's *Lace Ideas* picture presentation at the Granada, San Francisco where she displayed some real high kicking[40] before appearing in the Boris Petroff picture presentation of *Leap Year Fancies* at the Capitol New York in mid-1928.[41] Europe beckoned in late 1928, and she got a booking to appear at the salubrious Ambassadeurs restaurant at the Cannes Casino for January 1929 alongside the dancing duo of Jean Barry and David Fitzgibbon.[42]

After the South of France, Lee was engaged for Universum Picture House in Berlin before she gained the contract to appear in the Mistinguett show *Paris Miss* in Paris.[43]

Above: The Rocky Twins and Mona Lee, 1931

When the tour commenced is not clear, but they must have had a try-out in Paris in a private function or cabaret. Later reports suggested that the first port of call was Berlin and presumably this was in April 1931[44] and by May 1931 it was announced that the Rocky Twins and Mona Lee team was a success.[45]

Where they performed in Berlin and for whom is not known, but we must remember that in January 1930, they had been signed by Erik Charell to appear in Berlin in late 1930 in *White Horse Inn*, a revue-opera at the Grosses Schauspielhaus, but seemingly they did not take up the offer as they went to New York. The show was a big success and was still running in the Spring of 1931, so they may have been just added to the cast.[46]

However, a few years later there were references to the fact that they had been presented in Berlin and elsewhere in Max Reinhardt's Dorian Grey Ballet. There was, of course, a connection between Charell and Reinhardt as Charell had worked for Reinhardt and in 1924 had taken over the management of the Grosses Schauspielhaus that belonged to Reinhardt's theatre empire.[47] Equally, other venues might have booked them including the picture houses that gave presentations like the Universum where Mona Lee had appeared in 1929, or the Wintergarten or Scala Theatres that engaged variety acts.

By May 1931 they were in Oslo, partly to see their family but also to be part of a revue staged at the Red Mill (Rode Molle) from 17th May along with Al Val Reno (American stepdancer) and Les Koud Vor (Russian Dancer). The Red Mølle was established in 1920 and was an elegant dance restaurant, established by restaurateur Sigurd Paulsen in the area of Tivoli. The name Rode Molle came from the decorative red mill of the house (above the entrance), inspired by the French Moulin Rouge. There was a large dining hall arranged around a large central dance floor, and there was space for two orchestras at each end.[48]

After a few weeks, for some reason, they had to rush back to Paris and drove in their Graham Paige car and then drove from Paris to Copenhagen a distance of over 1,200 km taking at least 14 hours. In Copenhagen, they appeared in Oscar Holst's annual revue at the Apollo Theatre in June before returning to Oslo and another few weeks at the Red Mill in July. Thereafter, they visited Stockholm and were one of the dance attractions at Ernest Rolf's revue at the China Theater located at Berzelii Park next to the exclusive Berns Salonger restaurant.[49]

The multi-talented Rolf was described as 'the Ziegfeld of Sweden' but was also an actor, singer, lyricist and composer.[50] He opened the China theatre as a silent cinema in 1928, but from 1929 staged a series of annual summer revues with stars from all over Europe and the USA that made the venue internationally famous.

Above: An interior view of the Rode Molle, Oslo

Right: An advert for the Rode Molle, Oslo

Rolf's 1930 show, which ran from April through the summer, featured Jack Hylton's orchestra from London, the acrobatic dancing of Mitty and Tillio from Paris, the elegant dancing of Robert Quinault and the singer Josephine Hall from the Cotton Club in Harlem.

Variety thought the show was not so hot 'the Swedes have never gone in for revues of the pretentious style as known in America, which they call here variety or vaudeville. A revue in Stockholm is more of a topical revue. Rolf always spends much money on his revues, and his present one is equally gorgeous but too local with not enough choruses and dances and foreign acts and is therefore slow.'[51]

The 1931 show was equally dazzling and spectacular and full of extraordinary acts led by the popular local singer and dancer Karl Gerhard, who was much in the Maurice Chevalier mould.

There were also the decorous dancing Epp Sisters from Paris, the conjuror Giovanni, Tutta Rolf (the actress wife of Ernst Rolf), the acrobatic act of the four Malinoffs, an imitation of a little boy and girl act called Lillibror, three Greek male acrobats called Bonos Cesar and the 16 Jackson girls. Amongst the many production numbers, there was the spectacular 'Katarina 11' and a pirate finale. The incredible costumes and sets were designed by Zig from Paris, Gueye Rolf and Gunila Stierngranath. After the show, there was supper and dancing at the Midnight Follies in the Embassy Club, under the direction of Rolf and the Rolf's Orchestra, and perhaps many of the acts from the China theatre show doubled here.[52]

The Rocky Twins and Mona Lee would have been slotted into proceedings in Rolf's revue in late July - August as it was normal to change acts every so often during the run of a show to ensure freshness and novelty. Allegedly they were going to introduce a lot of new things, and one of their new dance numbers was a rain sketch. Unfortunately, one of the twins slipped and hurt his knee on 7th August and was hospitalised and it was thought he would have to remain there for a couple of weeks. The other brother took a plane to Paris to see about their forthcoming engagements.[53]

Despite reports that another American engagement was being considered, it was likely that they were offered to appear with Mistinguett in her next show that she was planning and materialised as *Paris Qui Brille* that followed Josephine Baker's show *Paris Qui Remue* at the Casino de Paris.

Back in Paris, and the injured brother fully recovered, the twins were having fun and enjoying the autumn nightlife. But hard times were afoot in the Paris nightclubs due to the effects of the Wall Street crash, dwindling American visitors and their spending power and the

Above: Ernest Rolf

onset of depression. Exceptions in Montmartre were the still thriving Abbaye de Theleme with its strong South American following, Florence's, described as 'the ritzy French and American spot' (run by the black singer Florence Jones) and Bricktop's. In Montparnasse, the exotic Martinique dancers were enjoying success at the Boule Blanche, and Train Bleu and the Lido (that had opened in 1928) was still doing good business on the Champs Elysees.[54]

An undisclosed new nightclub described as 'another Passy Boite' (meaning it was frequented by what was considered to be the rich, society set) opened in October. Presumably, somewhere in Montmartre, it was patronised by the Rocky Twins crowd, the Grand Ecart bar crowd and the Honore Palmer crowd, hence reinforcing that it was also a place favoured by men of a particular sort.[55] The same age as the Rocky Twins, Honore Palmer was an American millionaire from Chicago who had studied art in Paris and was a portrait artist and painter.

The Twins did not emerge in another Parisian show and instead accepted an offer from America. They dissolved their arrangement with Mona Lee who then partnered with Tommy Lad, another ex-Mistinguett dancing partner from the Casino de Paris and in the autumn of 1931 performed in St Jean de Luz and the Alhambra in Paris.[56]

Before they left for America, they went to see Mistinguett in *Paris Qui Brille* launched 17th October 1931 at the Casino de Paris accompanied by Josephine Baker. Billy Milton recalled 'Josephine, and the Rocky Twins sat in the box for the first half of the show, and Josephine came back and said to Mistinguett 'Darling you were wonderful. It's coming over beautifully' She kissed her on her two cheeks and took her entourage off. But when the curtain went up on the second act, her box was empty which was a tremendous insult to Mistinguett.'[57]

Billy Milton was Mistinguett's newest dancing partner and co-star in *Paris Qui Brille* and had met the twins in London in 1929. He went to a party thrown by the twins in Paris with Mistinguett at this time and said 'these sexy boys had now become the toast of Parisian high society. We arrived in the middle of an altercation between the tin millionaire Arturo Lopez and one of the twins. He had apparently refused to wear a costly pearl necklace, which Arturo had bought him at Cartier's under his shirt. 'It tickles me' he complained and removed it from his neck and put it down on the table. In a flash Miss, sizing up the situation picked up the necklace and said 'I don't like to see you both quarrelling like this. I will wear it until you make up.' At which point, she put it around her neck. No one saw that necklace again except in her private collection.'[58]

The Rocky Twins in smart suits from Paris, late 1920s or early 1930s

CHAPTER SIX
HOLLYWOOD, MGM AND THE PANSY CRAZE 1931-1932

As we know, the Rocky Twins loved their first stay in America and were very anxious to get back. Indeed, in the summer of 1931, when they were performing in Oslo, they announced that in the Autumn of 1931 they would return to New York to dance and sing in an operetta and that they were 'looking forward to playing comedy.'[1]

It would appear that two offers emerged, one for the stage in New York and the other a Hollywood film contract from Metro Goldwyn Mayer. The second American trip was an attempt to break the mould of what they had been doing before in Paris – in other words just dancing in a revue. They wanted to broaden their horizons and develop more rounded performance skills on the stage and not just dance but act and sing and change the way they were perceived. They also wanted to appear in more movies and break into the big time in Hollywood. Language problems may have been minimised as by this time they would have been able to converse in French, English and German following their stay not just in Paris, but London and Vienna, but their grasp of English and their accent may not have been entirely acceptable for an American audience.

It was later stated that the New York engagement was for the producer Max Gordon,[2] who had started off running the RKO vaudeville agency and was the agent for the Marx Brothers, before he embarked on stage production. Within a short space of time he had come to the forefront of legit producers on Broadway and by 1931 was making a big success and had two shows that were still doing good business: *Band Wagon* and *Three's a Crowd* starring Clifton Webb.

Gordon had visited London twice before in late 1930 and the summer of 1931. How he knew the Rocky Twins is not clear, but since the twins mentioned in June 1931 that they were going to appear in an operetta in New York, it is likely that Gordon must have seen them in New York in late 1930. He may have been keen to secure them for the romantic comedy-musical *Cat and the Fiddle* that he was to stage in late 1931 at the Globe Theatre.[3]

It is also important to note that, during Gordon's trip to Europe in July and August 1931, he went to see the rehearsals of, what was called, *Waltzes from Vienna* at the Alhambra in London and bought the American rights.[4] He was anxious to stage it in New York but was not sure where, or when, or how, as it was a big show mechanically and in personnel.

Despite these issues, he was in the process of casting in October and November before he finally announced in late November that he would have to delay production.[5] Gordon may well have initially secured the twins for *Cat and Fiddle* and may have been considering them for *Waltzes from Vienna* (which was eventually staged in 1934). They were not listed in the programmes for either the out of town tryout for *Cat and the Fiddle* or the launch in New York. So it would seem that in the end, they did not go to New York.

Interestingly, in later interviews they only referred to travelling to Hollywood in 1931 and not to New York. One report a year later, stated that they had been brought to the USA with a view to appearing in a New York show, but instead went to Hollywood.[6] Their travelling arrangements made their destination evident by the fact that they did not cross the Atlantic in the usual way from Cherbourg to New York. Instead they left France from the port of Saint-Nazaire, on the 21st October aboard the French liner SS Mexique travelling to Galveston, Texas on what was called the Mexican line.[7] The reason for this routing must have been because they felt that this was a more direct route to Los Angeles. From Galveston, they would have travelled the short distance to Houston to connect on the famed Sunset Limited train service run by the South Pacific Railroad from New Orleans to Los Angeles that took 42 hours. It was a deluxe service with dining and sleeping cars, club car and observation car to see the stunning scenery including the 120-mile trip over the Apache Trail and the Carriso Gorge.

They were in Hollywood in November 1931 because there was a report stating that they were 'poised to crash foreign talkers'[8] and another, that the West coast production combine of Fanchon and Marco were considering signing them.[9] The latter, a dynamic brother and sister duo, often simply called, F&M, created spectacular live stage shows for movie houses in California and across the country that were called 'Ideas'. Each 'Idea' centred on a theme like Montmartre, Mars, Aloha Circus and Jungles for example. They had lavish sets and costumes, teams of chorus girls and dancing and star acts.

The ex-dancing partner of the Rocky Twins, the American Mona Lee, had come from the West Coast and had been part of an F&M 'ideas' picture presentation called *Lace* in early 1928. She must have given them some advice about dancing opportunities in California including F&M.[10] Sadly, nothing transpired with F&M perhaps because they could not commit to an extended tour across the country because of their film contract.

Film-making was not immune to the general depression following the Wall Street crash in 1929, and things were not a bed of roses. Although many studios were suffering financially, MGM weathered the storm and even made a profit.

But another big storm was brewing regarding censorship, and one of the most significant issues became how to adapt talkies into foreign languages. The Hollywood contract from MGM and had been evolving for sometime before the twins finally went to Los Angeles in late 1931. With the advent of the talkies in the late 1920s, many of the Hollywood studios were grappling with the vexing issue of language. For many, the conclusion was to create several versions of each film primarily in English, Spanish, French, German and Italian. MGM had been vigorous in its plans to follow this route, which was under discussion during 1929.

The issue of how the Hollywood deal came about may have arisen in late 1929 when the Rocky Twins were in London with Mistinguett where it was announced that Mistinguett was discussing the idea for her to star in American talking films.[11] Then in early 1930, there were more reports that she had indeed signed a contract.[12] Given the closeness of Mistinguett and the twins at the time and their long run in *Paris-Miss* through 1930, the idea of the twins appearing with Miss on the screen would have been a promising idea by Hollywood executives. And, although the name of the studio is not given, it must have been either MGM or Paramount, as these were the two emerging players in foreign language film production.

The twins did say that one of MGM's agents (either Allen Byre MGM's chief in France or the Paris representative Joseph K. Freeman) saw them perform in Paris in *Paris-Miss* during 1930 and an offer was made for them to appear in foreign language films to be created in Culver City.[13] Because of other commitments or because MGM stalled, they were not able to travel to Hollywood until late 1931. There were several possible reasons for their contract - first, they were part of MGM's policy to engage foreign speakers, they had the advantage of already having appeared in some European films, and MGM wanted dancers as they were expanding their concept of the all sound musical.

The development of foreign language film versions became a big issue once the talkies had been established and became popular and the trend for wiring movie theatres to sound accelerated. It all happened very quickly in the space of a few years. At first, it was thought that foreigners were glad to hear the voices of English stars speaking English, but they subsequently demanded that the product should be given in their native language. Despite the cost, it was felt the only option, to ensure dominance in foreign markets, was to create several versions of each movie in several different languages.

In late 1929, following a conference between MGM chief Louis B. Mayer, Irving Thalberg (head of production), Arthur Lowe (head of MGM's foreign department) and other executives, MGM announced that they would produce all of its notable talking films in English and other languages. Lowe also said that he could foresee a foreign film race with complete foreign talking versions of many important movies. He stressed that the plan was to employ separate casts and use stars like Greta Garbo who spoke several languages in the different versions as central figures. The new operation went into effect immediately, and the first picture that emerged was *Die Sehnsucht Jeder Frau* or *A Lady to Love* (*Sunkissed*), starring Vilma Banky made in German and English.[14] This was followed by *Le Specter Vert* or *The Unholy Night* (in French) directed by Jacques Feyder with Andre Luquet.

MGM invested between $4-5 million in foreign productions in Hollywood through the period 1929-1932 and in addition to foreign speakers already on the lot at Culver City, they secured a vast number of performers from Europe and many production people like the French director Jacques Feyder.

Arthur Loew and associates sailed for Europe in the Spring of 1930 for a 6-week tour of MGM's offices and to assess the impact of sound and MGM's plans for foreign language versions of their films. It is likely that during their stay in Paris the MGM team began signing up relevant performers and production personnel and this may well have been when the Rocky Twins were approached about a contract.[15]

On his return from Europe, Arthur Loew said that the stars of the future would be linguists.[16] By November 1930 MGM was saying that it was planning to have foreign versions of each English dialogue film. 50 Foreign talkers were added to the schedule for the coming year, with the majority in German, French and Spanish and 46 foreign workers under contract with 15 more on the way to Culver City from Europe.[17]

An example of MGM's prowess in creating big musicals and thinking about foreign language adaptations was a monolithic project initially called *From Broadway to Heaven* but renamed *The March of Time*. It was not only a vast project but also a colossal disaster. A part-technicolour cavalcade of the entertainment business from the 1890s to the present, filming began in December 1929. But in the spring of 1930, the American Dodge Sisters were added to the cast. The Dodge Sisters had scored a big success in London, Paris and New York[18] and MGM had affirmed that it was keen to corner the market infamous 'teams' from the stage.[19] When filming was complete in June 1930, there were concerns that many of the vaudeville performers lacked screen technique, but also it was perceived that there had been a decline in audience interest in musical films.

MGM decided against a release and planned instead to cut up the musical numbers for interpolation in musical shorts. At the end of March 1931, they released a German Version of the film called *Wir Schalten Un Auf Hollywood* (*We Are Switching Gears to Hollywood*) containing three episodes with the Dodge Sisters and the Albertina Rasch Girls.

THE AMBASSADOR CRYSTAL PLUNGE and SUNTAN BEACH, LOS ANGELES, CALIFORNIA

Above: A view of the pool and beach area at the Ambassador's Hotel
Below right: An impression of the Cocoanut Grove nightclub in the Ambassador Hotel

Then in 1933, MGM revived the production with a new cast playing the original characters, and some of the original footage retained. It was released as *Broadway to Hollywood* in September 1933.

The Rocky Twins were appointed by MGM in the midst of all these developments primarily as performers for foreign talkies but also as part of a determined policy to acquire well-known 'team' dancing acts. They were part of a mass engagement of foreign talent at the time, which might explain why there were no announcements of their arrival at MGM or any indication of what specific plans MGM had for them.

The twins were of course somewhat arrogant and full of their own self-importance. In many ways, they were narcissists with a deep desire to be admired and loved. They craved applause and attention and wanted to be centre stage. They believed that they would 'become the company's new stars' and 'the world's 8th wonders.'[20] Nothing was further from the truth, and in fact, things did not go exactly as they had planned.

On arrival in Hollywood the twins were 'full of money' and with smiling faces checked into the salubrious Ambassador Hotel, a 22-acre playground in the heart of the city at 3400 Wilshire Boulevard.[21] The hotel had been built in 1921 as a deluxe resort with 400 rooms and bungalows, complete with shady gardens, bridle paths, stables, a bowling alley, miniature golf course, open-air palm court restaurant and a post office and furrier. There was also an Olympic-sized swimming pool and a lido with suntan sand bathing beach. It had also become a mecca for smart society and cinema stars, who mingled nightly at the world famous Coconut Grove nightclub to dance the night away.

With these endless opportunities for varied recreational activities, stunning location and immediate access to the cream of Hollywood society, this was the perfect place for the Rocky Twins to exert their magic and mingle and network as they had done in Paris. This was all they did because although they had what was called a 'somewhat advantageous contract with Metro Goldwyn Mayer'[22] the weeks and months rolled by with no film assignments. They were not the only ones in this predicament. For example, by May 1932 the French film director Jacques Feyder had had no assignments for several months.[23]

The Rocky Twins must have visited the MGM studio in Culver City for meetings, but they spent most of their time enjoying the Californian sunshine and had 'plenty of opportunities to do touring, travelling and social activities.'[24] They also decided to take English lessons[25] and maintained their usual rigorous exercise regime to keep them fit and in tip-top shape.

Through their socialising they discovered that the depression was exerting a severe effect on many people and their wealth became quite an asset having brought money with them and being on MGM's payroll. At some point, a movie star, whom they had met, offered to sell them a Beverly Hills mansion and they also acquired a Rolls Royce from another star. The mansion had 22 rooms and was not vast or apparently ostentatious, but it was beautiful, and on the spacious porch, there were wonderful views of Hollywood, and there must have been a pool.[26]

Besides the attractions of the Ambassador hotel and the Coconut Grove nightspot, the Rocky Twins would have wasted no time in sampling the varied nightlife of Hollywood. There were at least 15 class cafes and dancing places, half of which were offering floorshows, and all enjoyed good business with the depression getting the credit because 'customers are loosening the purse strings to rid themselves of the blues.' The main places getting the best crowds were the Frolics (formerly George Olsen's), Sebastian's Cotton Club and the Paris Inn. Other venues included the Bohemian Cafe (formerly Pom Pom), the Biltmore Hotel, the Roosevelt hotel, the Pyramid Cafe, the Silver Slipper, Fiesta, Club Royale and Jahnkes Tavern. Club Alabama and Show Boat were what was called black and tan spots like the Cotton Club in Haarlem but were located south of downtown in the Los Angeles Harlem district.[27]

At the same time the Pansy Craze, that had swept New York the previous year when the Rocky Twins were in the city began in Los Angeles. Like New York, the nightclub crowd in Hollywood had an appetite for something different and thrilling, and as the writer, Daniel Hurewitz said they had a 'curiosity about perversity' that attracted them to see the pansy shows.

The Rocky Twins in their flash car outside their Beverly Hills mansion
Courtesy of the Wisconsin Center for Film and Theater Research / Wisconsin Historical Society

Indeed, 'perhaps some of the audiences actually found the fairies genuinely erotic and sexy.' The allure of the fairies or pansies often in drag as outré performers became a big draw and club managers scrambled to make the most of this new trend.[28]

Allegedly, one of the first pansy floor-shows was at a venue called BBB's at 1651 Cosmo Street and named after Bobby Burns Berman the owner, who had made a name for himself on the East coast in the mid-1920 before moving West. BBB's had been floundering in bankruptcy but was re-opened under financial guidance of Al Rosen, an agent, in early April 1932. It was a tiny, dark, noisy cellar with a postage stamp sized dance floor but had the wildest entertainment in town. With BBB as the outrageous Master-of-Ceremonies and Harold Howard's 7-piece band, there was a pansy floorshow comprising 10 gorgeous female impersonators. The novelty proved highly popular and the profits huge, but police interference was expected. Nevertheless, it attracted a high profile clientele and at various times throughout 1932 guests included Tallulah Bankhead, Marlene Dietrich, Billy Haines, Jean Harlow, Ethel Barrymore and even Howard Hughes with Cary Grant dropped in two nights in a row.[29] BBB's became such a draw that Jean Morgan planned a second pansy floor-show at the Pyramid Club.[30]

By the spring of 1932, despite their nocturnal excursions, the Twins may well have been getting somewhat bored professionally. Thankfully, they renewed their friendship with the screen actress and dancer Julanne Johnston, whom they had met in Vienna in late 1928, and she was to play a pivotal role in their Hollywood sojourn.

Johnston had studied dancing at the Denishawn dancing School and played two seasons with the Hollywood Community Theatre before she went on a vaudeville tour as part of Paisley Noon dancing act.[31] With golden brown hair and 5 foot 6 inches tall, she was also regarded as a graceful beauty and had been a model for numerous photographers.[32]

Living in Hollywood, she naturally drifted into movies with small parts from 1917 onwards, until she gained the coveted role of the Princess in the *Thief of Bagdad* (1924) with Douglas Fairbanks. After that, she travelled to Europe and made some films in London and Berlin, before resuming her career in Hollywood through to 1930. Throughout she had the advantage of also being able to continue a career as a professional dancer. For example, in early 1930 she teamed up with Danny Dowling, a handsome, film extra man and professional dancer, and they were seen at the Cocoanut Grove and in a hotel in San Francisco. They also gained a contract to appear at the Roosevelt Hotel but Dowling fell in rehearsals, and an x-ray revealed he would never dance again[33]

Left: A portrait of Julanne Johnston, late 1920s

By late 1931 Johnston had teamed up with Charles Baron and danced in the Blossom Room of the Hotel Roosevelt and appeared in a stage show called *Chevalier Impressions* at the Paramount Theatre.[34]

Dreamy and imaginative she liked jazz and parties and was a social butterfly with many high profile friends in the movie industry and was closest with the actresses Colleen Moore and Virginia Valli (the latter married Charles Farrell and moved to Palm Springs where they became firm social fixtures and popularised the resort).

In early March 1932, Julanne Johnston teamed up with the Rocky Twins. Girlish, quaint and lovely, Johnston would have made a beautifully decorous dancing partner. The trio offered a series of spectacular dance numbers in the Garden room of the Biltmore Hotel for their Tuesday night dance parties. The Biltmore opened in 1923 and had become another grand, and iconic landmark in Los Angeles and its various function rooms became an important rendezvous in the Hollywood social scene.[35]

Although no other credits are forthcoming, it must be a foregone conclusion that due to Johnston's extensive contacts the trio danced in other nightspots in Los Angeles over the next couple of months. Since she was well connected with an extensive social circle, she would have indeed introduced the twins to many leading Hollywood celebrities.

In April 1932, the Rocky Twins appeared on the vaudeville bill of the famous Paramount theatre in Los Angeles.[36] The Paramount Theatre opened in 1923 as Grauman's Metropolitan Theatre and was built by impresario Sid Grauman, best remembered for his two movie palaces, Grauman's Chinese Theatre and Grauman's Egyptian Theatre. It was the largest movie theatre ever built in Los Angeles but was acquired by the exhibition arm of Paramount Pictures in 1924 and renamed in 1929.

The theatre was located at 6th and Hill Streets, one block west of Broadway, where most of the city's major theatres were located. In August 1931 it was relinquished from the Paramount chain and came under the umbrella of the independent picture house circuit called Hughes-Franklin ran by Harold B. Franklin (former president of the Fox-West coast circuit) and Howard Hughes. It didn't last long, and by late 1931 it had disbanded, and Franklin devoted himself to the Paramount and one other Los Angeles theatre, and at the same time became general manager of RKO-Radio.

In the spring of 1932 Franklin experimenting with different types of stage shows at the Paramount and finally, on 21st April he gave a more typical variety line-up. The opening was a bacchanale act with Leo Danny as a satyr, Isabel Mack and 16 nymphs followed by Takiami, a Japanese top spinner, a female trio billed as Three Shades of Blue working around a piano and an adagio quartet called the Olympic Four.

The Rocky Twins did a song in French that, according to *Variety*, meant nothing but the routine of mirror gestures kept it from dragging. They followed this by a matched stepping routine of the continental type and a finale with faster eccentric steps.[37] Whether the week at the Paramount was the total of their vaudeville experience at this time is not known as no further listings can be found.

There was another suggestion that about this time they may have also performed in cabaret at the Ship Café in Venice beach, which was regarded as the most unique beach resort in the world. The author Mark A. Vieira claimed that they had become the 'establishment's celebrated drag act' and that MGM's British director Edmund Goulding, who was a regular habitué, decided on seeing them perform, that he wanted the twins in his forthcoming movie *Blondie of the Follies*.[38]

Above: The exterior of the Ship Cafe on Venice Beach
Below: The interior of the Ship Cafe on Venice Beach

Baron Long's Ship Café was built in 1905 and fashioned after a Spanish galleon. It featured high priced cuisine and booze during prohibition, private salons on the second deck and staff dressed as 16th-century naval officers. After a period of closure in the early 1930s, it was re-opened by Tommy Jacobs in April 1932, and it still retained its original allure as a top Hollywood nightspot. The situation with Goulding was in fact slightly more complicated in the sense that what Vieira didn't know was that MGM had the twins under contract and so it might have been incumbent on Goulding to use them.

At last, after what must have been over 6 months of languishing in the sun and socialising, the twins were finally cast in the Marion Davies movie *Blondie of the Follies*. Planning began in the spring and filming took place during June-July with a release on 21st September 1932. At the time, Goulding, 'a sensitive, dedicated craftsman'[39] was riding high on the success of *Grand Hotel*, but his tenure at MGM was strange since Louis B. Meyer did not approve of him and yet he was admired and promoted by Irving Thalberg.

Goulding also harboured dark secrets since he was rumoured to be homosexual and a voyeur, tendencies that eventually got him into hot water. To disguise his various proclivities, he married the British ballroom dancer Marjorie Moss in November 1931, in what many described as a 'lavender' marriage of convenience.[40]

Blondie of the Follies was a backstage musical of two showgirls competing for the same man. Blondie (Marion Davies) and Lottie (Billie Dove) are best friends from a New York tenement district. When Lottie joins the cast of a big Broadway show, Blondie follows. But the friendship goes sour when Lottie's sweetheart, wealthy Larry Belmont (Robert Montgomery), falls for Blondie. Since Davies and Dove were ex-Follies girls, they were both familiar with the territory and perfect for their respective roles.

The blonde and beautiful Marion Davies had started out in the chorus of Broadway musicals from 1914 and became a sought-after model. After appearing in the *Ziegfeld Follies of 1916*, she met the newspaper magnate William Randolph Hearst, one of the wealthiest and most powerful men in the country, who was also 30 years her senior and married. Mrs Hearst loathed Davies and refused to divorce.

Davies became Hearst's mistress, and Hearst took control of her professional destiny and created a film production company to make her one of Hollywood's greatest stars. Glamorous, kind and genuinely funny she appeared in numerous silent films and made the transition into sound. But her career as an actress and talented comedienne did suffer from Hearst's overbearing presence.

Goulding was chosen to direct *Blondie of the Follies* because of his charm, diplomacy and knack of dealing with big female stars. He needed all of his skills to deal with Hearst, and the production meetings were tense. There were too many people involved with too many opinions and ultimately everyone was under the control of Hearst who interfered relentlessly with the script and production details. The critics regarded the resulting film as being mediocre.[41]

The twins were under the impression that they were going to have significant parts in the movie in addition to their dancing contribution.[42] In fact, this must have been partly true since a lot of material and scenes were rejected at the planning stage or filmed sequences completely cut. For example at one point,

Goulding planned to introduce a funny routine where Davies (as Blondie) dressed as a Gendarme stops an argument between the Rocky Twins dressed up as girls.[43]

In the end, the Rocky Twins were only seen in one major dance scene with Davies in a pirate routine on stage in the Follies. They were also in a party scene with Davies and Jimmy Durante doing their spoof of *Grand Hotel*, and there was a further brief glimpse as they arrived on the stage in a car with Dove and Davies.

Their dance number in the party scene with Davies was cut, as was a sequence of them with Davies on a boat party and a Follies stage tableaux in a garden square with a fountain, where the twins were on either side of the chorus wearing shorts and feather boas![44]

During filming the Rocky Twins, who were called 'the charming princes of Beverley Hills,' were looked after by Marion Davies and Marjorie Moss (Mrs Goulding).[45] The twins said that Davies, was nice to work with and that she was 'very kind and helpful in every way possible.' She gave them a lot of advice and hints that came to their advantage during the recording of the film. They affirmed that she was indeed full of life and distinctly humorous in her work and in private.[46]

They were also accompanied in their free time and at the studio by the French journalist Rene Guetta described as 'one of the Parisian exiles in California,' who wrote for Marianne and Cinemagazine. He organised events each day for the twins that included giving small cocktail parties and a big dinner with the legendary actor Douglas Fairbanks.[47]

The Rocky Twins observed that film-making in Hollywood was on a larger scale than that in Europe with an abundance of technical aids and excellent equipment. They thought that there were lots of exciting things to see in Hollywood and they believed that the Americans had been very gracious to them and they felt that they had started well.[48]

However, they did say that sooner or later you became accustomed to the fact that a film contract also meant the end of one's private life. But what did a private life matter when you could earn thousands of dollars and have a magnificent house and a swimming pool.[49]

When filming, although she had a 14-room bungalow provided for her on the MGM lot, Marion Davies usually decamped to her 110 room Georgian beach house on the shores of the Pacific Ocean in Santa Monica. Here she would continue entertaining with her usual panache and throw fabulous parties, which must have included the Rocky twins as guests. She also made quick trips to William Randolph Hearst's San Simeon mansion via flights from Clover Field (today's Santa Monica Municipal Airport) to its rural counterpart.[50]

Above: The Rocky Twins and Marion Davies in the Pirate Number from *Blondie of the Follies* (1932)
Courtesy of the Wisconsin Center for Film and Theater Research / Wisconsin Historical Society

Above: The Rocky Twins and Marion Davies in *Blondie of the Follies* (1932)

Once *Blondie of the Follies* was completed in mid-July both Davies and Hearst moved back to their vast mansion located atop a hillside called La Cuesta Encantade (The Enchanted Hill) overlooking the stunning coastline of San Simeon and the Pacific.

Over the next few months, leading up to Christmas 1932, it was not unusual for up to 70 Hollywood guests to appear on the weekend or for more extended visits, transported from the city on Hearst's train[51] The Rocky Twins were frequently on the guest list with at least three known visits.

Immediately after the twins finished the recording of *Blonde of The Follies* they decamped with Marion Davies and, no doubt a vast entourage (one guest was the famous actress Constance Talmadge), to the San Simeon mansion - now often called simply Hearst Castle - for a lengthy three-week stay.[52]

It was a beautiful spot with a great view of the mountains and the ocean and everyone referred to it as the Ranch rather than the Castle. The train would leave Los Angeles at 8.15 pm and arrive at San Luis Obispo at 3 am, and then cars would transport all the rather sleepy guests up to the Ranch. According to the Rocky Twins, tall, netted fences surrounded the estate and all guest were given a unique passport that was inspected by the guards stationed at the entrance.

Some regarded the estate as more ostentatious than Versailles and it contained several large buildings constructed in a Mediterranean Revival style. The main house had 38 bedrooms, and three other annexes contained 20 further bedrooms. In the main house was the Refectory where guests dined under banners from Siena and other French tapestries.

Since Hearst was a passionate art collector the Ranch was 'equipped with an adventurous splendour'[53] containing amazing valuable works of art and other treasures. Lunch was at 2.30 and dinner at 8.30. There were 3 chefs, and the food and service was impeccable. Hearst banned hard liquor at all his parties although cocktails and wine were permitted and some quests would smuggle in alcohol for after dinner drinks in the guest bedrooms. Other rooms were designed for socialising and resting such as the billiard room, morning room and a huge movie screening room

There was a Roman indoor pool decorated with 18-carat gold filled tiles made in Venice and a lavish open-air Neptune pool with an old Grecian temple. There were also extensive gardens, and guests could enjoy a range of outdoor activities including tennis, horse riding, swimming (which the Rocky Twins would have more than enjoyed given their fondness for physical exercise) and sometimes there were picnics at the beach 5 miles up the coast toward San Francisco.

Above and below: Two views of Hearst Castle

The twins thought that the strangest thing in the Ranch was a kind of zoo with a menagerie of lions, tigers, leopards, bears, monkeys, camels, elephants, deer and zebra. They were impressed that the animals lived their natural life in complete freedom behind their respective enclosures, but had vast areas to live on a perfectly natural basis. They did add that as a consequence it could be a paradise for hunters, but only Hearst's very best friends were allowed to do this and only on special occasions.[54]

Regarding Hearst himself, the twins said that he was 'a very gracious and kindhearted man' and that he was 'a bit of an original' and added that he was cool 'as his taste' testified. During their first trip he was only there two days at a time, and while he was there, all his regulations had to be observed.

Before Hearst arrived, he would send a long telegram about what he wanted for dinner and how everything should be arranged, and all guests had to wait for him before eating. Although cocktails and wine were served, Hearst was not happy about overindulgence. According to the twins one night a lady at the table was far too animated, and Hearst immediately ordered the removal all the wine and all the glasses. He was so furious that he ordered the young lady to leave. Drinks were then not served for four days until a telegram from Los Angeles announced that drinks could be served again.[55]

Of course Hollywood was awash with other parties and functions that attracted official recognition in the press, and the Rocky Twins would have been on the guest lists for many of them. For example before their trip to San Simeon they were spotted at a tea party at the home of the screenwriter Polan Banks in early August, and even the famous Hollywood columnist Louella Parsons said you 'cant tell one from the other.'[56] In late September 1932, they were cavorting at tennis and tea in the home of the actress Colleen Moore (a close friend of Julanne Johnston) and Al Scott. Those that went 'athletic' were Kay Johnson, Mary Duncan, Jack Colt and Adeline Schulberg and the Rocky Twins, Julanne Johnston and Jean Malin did not.[57]

One significant news event in early October was that allegedly Leif secured a Swedish divorce from his wife.[58] If this is correct, Leif must have met and very quickly married a young Swedish lady during their tour of Scandinavia in the summer of 1931. In later interviews, it was noted that Leif had married three times and if this report was accurate, this must have been his first of three failed attempts at matrimony.[59]

Besides the official reports of their activities, there were the unofficial 'secret' parties. Some were alluded to at the time, but many have only been discussed in recent years. Underneath the so-called layer of respectability was another of sexual experimentation and wild excess. As the film industry grew Hollywood became a magnet for artistic talent such as actors, writers, directors, designers and other cinematic technicians. Most of the talent came from Broadway and Europe and according to the writers Lilian Faderman and Stuart Timmons 'they were accustomed to bohemian living unconfined by the narrow sexual strictures' and 'valued nonconformity and adventurous experimentation.' As a result, they mainly had a fluid view of sexuality and gender.[60]

The fabled writer and socialite Mercedes de Acosta said 'when I was in Hollywood (in the 1930s) it was considered a wild and, in a manner speaking, a morally 'lost' place. The whole world thought of it as a place of mad nightlife, riotous living, sexual orgies…. uncontrolled extravagances, unbridled love affairs and in a word – SIN.'[61]

Actually, de Acosta was wrong. Those in the know, like herself, could see that Hollywood was wild and perhaps morally lost but overall Hollywood's sexual libertarianism, extravagances and excesses were usually well hidden from the outside world. A mask had been created to keep all these secrets secret, and many of its players had learned to play the 'movie game' by creating more conventional public images as a smokescreen. Marriages of convenience or girlfriends, both for publicity purposes, disguised sexual freedom and open arrangements. Allegedly, one such prominent couple was the actor Edmund Lowe and his wife, Lilyan Tashman. However, many rebels refused to conform, and some like William Haines later suffered the consequences.[62]

De Acosta may have already been in the frame of the life of the Rocky Twins at the time because she had brought the dancer Marjorie Moss to Hollywood. Shortly after her arrival, Moss married the director Edmund Goulding, in one of these arrangements. De Acosta, who was quite upfront about her sexuality, had been involved with several prominent women including the actresses Alla Nazimova and Eva Le Gallienne and the dancer Isadora Duncan. In 1931 she met Greta Garbo and was close to her through 1932, but the exact nature of their relationship is still debatable.

Edmund Goulding's home became an unofficial club-house for British expats, mostly notable homosexuals, like his friends Noel Coward, Ivor Novello and Cecil Beaton. When he married Marjorie Moss on 28th November 1931, Ivor Novello was staying with him, and he gave the bride away since he was also an old friend of Marjorie's. Cecil Beaton stayed with them in early 1932, and this is where Beaton met Greta Garbo. Although Goulding and Moss lived together for a while in his Spanish style house in North Linden Drive, Beverley Hills, Goulding rented another place on Angelo Drive where he lived separately from his wife.[63] According to E.J. Fleming, Goulding was 'a sex addict and dedicated voyeur' who hosted weekly parties comprising a wide cross-section of participants.[64] His Angelo Drive house 'became the site of notorious clandestine orgies'[65] where both men and women would 'cavort in all-night revelries.'[66]

His rather bizarre social life did cause some consternation to many, but Goulding tried to be careful, and his discrete plan of marriage was useful camouflage at first, but then everything backfired, and one incident threatened to expose his secrets. Since the Rocky Twins were involved with Goulding and his extensive entourage they must have been aware if not involved in some of his activities.

Sometime in September 1932, Goulding staged one of his parties but as a result, two women were injured in a manner that recalled the ugly circumstances of the Fatty Arbuckle affair, and they ended up in hospital.

The story was 'so filthy' it couldn't be printed. But the women intended to press charges and reveal the names of the other participants, which allegedly included several MGM stars. To contain the crisis, Irving Thalberg asked Goulding to leave town, and he and his wife immediately went to London. He did not return until the matter had blown over, the women and police got paid off, and the necessary arrangements made with District Attorney Baron Fitts.[67]

Of course, this was an extreme event, and other well-known homosexuals gave their own parties at home that did not create such a furore. For example, the gourmet cook and MGM scenarist, Edgar Allan Woolf, who was described by MGM story editor Samuel Marx, as a 'wild, red-haired homosexual' was never happier than when his home was filled with guests. His Saturday night party-guests were a hodge-potch of stars, producers, writers, directors and new Hollywood settlers.

In one party in July 1932, he turned his patio into a peach orchard with boughs of peach blossom and outdoor dining. There was a considerable celebrity guest list including such luminaries as Grace la Rue, Mr and Mrs Stromberg, Mr and Mrs Louis B. Mayer, Mr and Mrs Edmund Goulding, Chico Marx, Theda Bara, Charles Brabin, Ernst Lubitsch, Ramon Novarro, Jeannette MacDonald and many others.[68]

The actor William Haines, the director George Cukor and the costume designer Howard Greer for example, also hosted parties like that of Edgar Allan Woolf with a mix of guests from all parts of society and not just Hollywood celebrities. But in each case, these parties would evolve as the night wore on, and often later, they became just a gay male oasis.

There were also other evenings that were explicitly a gay social outlet in a safe haven. These parties also created career opportunities for young men who were gay or playing gay that were capable of the utmost discretion. If you talked, the doors were closed. This was a well-known rule in tinsel-town 'when you've been in Hollywood long enough, you'll learn that Hollywood lives in a glass house and so doesn't throw stones. The eyes of the world are on this place. No one can afford to exploit their grievances openly.'[69] The producer Joseph Mankiwiecz said gays flocked to Cukor's parties because 'George was their access to the crème of Hollywood'.[70]

Although not 'A' list Hollywood celebrities, the Rocky Twins did have an MGM contract, they had connections with the 'A' list via Edmund Goulding, Marion Davies and Julanne Johnston and they also had the added benefit of youth (they were at the time only 23), good looks and fluid sexuality. With these advantages, they must have been able to gain access to many of the official social affairs and the unofficial private parties.

Left: A portrait of the female impersonator Francis Renault
Courtesy of J.B. Doyle Archives

By September 1932, Hollywood nightlife had taken a dramatic turn as the new Pansy Craze that had begun in the spring, erupted with full vigour in several locations for the autumn season. The underlying permissiveness and sexual freedom that pervaded the Hollywood elite found full expression in these nightclubs and cafes. At the same time some of the movie studios began to incorporate effeminate and fairy-like characters in their films and as Daniel Hurewitz pointed out by 1933 'homosexuality was alluded to more often than at anytime before.'[71]

Described as the 'whoops' or 'oo-la-la' phenomenon, the penchant for watching female impersonators had continued through the summer of 1932 with the pansy floor-show at BBB's. Here there was a line up of 10 guys in drag and individual performers like the prima donna Loyce Trent, but the high spot was still the clowning around of BBB himself.[72]

It was thought that the craze would build up and last over the winter even though it had already been and gone in most Eastern cities.

Indeed, in July and August 1932, the famous female impersonator Francis Renault appeared at EuJean Stark's Bohemina Café on Santa Monica Boulevard, followed by the Dome on Ocean Park, a week at the Pantages Theatre and a month at BBB's.[73]

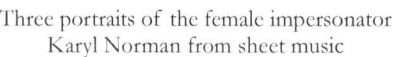

Three portraits of the female impersonator Karyl Norman from sheet music

In mid-September, there were two new openings with another sensational female impersonator Karyl Norman opening at La Boheme and Jean Malin at the Hotel Christie in what was called Club New Yorker along with the Rocky Twins. Also, the bawdy Rae Bourbon worked in drag at Jimmy's Back Yard and BBB's.[74]

La Boheme on Sunset Boulevard (later to become the Café Trocadero), just across the city border-line in the country, comprised a compact and atmospheric room with a capacity of 350 and staged one of the smartest and most entertaining floor-shows seen in Los Angeles for a long time.

Karyl Norman was seen in his 'Creole Fashion Plate' in three sections displaying his usual elegant, feminine attire and led a chorus of 6 girls with several other principals including La Verde, another female impersonator, who did the rumba. The show was admired because even though Norman was a female impersonator, it displayed nothing of the 'pansy' flavour. Showing grace and agility, Norman was classy and inoffensive in contrast to many other more bawdy performers. [75]

By far the biggest splash was made at the newly named Club New Yorker, which was formerly the Greenwich Village Café, situated in the basement of a building adjacent to the Christie Hotel, at 6724 Hollywood Boulevard. Run by Bernie Hyman formerly of BBB's Cellar, it was a dazzling new cafe in futuristic black and silver that promised to become a new gathering place for the great and near-great of the motion picture world.

The Christie Hotel was Hollywood's first deluxe high rise hotel built in 1923 and closest to all the Hollywood studios and swiftly became a well-known landmark and its grill room and cocktail bar a firm favourite with the movie colony. Marlene Dietrich and her husband Joe Seiber dined there, and Gloria Swanson was a frequent visitor[76]

With a cosy capacity of 250, Club New Yorker, opened mid-September with Jean Malin as Master-of-Ceremonies, dressed in top hat and tails and a red rose in his buttonhole, with the Rocky Twins and Julanne Johnston leading the floor-show. Sophisticated and attractive, the place lived up to its name providing class entertainment and atmosphere with New York prices ($2 cover charge) and entertainment, and was 'the most authentic touch of New York...since Mayor Jimmy Walker dropped into town.'[77]

Left An advert for
Hotel Christie, Hollywood

Left: the exterior of the Club New Yorker, Hollywood, 1933

Below: the interior of the Club New Yorker, Hollywood, 1933

Courtesy of Bison Archives and Hollywood HistoricPhotos.com

Above: Jean Malin (left) in *Arizona to Broadway* (Fox 1933)
Courtesy of J.B. Doyle Archives

Jean Malin was a big success with his wisecracks and flip remarks, but he also took up half of the floor-show with his female impersonations. Malin was regarded as a class entertainer who showed the local café performers how it should be done and sang, danced and thrust sharp, cutting, witticisms at the cream of Hollywood. Malin was at his best being fed his lines by the likes of Jack Oakie, Polly Moran and William Haines.

The Rocky Twins, described as clever entertainers, were dressed as girls in one number and seen as pretty and dainty. Most of the time they danced with Julanne Johnston, who was thought to be beautiful but mostly decoration, although their dancing together was admired as being quite graceful. Other performers included the torch singer Eddie Adams, who worked alternately in male and female garb; Mona Ray, James Blair and Hal Wayne's 11-piece band furnished the music.

There was also a young 16-year-old Betty Grable, who was a great tap dancer with loads of personality and she became friends with the Rocky Twins. Grable, later to become the No.1 pin-up girl of the World War II era, had moved to Hollywood two years before and had appeared in the chorus line of Fox films and Goldwyn's pictures before joining RKO in 1932. After her appearance in Club New Yorker, she joined the cast of the stage show *Treasure Ships* at the Los Angeles Paramount Theatre.[78]

Club New Yorker hit the big time especially with the smart Hollywood set and the picture crowd. It was jammed nightly with celebrities who shrieked with delight at Jean Malin's quips, and one-night, notable guests included Marguerite Churchill dancing with Ricardo Cortez, Mary Brian and Dick Powell, Alice White and Cy Bartlett, Ben Lyon and Bebe Daniels, Joan Blondell and George Barnes, Madge Evans and Tom Galley.[79]

During the run of the show at Club New Yorker, the Rocky Twins gained high praise for their dancing of the Zwel Hertzen with Julanne Johnston described as 'the loveliest thing in motion.'[80]

The twins were also asked to perform as part of a special entertainment at the Masquers Club on 16th October 1932 and scored a big hit with their dancing. Located in a converted building at 1765 Sycamore Avenue, the Masquers Club was a private social venue for actors in Los Angeles created in 1925 by actors from New York City who had left Broadway to act in motion pictures.[81] At this time Paal Rocky was seen in the company of Kitty Curtiz (aged 17) at the opening of the new supper club – the Biltmore Garden Room - fuelling rumours of a romance.[82]

Kitty was the daughter of the Hungarian born film director Michael Curtiz and actress Lucy Doraine and was worldly-wise but troubled. She was 'highly nervous and highly strung' as a result of a confused childhood having been farmed out to nannies, convents and boarding school. She had grown up under the erratic parenting of her mother in Europe and had moved to Hollywood to be with her father in 1930, but he was equally indifferent to her upbringing. She had been excited about beginning a new life in America, but her enthusiasm quickly faded.

She later said 'that happiness all but dissipated as soon as I learned my way around Hollywood. It was not the life I desired: on the one hand, the strenuous, fast-paced work, on the other hand, the excessive partying, and in that gap between the two, there is barely a break, a pause. I'd love to live a life more profound, more humane.' In 1933 she returned to Europe to try and establish a career for herself away from both parents, but two suicide attempts represented an unsurprising cry for help[83]

Despite all the fun and frivolity and the attractions of the Pansy Craze, the depression triggered a reactionary mood from the establishment against homosexuality that was viewed as evil.[84] The vice squad began to clamp down, and at the beginning of October 1932, there was a double raid on BBB's cellar and Jimmie's Back Yard, that was reported as an assault 'on the Nance and lesbian amusement places'. Bobby Burns Berman and Ray Wright (the manager of BBB's cellar) were charged with a violation of the prohibition act and released on $1,500 bail, and 7 patrons were also arrested on charges of being drunk and possessing liquor. Thomas B. Gannon proprietor of the Back Yard was charged with liquor possession and maintaining a nuisance.

The Pansy Craze was not closed down entirely by the police raids. Jean Malin continued at the Club New Yorker in a new edition of the floor-show from the end of November but minus the Rocky Twins.[86] Perhaps because of the police raids, BBB changed its show and the Boys Will be Girls revue was sent elsewhere. In its place, BBB presented a new show headed by the great mimic and imitator Fred Monroe directly from New York in mid-December.

Monroe's style was perhaps less bawdy as he was described as being clean minded and refined and gave numerous clever impersonations of the stars of stage and screen in an all-star variety show. A large number of famous film celebrities were in the opening night audience, and Monroe even imitated Jean Malin and Karyl Norman who were both there.[87]

In late 1932 the Twins were asked if they wanted to continue filming and they answered that they were still under contract to MGM and had not made a final decision. Perhaps after *Blondie of the Follies* MGM had further plans for them. But at the same time, Paramount Studios were discussing using them and most likely trying to arrange a loan of their services from MGM. They had also become friends with the striking blonde Norwegian film actress Greta Nissen, and they were discussing the possibility of doing something together.

Nissen was three years older than the twins and had started as a dancer but came to prominence in some Danish silent movies before she visited New York in a Danish ballet group. She appeared in several Paramount Pictures and on Broadway in *Beggar in Horseback* (1924) and the Ziegfeld revue *No Foolin* (1926) before being signed to Fox in 1927. By late 1932 her contract at Fox had expired, and Nissen had ditched her first husband, actor Weldon Heyburn. This might explain why she was keen to do something different. Nissen joined the agency Lyons, and Lyons[88] and the plan was to go on tour with the Rocky Twins as dancing partners and visit some of the more prominent cities in America. But they could not be too far from Los Angeles because the twins needed to be able to come back to film two movies, one of which was a big revue film that Paramount was planning with the twins acting and dancing.[89]

Right: A portrait of Greta Nissen from the early 1930s, Hollywood

For some reason, MGM kept the Rocky Twins on the payroll for a long time seemingly relinquishing their contract in late 1932. Following completion of *Blondie of the Follies*, it became apparent that their prime reason for being in Hollywood – to engage in foreign talkies – had evaporated. The foreign talkie films that MGM had made had not done well, and a lot of money had been lost.[90] Part of the problem for foreign language films was that European countries instigated a quota system that effectively caused havoc to distribution.[91]

In August 1932 Arthur Loew at MGM announced that it would discontinue the filming of all foreign language pictures upon the completion of 10 foreign versions currently in production as a protest against the quota laws and other restrictions on the exporting of their American films. At the same time, the development of the less expensive practice of dubbing took over. Loew claimed that hundreds of foreign players would be thrown out of work within the next few weeks. This may have included the Rocky Twins.[92]

When Leif was interviewed in 1963 about his stay in Hollywood, the journalist claimed that he had heard a few times that the Rocky Twins did not have any character or personality. He argued that it was not exactly that way. 'In their own safe environment at home in Norway, they probably would have done well. But they did not live in their own safe environment. On the contrary, they ended up in an environment where if you wanted to make it you had to be made of stone and whatever you could say about the boys - stones they were not. It is admirable that they took their work as seriously as they did. Even though they could drink to the early morning, take part in late night parties they continued with a really strenuous training programme, which is a good example of strong character and virtue.'[93] However, the journalist at the same time said that they had become 'conceited and full of themselves.' They had taken both the fame and big income as something natural and believed that fate had chosen them for greatness.[94]

Despite that fact that they were conscientious and maintained their training programme, their failure to appear in one single foreign language film and their only film appearance in *Blondie of the Follies* meant that their MGM contract was a huge disappointment.

Whatever the reasons for their failure - language, unsuitable character, limited range and acting ability and the fact that probably MGM did not know what to do with them - it was thought that they had reached their peak and were now in decline. A few years later, a press report said that they had 'failed to make the grade' in Hollywood.[95] In short, they did not have the breakthrough that they so earnestly sought and somewhat arrogantly believed they deserved. As the Norwegian foreign diplomat in Paris - Fritz Wedel Jarlsberg – once feared - the black orchids had started to wilt and fade.[96]

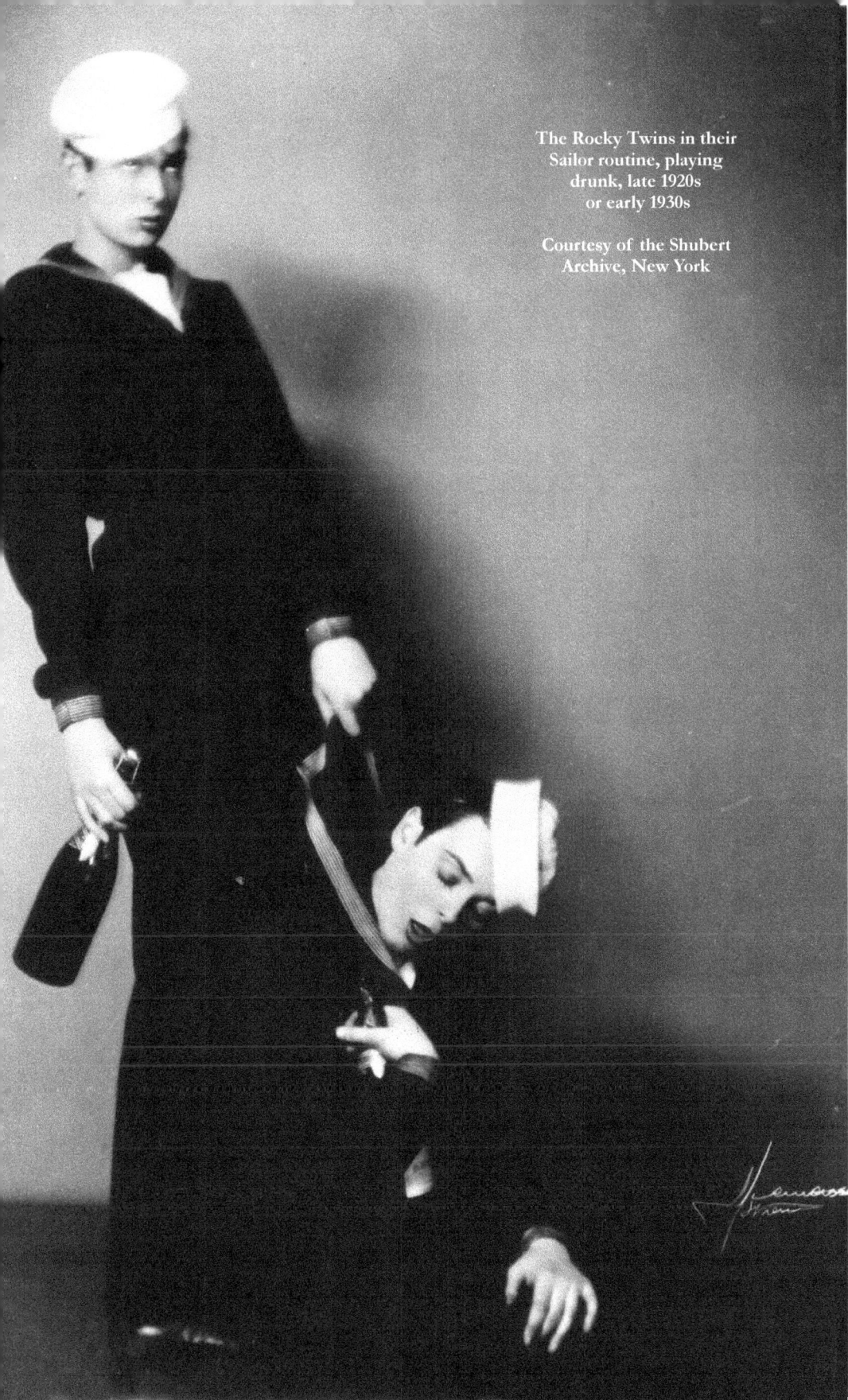

The Rocky Twins in their Sailor routine, playing drunk, late 1920s or early 1930s

Courtesy of the Shubert Archive, New York

CHAPTER SEVEN
LARRY HART AND LOW AND BEHOLD
1932-1933

Instead of appearing in the second edition of Jean Malin's floor-show at Club New Yorker, the Rocky Twins skipped off for a break with Marion Davies and William Randolph Hearst to San Simeon at the end of November 1932. Described as a Christmas party, guests included Charlie Chaplin, Mary Pickford, Norma Shearer and Greta Garbo.[1]

In later years Paal would say that Hearst did not tolerate his private life being mentioned. When someone spoke about Hearst, it was in the same way as talking about Hitler in Germany before the second world war - softly and carefully as if there were a dying man in the room next door. Paal claimed that at this time, Leif said a somewhat innocent remark about San Simeon to a correspondent from the Paris Soir and a few days later they were dismissed from MGM (Hearst's own private production company Cosmopolitan films was part of Metro) indicating that Hearst was not happy.

This story is likely an embellishment on Paal's behalf. There were no interviews in Paris Soir nor any of the French press about San Simeon at this time. MGM simply released the Rocky Twins from their contract as they could not find something suitable for them to do and the original reason for their contract had ended. Equally, if Hearst was unhappy with them in late 1932 why did he invite them to San Simeon in early 1933?

Paal did recount, rather amusingly that at dinner the most beautiful women in the world displayed their jewels and expensive toilettes and their gowns were so low cut, both in back and front, that one saw almost everything of everything. At the table, Leif was sat next to an unknown beauty - but a very forward blonde, named Sandra Rambeau.

It was whispered that she was seen daily in Chaplin's Rolls-Royce. She had never had a part in a Chaplin film but played the leading role on board his luxury yacht for several short weeks, until another blonde and now brunette, Miss Paulette Goddard, took over. Rambeau, who became known as an international glamour girl, led a colourful life and moved through an American playboy, a royal prince of England, a Hindu prince, a French-Argentine multi-millionaire, the president of Mexico and General von Epp, Nazi super-strategist.

Paal was also disparaging of his Hollywood sojourn. 'I was pumped full of stories that Hollywood is not as bad as its reputation. Nonsense and baloney. It is much worse.' After the dinner, he lay the next morning with a cold-water compress over his forehead and felt as if he had come as far out in the world as he would like to. He longed for the anonymous fellowship of little quiet Oslo and a Christmas with hobgoblins and lead cake instead of a Hollywood Christmas without all the glistening diamonds and firecrackers. But this was America Paal said 'the symbol of the worse and the best, the most naive and the most fanatic.'[2]

Paal was not the only one to be critical of tinsel town, and Max Gordon, who had been associated with the Rocky Twins in late 1931 also spent some time in Hollywood and said 'there was an insularity among its inhabitants, a remoteness from the realities of life and an overindulgence in luxury.'[3]

On their return from Hearst Castle in early December, the Rocky Twins appeared with Julanne Johnston in a charity show organised by the Los Angeles Examiner and staged at the Shrine Auditorium on 15th December. It was a mammoth undertaking including a Fanchon and Marco revue, Bebe Daniels, Ben Lyon, Tom Mix, Barbara Stanwyck, Frank Fay, Wheeler and Woolsey, Billie Dove, Jackie Cooper and dozens more stars. Shortly afterwards they began rehearsals for their first stage show on the West Coast in Felix Young's *Tattle Tales*. This contract for a legitimate stage show did indeed indicate that MGM had just terminated their movie contract enabling them to do something more substantial.[4]

Felix Young had a chequered history and was hardly reliable or consistent. He had started off as a performer and then turned to stage and cabaret production. At one time he was part owner of Ciro's nightclub in New York (1925), but he was also a casting agent and in 1926 entered the Picture business and looked after Paramount's stock company. In 1928 he was arrested on fraud charges.[5]

Young was a gambler and lived the high-life. He was once described as 'a dandy with a breezy but polished style' and he 'could sweet talk a cardinal out of his red hat.'[6] From the late 1920s to early 1930s, he flitted from stage production, film production and casting. But despite his foibles, Young was a good showman had assembled a glittering array of talent for his lavish and extravagant 'sophisticated musical revue' *Tattle Tales*. Young had great plans for the show and hoped its success would make it a national institution like *Earl Carroll's Vanities*.[7]

The star of the show was Frank Fay, who not only performed his routines but was also the Master-of-Ceremonies. Fay was a popular variety artist and comedian with a risqué humour. But he was also well-known for his abrasive personality, and was dismissive and unpleasant and disliked by most of his peers. Fay was also an alcoholic and had a troubled marriage to the actress Barbara Stanwyck.[8]

There were 125 featured artists in the show that included Janet Reade (singing star of Ziegfeld's, *Whoopee* and *Hot Cha*), Guy Robertson (noted tenor of Broadway musical and operatic hits) Miller and Black, Florence Robinson, The Three Blue Blazes, Don Cummings, Luis Arnold, Nick Copeland, the 20 jubilee singers and a chorus of 32. Grace Poggi, who had achieved recognition in *The Kid From Spain*, danced with the Rocky Twins. The twins were seen as 'good-looking boys' and were 'shrewd enough to finish their so-so dancing with high kicks and spectacular bits to good reaction.'[9] Another noted addition was a 16-year-old Betty Grable who had already worked alongside the Rocky Twins in the Club New Yorker show and was seemingly enamoured with Paal. Although Grable was very young, Paal made it clear in later interviews that he was romantically involved with Grable at the time and went so far as to say that they were 'almost engaged' and were together for a few months.[10]

Given, the strange and volatile combination of two difficult characters with Young and Fay, it was probably a foregone conclusion that it was not going to be a smooth ride. *Tattle Tales* previewed in Santa Barbara at the Lobero Theatre 3 days before the opening in Los Angeles. It was meant to open at the Belasco Theatre on Christmas day 1932, but it was delayed for 4 days. It was, however, well received as 'the best west-coast revue presented in the past five years'[11] and 'the best show of its kind that has been staged here in several seasons, made so because it has plenty of clever people, some exceptionally good numbers and the ever-resourceful Frank Fay as its stellar personality.'[12]

Sure enough, problems emerged. Fay was drinking heavily and following arguments Fay was replaced and stayed out of the show for 2 weeks. But when the show moved to the Hollywood Playhouse on 14th January 1933 for two weeks, Fay returned and effectively took over as producer and added Stanwyck.

The dancer Nitza Vernille was also added to the cast and was matched with the Rocky Twins, and they did an exotic waltz together. Although Variety reported in mid-January that Paal Rocky was at the Good Samaritan Hospital for treatment of jaundice, the show did go on, and somehow Paal continued. *Tattle Tales* then went to the Curran Theatre in San Francisco, but Fay's drinking was so out of hand he couldn't appear. Eventually, Stanwyck closed the show.[13]

After the escapades of *Tattle Tales,* the Rocky Twins relocated to San Simeon to see Marion Davies and William Randolf Hearst again. Over one weekend the correspondent of Le Matin, was a guest with 50-60 others including the French screenwriter and director, Harry Abadie of D'arrast, Douglas Fairbanks, Princess of Kapurthala (who had been a Spanish flamenco dancer and singer who married the Indian Maharaja of Kapurthala in 1908) and the businessman and navigator Baron Empain. Another guest was the suave and debonair actor Adolphe Menjou along with someone he called 'his new wife.' But Menjou married Verree Teasdale in late 1934, so perhaps she was there and being discretely touted as the next Mrs Menjou.[14]

The Twins in the meantime teamed up with the blond, statuesque beauty Nitza Vernille following their pairing in *Tattle Tales*. Vernille had been born in Alameda, San Francisco in 1902 with the name Eunice and so was 7 years senior to the twins and had already enjoyed an illustrious career. In 1920 she won a popularity contest in San Francisco for the most beautiful subject for motion pictures and was allegedly given a role in a Mildred Harris Chaplin picture.[15] But dancing was her primary interest, and in 1921 she appeared in cabaret at Tait's restaurant in San Francisco. She was described as tall, beautiful and graceful.[16]

After that, Vernille toured in vaudeville and cabaret and appeared in the Shubert show *Spice of 1922* and John Cort's *Go Go* (1923) and *Sharlee* (1923).[17] In 1925 she signed to play 15 weeks on the Orpheum Vaudeville Circuit and 25 in the Keith-Albee houses.[18] After more vaudeville tours she went to London in late 1928 to appear in the *Lilac Domino* and also danced at Verrey's restaurant in cabaret.[19]

Nitza Vernille in the late 1920s

From London, Vernille went to France and danced with Jack Holland, first at the Casino Municipal in Cannes[20] and then in a Paramount stage show in Paris.[21] On returning to New York, she teamed with Cesar Romero at Charlie Journal's Montmartre Club[22] and then migrated west back to California where in late 1932 she was part of a floor-show at Lee Moore's Frolics Café, where she became a 'sensation nightly.'[23]

Like their other partner, Julanne Johnston, Nitza Vernille was a perfect choice since she was a very experienced dancer and apparently had a good reputation and contacts. The twins had also met Vernille in Paris when she was dancing with Jack Holland at the Paramount theatre in 1929 – perhaps in May after their return from London and before they went home to Oslo.[24]

The three dancers became the highlight of a new vaudeville show staged by Ben Black called *Tip Top* that was staged at the Golden Gate Theatre in San Francisco in mid-March 1933 and may well have toured for a while in the area. The show also comprised 8 chorus girls, Claudia Coleman (impressions), Boyce Coombs, Allen Bernard and Stewart (a piano act), Nathan Stewart (baritone singer) and the Olympic Four (a mixed acrobatic combo).[25] A reporter from Paris treated their appearance in vaudeville with some disdain claiming they had appeared in a second-rate cinema, five times a day with a whole troupe where they were not even the stars. As a result, it was thought they were losing their magical allure.[26]

The engagement did not last long because by early April the twins were back in Hollywood. The usual night-spots in Los Angeles continued unabated with the favourite spots of the Ambassadors (Cocoanut Grove), Roosevelt Hotel Patio Roof, The Biltmore Garden Room, Stark's Bohemian Café, The Paris Inn, Sebastian's Cotton Club and The Frolics Garden leading the way [27]

The Pansy Craze, that had flowered in 1932, but had been disrupted by the vice squad and the police in late 1932, seemingly continued unabated. One new venue was the Hollywood Barn that had opened in late 1932 and where the novel décor made you think you were in a barn. Situated at Cahuenga and Sunset Boulevards, the Barn was the brainchild of the famous band-leader Buddy Fisher, and on 11th February 1933 Jimmie Holmes staged the *Topsy Turvy Revue* with 20 men and women in a 'modern masquerading novelty' that offered 'one of the freakiest and most novel shows in town.'[28] It was most definitely a girls will be boys and boys will be girls variety show and it was thought that suggestiveness and overacting could have easily spoiled it but maintained a good balance of fun and was, therefore, a unique show that ran for several months.[29]

At about the same time Frank Sebastian's Cotton Club engaged another female impersonator called Leon Le Verde who became the centre-piece of a series of shows that ran through early 1933.[30] Le Verde gave imitations of famous women of the stage and screen and wearing striking costumes was described as 'the greatest female impersonator in the business' and moved in May 1933 to Club Ballyhoo and danced with Maxine Lewis.[31]

In the meantime the ever popular 'gay' hangout BBBs cellar, which had been raided in late 1932, reverted to a 'girlie' show called *Cellarettes* in February 1933 with 8 chorus girls and BBB acting as MOC but also giving new songs and dances and Jean Malin providing some impromptu stuff.[32] However, by April 1933 BBB went into the show at the Barn,[33] and his Cellar went back to its old ways with Ray Bourbon and a new pansy revue.[34] This show was transplanted to Tait's Café in San Francisco in May 1933[35] but suffered four nightly raids from 'great big gorgeous policeman', and 7 members of the troupe including Rae Bourbon were carted off to jail. The police raids threatened to close Tait's, so the show was abandoned.[36]

The intimidation and police harassment did not deter specific cafes from continuing with the vogue for female impersonation, and some got away with it while others did not. The most prominent opening was in April 1933 at the Club New Yorker with Jean Malin and the Rocky Twins, although whether Malin and the Rocky Twins performed in drag is not clear. The show that opened 6th April was called *New Yorker Nites*, and the twins danced once again with Julanne Johnston. Other acts included Doris Roche, Gloria Gilbert (star of *Ballyhoo* and appearing at the Chinese Theatre), Johnny Kindo (a sensational accordionist) and Ted Dahl and his orchestra providing the dance music.[37]

During the run of the show, there was a comedy of errors when the Rocky Twins were stopped by the police one night for double parking and were arrested since they didn't have a driving license and no proof that the car they were driving was their own. They were also unable to satisfy the police officers about why they had a large quantity of jewellery and a lot of women's clothes in the car. So they were yanked off to jail and kept there overnight. The jewellery was theirs, but the clothes belonged to their dancing partner Julanne Johnston, or so we are told, but perhaps some were theirs.[38]

However, the show did not last more than a month because by mid May, Barnett Hyman, the owner, was declared bankrupt and Club New Yorker closed.[39] In the meantime, Jean Malin was signed by MGM to appear in the Joan Crawford vehicle *Dancing Lady* [40] and popped up in May at the Barn in another cross-dressing revue.[41]

One significant person that loomed large in the life of the Rocky Twins during their stay in Hollywood was the lyricist Larry (Lorenz) Hart part of the famous songwriting duo of Rodgers and Hart based in New York.

Hart was a complex character. Short at 5 foot tall, he felt physically unattractive and concealed his true feelings by being exuberant and wild so that outward humour masked his inner turmoil. Hart was intelligent, witty, generous to a fault and a complete charmer, but he was also restless, nervous, impatient and uncontrollable. With a cherubic, pixie-like face he liked to indulge in little private jokes. For some, he was the saddest man because they thought that he felt lonely in the crowds that he sought and collected. He was, it would appear, also at odds with his homosexuality, but loved going out and partying to the early hours and drank heavily.[42]

Richard Rodgers and Larry Hart arrived in Hollywood from New York in November 1931 after signing a contract with Paramount and set about writing the songs for the next Maurice Chevalier, and Jeannette Macdonald film *Love Me Tonight* (1932). Afterwards, they worked on *Phantom President* and the Al Jolson movie *Hallelujah, I'm a Bum*.[43] At first, Larry lived at Rodger's new home in Beverley Hills, but in May 1932, he rented a property nearby with a 60-foot swimming pool. In no time at all both households were soon on the Hollywood party circuit[44] and Hart was spotted several times at theatrical openings, and felt at home in Hollywood.[45]

Above: Richard Rodgers and Lorenz Hart
Courtesy of Library of Congress Prints and Photographs Division

But by September 1933, the contract with Paramount was not renewed, and they moved to MGM. Here they were assigned to work on the movie *I Married an Angel* designed to be the first Jeannette Macdonald film for MGM. But due to objections about the story by the Hays office, it was abandoned.[46]

Exactly when Hart and the Rocky Twins met is not clear but since they arrived in Hollywood at about the same time – in late 1931 - and gradually visited the same places, especially those venues that catered for a more gay audience like BBBs cellar and Jimmie's Back Yard, not to mention private parties, their paths must have crossed during the period mid to late 1932. Indeed, it has been noted, that Hart loved the Club New Yorker, which was regarded at the time as the 'in' place to go and he was a regular patron from when the first show was staged in September 1932. Hart usually started out the night here, picking up the tab for everyone and often joined the star of the show Jean Malin, and his entourage who accompanied him to his home after the show, where the party continued.[47]

The Rocky Twins must have been part of this 'select' group of night-time revellers, and as Samuel Marx said they 'joined the entourage that accompanied Larry around the town, to the private parties and the late-night clubs. The Rocky twins became closely involved with Larry.'[48]

Just like the Rocky Twins, Hart had two lives attending both the above board parties and social functions and the more overtly gay places and secret parties. He did the social rounds with studio people and mutual friends and because of his reputation doors would have been opened to him. Rodgers and Hart rarely went to same Hollywood parties, but in mid-1933 they were party guests at Ernst Lubitsch's house,[49] and they both enjoyed visiting the home of writer Edgar Allan Woolf. His Saturday night guests were a mix of stars, producers, writers, directors and new arrivals. Hart would often go the parties with his mother and then leave her there while he prowled the late night-spots.[50]

One of Hart's closest friends was also the most colourful and for some the most distasteful. Dr Milton Bender was a graduate of the New York University School of Dentistry but was attracted to the delights of the stage. When he started out in practice, Larry Hart came to his office as a patient and a close friendship developed with Bender giving up his practice to become personal agent for Hart. Later, his association with Hart gave him access to many people he would not have had otherwise. Bender also tried his luck as a theatrical producer and lyricist and worked with Rodgers in 1917 on *One Minute Please*, a benefit show in 1917 and then with Hart in *You'd Be Surprised* in 1920. Later, he also produced a show called *The New Yorkers* in 1927 before he branched out as a theatrical agent of sorts.[51]

Wherever Larry Hart went, Bender followed, and he was soon in Hollywood.[52] Bender was described as a 'strange individual' who was an 'uninhibited swinger of his day' and 'gross.'[53] Leonard Spigelgass added 'he was a kind of comic, also a producer, pimp, arranger. I simply ignored him. To me, he was something slimy, a worm.'[54]

Tall and balding, Bender was also seen as 'a leech and a procurer.' He was unashamed about his homosexuality, but his lifestyle and sexual appetite was labelled as 'debauched' and 'salacious' both rather self-righteous labels and thus a matter of prejudice or perspective. On the other hand, he could have been simply enjoying the pleasures of life. He mixed with a large number of homosexuals both in New York and Hollywood, and this provided a huge appeal to Hart who was always amused by his antics. Hart also had an open invitation to Bender's regular parties at which we are told 'orgiastic sex and perversions were chic' – once again rather sensational and judgemental words.[55] Rodgers and his family, understandably loathed Bender and most of Hart's friends felt the same way. Their aversion was partly due to his overt homosexual lifestyle and the fact that Hart, a most generous man, basically subsided Bender's outgoings in return for obvious diversions.

The Rocky Twins were described at the time as professional dancers usually performing in drag who were 'incredibly handsome identical twins' admired as male courtesans and 'pursued by international swingers of the day.'[56] Actor-dancer Bennett Green said 'they were beautiful boys but absolute madmen' as they loved to play un-funny jokes, phoning people all hours of the night just to annoy them.[57] Many friends of Hart described them as wild, and Irving Eisman said they were both wild and brazen.[58]

Their madcap attitude and love of life made them the toast of a rather bizarre group who loved the Rocky Twins so much that when they performed, they flung diamond jewellery at their feet in the form of rings and bracelets. For some, the twins had become prized possessions. Larry Hart squandered money and gave various people lavish gifts purchased from Tiffany or Cartier and Lee Gershwin (wife of lyricist Ira Gershwin) recalled seeing Hart giving the twins expensive gold cigarette cases. 'How they danced around the room' she remarked.[59]

Irving Eisman insisted that Milton Bender was in love with them, but Hart just thought they were wonderful and took them everywhere enjoying their tremendous notoriety. 'They hit the bars, they hit the clubs, they went to parties.'[60] Of significance, at some point in 1932, the Rocky Twins decided to take Milton Bender on as their theatrical agent.[61]

At the end of 1932, Larry Hart made a new friend with a young producer named Leonard Sillman, who accompanied him on his nightly rounds of all the Hollywood cafes and gay haunts. Sillman was looking for new talent for a revue he was planning that was to be called *Low and Behold*, a show that in the end included the Rocky Twins.[62]

Born in 1908, Sillman was therefore about the same age as the twins and had a lot in common with them. Not only was he energetic, colourful and handsome, but he had also started out as a dancer and was without question homosexual. Sam Irvin

Above: Leonard Sillman in the early 1930s

commented that perhaps he had never been asked if he was homosexual simply because everyone already knew the answer.[63]

Sillman had been obsessed with the stage from an early age and with his distinctive resolve became relentless in his objective of making his way in the theatre. It helped that as a young man he was suave, debonair and self-assured, but for some, his confidence was perhaps too forthright and brash. When he was 12, his family visited Hollywood, and unsurprisingly he was able to meet many movie stars. Three years later he assaulted Broadway and met many of the great producers and became quite the social butterfly mixing with aplomb with the good and the great. He did classes with the dance instructor Ned Wayburn and got small parts in a show produced by Lew Fields and even with Wayburn himself. He then went into vaudeville with Imogene Coca before replacing Fred Astaire in the touring company of *Lady Be Good* and toured in John Murray Anderson's *Greenwich Village Follies*. He did more vaudeville with Frances Gershwin, sister of George and Ira, and appeared in several Broadway shows including *Loud Speaker* (1927), *Merry-Go-Round* (1927), and *Polly* (1929).

Sillman then headed to Hollywood where he taught dance to movie people (including Ruby Keeler), had bit parts in some films and appeared in two stage shows *Temptations* and *Hullabaloo* (1932).[64] He was extraordinarily well connected and acquired an impressive list of celebrity friends from New York and Hollywood that included Tallulah Bankhead and Clifton Webb. As Sillman himself said 'no theatrical celebrity of any stature was safe from my assiduous wooing.'[65] His high-profile parties in his swish Hollywood apartment highlighted his social prowess and status. In mid 1931 he gave a Sunday afternoon tea party for George Gershwin and his brother Ira with guests including the playwright and producer Edgar Selwyn, Julanne Johnston (a friend of the Rocky Twins), Mary Miles Minter, Ramon Novarro (another member of the elite gay Hollywood enclave), Laura La Plante, Grace LaRue, and ZaSu Pitts. There were also the German dancer's Sisters G, the stars of John Murray Anderson's film *King of Jazz*. The Twins had performed with them for nearly 5 months in the Emil Schwarz revue *You Will Laugh! (Sie Werden Lachen)* at the Stadt Theatre in Vienna in 1928/1929 and so would have been on good terms.[66] Given all the connections it is not inconceivable that the Rocky Twins were also present.

In late 1931 Sillman gave a party for actress Dorothy Mackaill who had just returned from Honolulu got her to dance the hula with him and sing native songs. Here the guests included Roman Navarro, Laura La Plante, John Murray Anderson, Carmel Myers, Edgar Allan Woolf, the Sisters G and a host of other Hollywood celebrities.[67] It was interesting that Ramon Novarro was a frequent guest at Sillman's parties. Novarro was at the time – in 1931- one of MGM's biggest box-office stars, but he was another one of the Hollywood heart-throbs that tried to keep his sexuality secret, and he was most definitely gay.[68]

Perhaps Sillman's stage career was floundering. Part of the reason was that he was on the short side at only 5 foot 6 inches tall, and although he made a good juvenile, he had little future as a leading man. According to Charles Walters, he had also been blacklisted because of his volatile temperament and so 'he decided the only way to get a job was to become a producer and hire himself.'[69] Sillman, of course, suggested that it was a natural progression.[70]

By March 1933 Sillman was reported to be assembling the cast for a new type of revue patterned after the original Russian *Chauve Souris* called *Low and Behold* as a gala attraction that was to inaugurate the summer season at the Pasadena Community Playhouse.[71] Rehearsals began in mid-March 1933, but the Rocky Twins were already busy in vaudeville and may not have joined proceedings until later when they began to appear in the new show at Club Yorker in April.

Sillman promised that most of the cast would be 'talent that I definitely feel has great brilliance and unfound qualities: young and experienced people that have not had anyone to take them and bring them out the way they should have been brought out.'[72]

He was keen to include the Rocky Twins and said that when he asked them if they'd like to be in a sophisticated revue, he was planning, they leapt at the chance. He said 'they were young, incredibly handsome and rich.' But rather scathingly added 'talent they had not, but they were fairly bursting with boyish charm.' This comment must be why Gary Marmorstein said of them 'their talent, beyond their impersonations, were elusive.'[73] It is odd that Sillman thought they had no talent and yet their dancing numbers in *Low and Behold* were regarded as the best ones and they were seen as the leading lights of his show.[74]

Sillman added that after being headliners in European vaudeville, the Rocky Twins had landed in Hollywood 'to conquer new worlds.' He described their huge villa in Beverly Hills and said that they 'proceeded to give the most gilded parties since the great days of the wild, or silent era when a party was a party. The Rocky Twins parties were always climaxed by a mass visit to their bedroom where the twins would display their jewellery.' Sillman claimed that they had scores of diamonds and gold ornaments that were gifts to them from, they said, various crowned heads of Europe. He believed that they gave these parties in the hope of making a dent in Hollywood social life so they would be signed to movie contracts. 'Everybody came to the parties, but nobody gave them any contracts.'[75]

Low and Behold had its premiere on 16th May 1933, and many movie favourites attended including Tom Brown, Anita Louise, Frank Morgan, Edmund Goulding.[76] The dress rehearsal contained a staggering 75 numbers (the average show had 25) with 27 performers and ran from 8.30-2am. As a consequence, the show was pruned by an hour and a half for the actual launch. The principals included Sillman himself, Marguerite Namara (a recent arrival from London who had played in Noel Coward's *Words and Music*), the comedienne Lulo, the dark elegance, abundant sex appeal and glorious voice of Marguerite Namara, a gifted prima donna of the Paris Opera Comique and the Chicago Opera company plus the American beauty June Lang.

There were also such unknowns as Eve Arden (billed as Eunice Quendens), Teddy Hart (brother of lyricist Lorenz Hart), the young dancer Charles Walters (who became a top choreographer and director at MGM), the singer and actress Kay Thompson, Lois January (later appeared in the *Wizard of Oz*), the 6 foot blonde and beautiful Betzi Beaton (daughter of well-known writer Kenneth C. Beaton) and Sillman's hunky 19 year old chauffeur Tyrone Power.

Lorenz Hart was smitten by Power, who was having trouble getting a screen test despite his good looks. Hart tried to help him out, but even his influence, at the time, did little to yield any results.[77]

According to Sam Irvin *Low and Behold* 'had a surprisingly progressive queer eye' that had been 'unabashedly cultivated by its flamboyant creator.'[78] This was evident with a fat 300-pound bootlegger called Larry Armstrong who had a face like a quince but a wild gift for female impersonation. However, the stars of the show were undoubtedly the Rocky Twins, who also received the highest salaries of $14 each per week and were perhaps even more provocative than Armstrong.[79] How Sillman got away with showing female impersonators on the stage, given the circumstances at the time, is a mystery.

The Rocky Twins first appeared in the scene Service with a Smile, then Leif danced with Betzi Beaton in I've been Propositioned, they both did the Waltz with Peggy Neary, and then they did a high-class literary number with a musical version of the Picture of Dorian Gray.[80] Their piece de resistance, however, was The Dolly's and the Collies where they appeared in drag doing a burlesque of the Dolly Sisters, which Sillman described as 'a tasty little number.' This scene was 'in your face bravado' on behalf of Sillman, who was riding the crest of the wave with the Pansy Craze and revealed an audacious homocentric theme given that the Rocky Twins were regarded as 'notorious gay courtesans from Europe.'[81]

The Dolly sisters had made this one of their signature dances, first in *League of Notions* in 1921 in London, and then later in Paris. The Rocky Twins led a pair of Russian wolfhounds down a staircase in the opening of the number and then pirouetted about the stage, imitating the Dolly Sisters with the same movements, the same elaborate costumes, wide feathered hats and tall, thin walking canes. The result must have been sensational and humorous and became the highlight of the show.[82]

Low and Behold was received well and was thought to be 'mirthful, tuneful, saucy and satirical'[83] and 'about the classiest musical show to hit in this area for a long time.'[84] As word spread among the bohemian Hollywood elite, *Low and Behold* sold out, and it had to be extended from one to three weeks until its closure on 3rd June. But Sillman persisted and revived the show at Hollywood's Music Box Theatre from 10th July, but it did not last long and was closed by 12th August, in part due to the heat wave in Los Angeles.[85]

During this period Sillman discovered that the New York theatrical producer Lee Shubert was in town and invited him to see the show. Sillman said that backstage Shubert told Betzi Beaton and Eve Arden that he wanted to sign them to his forthcoming edition of the *Ziegfeld Follies* in 1934.[86] What he didn't say was that at the same Shubert also signed the Rocky Twins. Shubert also told Sillman he liked *Low and Behold* and wanted to put it into one of his theatres in New York.

As a result Sillman went to New York and evolved the concept of *New Faces*, but it was financed and staged without Lee Shubert in March 1934. Due to financial constraints, Sillman did away with lavish decor and costumes and created something basic and intimate and in a way reinvented revue.

During the production and staging of *Low and Behold*, Sillman's mother cooked wholesome spaghetti dinners for the cast and crew each evening. Afterward, the more adventurous members of the troupe would migrate to the Rocky Twin's Beverley Hills mansion, where we are told 'moderation and clothes were checked at the door.'[87] There were also late night excursions to various cafes including the Club New Yorker in April (before the launch of the show) where the Rocky Twins were performing with Jean Malin. Sillman and Lorenz Hart escorted Charlie Waters and Tyrone Power to see Malin and later, the revelry continued either at Malin's home or the Rocky Twins mansion. Walters said that Hart was the life and soul of the party and the soul of generosity.[88]

According to Charlie Waters and Samuel Marx, another favourite private place that summer was the Malibu beach house of actor Lew Cody and apparently another secret homosexual or voyeur like Edmund Goulding. Cody had been a very popular silent film star and was known as one of Hollywood's urbane screen villains and was regarded as a male vamp.[89] In 1926, on a whim, he married the actress Mabel Normand but the marriage was inexplicable, and they never lived together with Cody being labelled 'a heavy drinking disaster of a man.'[90]

Above: Lew Cody's Malibu mansion previously owned by Pauline Frederick

Cody was friends with Edmund Goulding and attended his wedding to Marjorie Moss in late 1931.[91] His impressive beach house at Trancas Beach, about ten miles north of Malibu, had been the home of the actress Pauline Fredrick. The mansion included a boathouse and a lighthouse tower 'that served as a beacon to attract transvestites, homosexuals in drag and lesbians in mannish outfits.' Many of whom were world famous.[92]

A male dancer who accompanied Lorenz Hart there said that 'they weren't orgies' and 'nobody got raped … if someone showed up and was shocked by what was going on, he left.' These clandestine late night evening parties, however, were not to be discussed the next day.[93]

Another chorus boy commented that 'if someone showed up and was shocked by what was going on, he left. You slept only with the person you wanted. It was understood that everything that went on was confidential and you never saw a hint of anything in Louella Parson's or any other gossip column.'[94] Sadly, after one of his Malibu beach parties in June 1934, Cody returned to his Beverley Hills home in the early hours of the morning and died of a heart attack aged 47.[95]

In the midst of appearing in cabaret at Club New Yorker with Jean Main and rehearsals for *Low and Behold*, the Rocky Twins and Julanne Johnston were signed to a contract with Paramount Pictures and were cast in the film *Midnight Club*, which was filmed in May 1933.[96]

A crime drama set in London, *Midnight Club* was about a gang of jewel thieves headed by slick criminal mastermind Colin Grant (Clive Brook) who had developed an ingenious method of creating alibis by creating exact doubles of the criminals making it impossible for the Scotland Yard Commissioner of police to arrest them. But the 'Midnight Club' gang was infiltrated by an undercover agent (George Raft), who falls for the gang leader's sweetheart (Helen Vinson) before he finally exposed the racket.[97] The Rocky Twins were shown rather fleetingly as the dancing act in the venue the Midnight Club itself along with Julanne Johnston doing an interesting ménage a trois waltz with the decorous Johnston looking quite adoringly at each of them in turn.

According to an interview with Paal Rocky in 1963, he said they were also involved in other film projects, including a film with Rita Hayworth and a film where Leif played alongside Errol Flynn as his younger brother. In one photograph they were shown seated on either side of a young Rita Hayworth, wearing striped shirts underneath jackets and it was made clear that they danced with her in a 'show movie' presumably meaning a movie musical.[98]

Rita Hayworth (at the time in 1933 still Rita Cansino) had been born into a dancing family and had become a regular part of her parent's stage act as 'The Dancing Cansinos'.

Chapter Seven: Larry Hart and Low and Behold, 1932-1933

Above: Paal Rocky in the early 1930s, post MGM and during
the time the Rocky Twins were associated with Rita Hayworth (Rita Cansino)

In 1933 Hayworth was being groomed at Warner Brothers and presumably it was in a Warner Brother's movie that she appeared with the Rocky Twins. This may have been in *Gold Diggers of 1933* or one of the Busby Berkley musicals such as *42nd Street* (1933) or *Footlight Parade* (1933), although their contribution was uncredited and was perhaps even cut from the final film.

After his fleeting appearance at Club New Yorker in April, Jean Malin moved to the Ship Café at Venice Pier for a few weeks in July and August.[99] His devoted fans followed him. Samuel Marx said that he did female impersonations 'powdered and rouged in stunning wigs and glittering sequined dresses. He mimicked prominent movie actresses so adroitly that he enraptured those who gathered at the ringside.'[100]

Pansy shows continued elsewhere, and Leon Le Verde appeared in a new show at the Hollywood Barn in June and July and then went back to Club Ballyhoo in August, while Karyl Norman became MOC at Frank Sebastian's Cotton Club and gave imitations of Mae West.[101]

Malin also regularly visited the Hollywood Barn and gave an impromptu act late at night. On his closing night at the Ship Cafe on 10th August, Malin gave a sensational performance. He climbed into his car with comedienne Patsy Kelly and his partner Jimmy Forlenza to go to a farewell party at the Hollywood Barn and tried to reverse away from the pier edge but accidentally shifted gear into forward and plunged 18 foot through the low barricade and into the ocean. The car landed upside down in four feet of water and Malin was pinned down by the broken steering wheel and drowned. Patsy and Jimmy were rescued and recovered.[102]

Leon Le Verde took Malin's place at the Ship Café and caused a furore with his female impersonations[103] and then went to Café de Paree (formerly Café Lafayette) as part of a snappy floor-show staged by Buddy Fisher.[104] However, with Malin's death, this was the end of an era, and the Pansy Craze gradually fizzled out.

According to Variety, with the end of Prohibition in late 1933, Hollywood's new fad was beer dens and Gay Nineties café's. Due to the vigilance of the local police, all the pansy joints had been closed because 'they had discovered an ordinance, which prohibited the appearance of anyone in a cafe in drag unless employed by the cafe. That killed the lavender spots.'[105] This may be the case, but every now and again brave souls re-interpreted the law and ignored the threat of police action. For example, in October the female impersonator Jackie Maye, staged a vaudeville act on the Orpheum circuit out of New York[106] and when the Rocky Twins moved back to New York in late 1933, they also staged their famous imitation of the Dolly Sisters.

Later, during the period 1935-1940, the composer and singer Bruz Fletcher entertained with gay double-entendres at Bali Nightclub on Sunset Strip in Los Angeles.[107]

Various observers have tried to explain the demise of the Pansy Craze. Most believe that the hostility toward any depiction of homosexuality was due to changing social attitudes as a result of the depression with a growing intolerance toward excess, unconformity or frivolity. Indeed, in Hollywood itself, religious pressure groups forced the studios to adopt the strict edicts of the Hays Production Code that dictated what could be shown in films and the conduct of actors themselves.[108] Equally damning to any form of understanding and tolerance was the book *Strange Loves: A Study of Sexual Abnormalities* published in late 1933 that exposed, what the author described as 'abnormals' and the great social evil of the third sex [109]

Across the Atlantic and back home in Oslo, their old dancing partner Mistinguett arrived toward the end of her European tour for an extended appearance at the Chat Noir cabaret in late May 1933 and was greeted at the railway station by Gudrun Roschberg, the mother of the Rocky Twins.[110] We are told that she also met their father, Colonel Adolf Roschberg. David Brett claims that Mistinguett's dancing partner Earl Leslie sought him out and contrived to have him waiting in her dressing room after the show, perhaps in an attempt to unnerve her as their professional relationship was at the time strained. Allegedly Father Roschberg had been, furious at finding out that his sons 'were not only homosexual but transvestites as well' and had threatened to sue Mistinguett until the twins sent him a portion of their rather considerable salary. But, instead of any disagreement, he merely took her out for dinner.[111]

The Rocky Twins wearing tuxedo's and top hats and carrying canes from Paris in 1930. A typical pose which would have found favour in the cabarets of New York in the 1930s

CHAPTER EIGHT
NEW YORK CABARET 1933-1936

The Rocky Twins left Los Angeles for New York in early August 1933 and checked into the Elysee Hotel where they had stayed on their first trip to New York. The reason for their relocation was because they had been offered parts in the new *Ziegfeld Follies*. Following the death of the great theatrical impresario Florenz Ziegfeld in July 1932, the Shubert brothers, famous New York theatrical producers, struck a deal with the Ziegfeld estate to revive the Follies.[1]

As early as June 1933, there was an announcement that Bobby Connelly would direct the new Follies[2] and by August it was jokingly revealed that almost everyone had been mentioned for inclusion in the new show.[3] Lee Shubert had seen the Rocky Twins in *Low and Behold* and most likely wanted them to do their imitation of the Dolly Sisters in their Dollies and Collies routine and perhaps the Dorian Grey ballet in the new *Follies*. It was also muted that they would dance with Betzi Beaton, who had also been signed[4] and there were rumours that Beaton and one of the twins – most likely Leif – were attached and serious.[5]

The Rocky Twins rehearsed for the show sometime in September or early October because in mid-October there was an announcement that in fact they had been denied permission to appear in the *Follies* by the Council of the Actors Equity Association on the grounds that, as aliens or foreigners, they had recently been in legitimate theatrical productions on the west coast and must await the expiration of a 6 month period before entering another production.[6]

As a consequence, they missed appearing in the premiere at the Shubert Theatre in Boston on the 30th October[7] and a further tryout in Newark in December before the launch at the Winter Garden Theatre in New York in early January 1934.[8] They subsequently embarked on a court case against the Shubert's claiming two weeks salary for rehearsals via the American Arbitration Association. But the plea was denied on the basis that they had not informed the producers properly about their standing with the Actors Equity Association and that the Shuberts' were not responsible when Equity forced them to withdraw from the show.[9]

It was a great shame that they were denied the chance to appear in the *Follies*. Not only would it have given them secure employment for the 6-month run, it would have been the re-making of them in New York. More importantly, it would have put them firmly in the limelight providing a platform for future contracts. As a consequence, although they triumphed in cabaret and a few other stage shows, they did not reach the great heights that they sought.

At the time, the extent of their friendship with the American actress Tallulah Bankhead became apparent. She was seen at a party in the famous Colony restaurant in mid-August 1933 with Leif Rocky, Peggy Fears and Blythe Daly, but one wonders - where was Paal?[10] The Colony was founded in 1923 and located on Sixty-first Street, off Madison Avenue and was protected from police raids by Mayor Jimmy Walker. It was hugely upmarket and full of stylish well-connected and affluent people.

Both Fears and Daly were interesting characters and well known as part of Bankhead's menagerie of friends with lesbian leanings, so it must have been an interesting party. The glamorous Peggy Fears had been married to the millionaire A.C. Blumenthal but was known to have been close to the actress Louise Brooks. Later in life, she helped developed the gay resorts of Fire Island's Cherry Grove and the Pines. Blyth Daly was British and coming from a well-off background became one of the bright young things in 1920s London. She became an actress but her acting career never really took off, and she was better known for her society antics.

Glamorous, beautiful and outrageous with her distinctive husky voice and sharp wit, Tallulah Bankhead had been a sensation on the London stage in the 1920s. In January 1931 she arrived in New York with a film contract from Paramount and made three films at their New York Astoria studio during 1931. She checked into the Elysee Hotel – where the Rocky Twins also stayed during their first trip to the USA from September 1931 to February 1932, and one wonders if, given the fact they were staying in the same hotel in late 1931, that this is where they first met.[11]

Above: A portrait of Tallulah Bankhead

In mid-December 1931, Bankhead went to Hollywood and made another three films, two for Paramount and one for MGM during 1932. She arrived in Los Angeles a few weeks after the Rocky Twins (they arrived in late October 1931) so there is a strong possibility that they met socially before she left once again for New York in December 1932. She was known to have visited some of the more alternative cafes including BBB's Cellar and may well have enjoyed the Club New Yorker show with Jean Malin and the Rocky Twins in September 1932.[12]

Back in New York, in December 1932, Bankhead appeared in the play *Forsaking All Others* that was staged in early 1933. During the run of the show, she spent a lot of time visiting the late night-spots in Harlem including the famous Cotton Club. In May she even went to a drag ball with her friend the Hollywood agent Minna Wallis, Irene Barrymore (wife of Lionel) and the actor Andy (Anderson) Lawler. They had a box and must have been dazzled at the sights.[13] Lawler was friends with William Haines and George Cukor and was also part of the clandestine gay circle in Hollywood and lived with Gary Cooper (Bankhead had appeared with Cooper in the film *The Devil and the Deep*) until the Hays production code forced them to change their lives.[14]

Minna Wallis was also rather cock-a-hoop because she had just found that the talented British lyricist and writer Rowland Leigh was in town and had immediately signed him under the noses of every other important agent.[15] Leigh was riding high on his success with the German film *Congress Dances* (1932) directed by Erik Charell and the operetta *The Dubarry* (1932). He had worked with the extraordinary British cabaret entertainer Rex Evans in London, and both visited New York and Hollywood. They were also part of the clandestine secret gay circle.

Bankhead returned to Hollywood in July 1933 for a vacation and to see what might be on offer and was known to have visited the Ship Café at Venice beach to see Jean Malin before his death. But she was back in New York in August 1933. Sadly, she was feeling unwell with stomach pains and checked into a hospital. By November 1933, she had to cancel the production of her next stage project *Jezebel* as she was forced to have a hysterectomy due to the ravages of gonorrhoea. On release, she returned to her suite at the Elysee Hotel and went to recuperate at her family home in Jasper, Alabama for Christmas[16]

Years later, Paal revealed in interviews that he was engaged for a while to Bankhead.[17] A press report from February 1934 corroborates his story which said that they had been license hunting but that she had called it off.[18] Shortly before this report, Irene Barrymore gave a lunch and cocktail party for Bankhead, Peggy Fears, Rowland Leigh and Tom Douglas amongst others. One must assume that, given the circumstances, the Rocky Twins were also on the guest list.[19] Also, a photograph of Paal and Bankhead together exists in the Hearst newspaper archive dated 15th March 1934 saying they were about to see Leonard Sillman's new show *The New Faces* at the Fulton Theatre[20] Whatever happened between them, it was over quickly because Bankhead returned to London at the end of March 1934.

The New York cabaret scene in late 1933 was hugely vibrant with around 30 venues that provided dinner, dancing, a top rate orchestra and usually a dancing act. Some of the more prestigious places included the Ambassador Grill, Central Park Casino, Chapeau Rouge, the Continental Grill at St Moritz Hotel, the Paramount Grill, the Pennsylvania Grill, Place Piquale, Park Central Coconut Grove, the Hollywood, the Mayfair Yacht Club and the Roosevelt Grill, the El Garron not to mention the famous Cotton Club in Harlem.[21]

However, there was a significant development with the reconstruction of theatres into large theatre-restaurants. The first and most important was the old New Yorker Theatre that had its seating ripped out and became the Casino de Paree. Modelled on the lines of the Folies Bergere in Paris it had two, terraced café floors, a restaurant and promenade with dance pavilion and a sensational floor-show.[22] But it had a bumpy ride due to the lack of a liquor license, and so initial traffic was light, but when a license was granted in December 1933, things took off. A new show devised by Billy Rose had 40 showgirls and new headliners every month.[23]

Without the *Ziegfeld Follies* appearance, cabaret would be a natural alternative for the Rocky Twins, and in early November 1933, they were snapped up by the astute nightclub maestro, Charlie Journal, for the newly re-opened Club Montmartre. One of the oldest nightclubs in New York, it had had an illustrious career having a central location in the Shuberts' Winter Garden Theatre building at 205 West 50th Street between 7th Avenue and Broadway. It had always been a class venue, and the gathering place for the elite of New York had lasted throughout the 1920s, previously hosting a range of other clubs that were named the Casa Lopez, Plantation Club and the Broadwalk.

Variety stated that it was 'always snooty' and catered to the class that liked the policy of formal evening dress.[24] For the journalist O.O. McIntyre, who wrote about New York nightlife, it had been the best nightclub in the prohibition era.[25] McIntyre said that Journal was one of 'silken rope greeters of Broadways elite' and said of the Montmartre and Journal 'the music, the lights, the conversation were pianissimo. Journal had a method of turning undesirables away without offence and dressed his conspicuous tables with the choice of his carefully selected clientele. Anybody who drank too much never got in again, and showoffs were so deftly jockeyed behind palms and smack against the bass drum they did not come back.'[26]

The famous journalist Walter Winchell called Charlie Journal the 'most affable of the headwaiters during prohibition,'[27] but he was also rather scathing called just a 'glorified head-waiter' by Variety.[28] He was more accurately described by Gilbert Swain in his New York column as a suave, discreet and wise gentleman of the world who had been 'the most trusted and socially accepted figure in New York's night-world.'[29]

Charlie Journal's return to Broadway after an absence of 2 years was marked with the re-opening of the Montmartre. He said that he had left the cabaret business when it became 'too shoddy and Coney Island-ish.' He believed that with the repeal of prohibition, which took place on 5th December 1933, it would bring back the old days and the old ways.[30] He was attempting to return the prestige that the Montmartre once held in nitery circles.[31]

The show, which was staged at the beginning of November, was seen as being not too long and went for a more intimate, swankier touch, rather than being floor-showish with a lot of girls and there was also no Master-of-Ceremonies to clutter up the premises.[32] The Rocky Twins headed the entertainment and were thought to 'impress as being French rather than Norwegian but in their tricky accents have an asset that's important to them.' Their first dance was 'concededly very different', and a little later they performed a special song about the strangeness of some American expressions concluding with a dance routine with Patricia Palmer.

Right: The Dolly Sisters in their Dollies and the Collies routine that was emulated by the Rocky Twins

However, their surprise hit was when they dressed up as the Dolly Sisters doing their very amusing dance that included two collie dogs on a leash, which were trained to mix into the routine. Other entertainers included Louise Henry (from the Andre Charlot revues and the Kit Kat Club in London). She was thought to be a real looker with a great deal of personality and charm who offered a Beatrice Lillie type of song.[33]

The Dollies and the Collies sketch had been seen in *Low and Behold* in Hollywood and was a big draw so much so that it was thought that the 'Rocky's are bound to be a hit novelty.'[34] However, it is interesting to speculate how they got away with appearing in drag in cabaret in New York when allegedly men appearing as female impersonators had been banned.

A few days after the opening night, a remarkable incident occurred, when the twins were doing the Dollies and Collie's number. Suddenly there was a commotion at a ringside table, and a glamorous women in an elegant gold gown cried out 'those are my dogs.' It was Rosie Dolly of the famous Dolly Sisters herself, newly married in 1932 to millionaire Irving Netcher and en-route to Hollywood.

When the twins finished their dance, Rosie rushed out and embraced the dogs. 'These are same dogs we danced with' she told the Rocky Twins 'oh how I have missed them. You don't know how much I love them' she said and sat on the floor romping with them. The twins told her that it was John Murray Anderson who helped them get the dogs from their owner Jud Brady. The next day the twins brought the dogs to her hotel room.[35] One can only imagine how the Rocky Twins felt - first their surprise and then their delight - that Rosie was in the audience. But sadly we are not told what Rosie thought about their imitation of the Dolly Sisters nor did Paal or Leif reveal anything about the encounter in later interviews.

In early December the twin introduced a timely new routine called La Valse Intoxicante.[36] They proved to be such a big hit that Charlie Journal signed them for another 20 weeks or 5 months[37] and yet in the Variety cabaret listings for early 1934, they are not mentioned, but presumably, they carried on until about April 1934.

At the beginning of December 1933, the Rocky Twins were part of the County Fair Ball, one of the largest and most ingeniously conducted charity parties of the season that took place in the ballroom suite of the Waldorf Astoria with 2,000 guests. Bright green artificial grass carpeted the floor space not give over to dancing, and supper tables were draped with canary yellow cloth behind quant white picket fences. At one side of the room was a real waterfall cascading down the slopes of a huge rock formation. There were dozens of concession booths and sideshows, and decorative effects included hundreds of coloured balloons. At 11.30 came the first in a series of elaborate entertainments under the direction of Julius Walsh with a carnival entertainment that included clowns, acrobats, adagio dancers and performing dogs. There was dancing until 1 am and then a second floor-show with a delegation of Broadway stars that included Marilyn Miller, Clifton Webb, Harriet Hoctor, Tom Patricola, Inez Courtney and Jack Powell and the Rocky Twins. Other famous guests included Katherine Hepburn, Helen Hayes and William Gaxton.[38]

In mid-December, a story circulated about Dr Milton Bender, the manager for the Rocky Twins, who assisted in the supply of liquor for a party but had an altercation with the bootlegger and ended up with what was called 'battling Siki lips.' In other words, he had got punched! The party was given for the twins by Clara Belle Walsh, the millionaire socialite widow of Julius Sylvester Walsh (the son of a wealthy Kentucky family) in her lavish suite at her home in the Plaza Hotel. She was a tall blond of Wagnerian proportions at nearly 6 feet tall and was internationally famous as a hostess and theatre and music patron. Legend had it that she was the first to host a cocktail party in St Louis in 1917.[39] No doubt there were many other society parties that Rocky Twins enjoyed at this time like they had done before when they had first arrived in New York in late 1930 and early 1931.

They also found time to socialise with new friends, including Rowland Leigh, who, as we have seen, had become part of Tallulah Bankhead's set via her friend Minna Wallis. They all went to lunch in early December, and Leigh said 'they still look so much alike it is almost impossible to distinguish one from the other', but it was thought that they carried their identity beyond physical resemblance as 'they really think of themselves as a single person.' In conversation, Leigh asked 'did you two really want to go into the theatre… or what were your first ambitions?' They replied in unison 'well at first our father wanted us to be a General.'[40]

Of course, the most important event took place on 22nd December 1933, when the mother of the Rocky Twins, Gudrun Roschberg, arrived in New York, directly from Oslo aboard the liner Bergensfjord. [41] She stayed with her sons in the salubrious Elysee Hotel for about two months, and it must have been a wonderful reunion since they had not seen each other for two years. One can only wonder if Mrs Roschberg attended a performance of her sons at Club Montmartre and what she made of them dressed up as the Dolly Sisters!

Interestingly, in February 1934, there were press reports that the Rocky Twins were, in fact, going to split up as an act and Paal was returning to Europe with his mother and would be going to Paris.[42] It was observed later in an interview that looking back to these times it was impossible to decide when things started going downhill.

The Twins were still on the hill and were dancing maybe better than ever, 'and yet some sort of dissolution process was in progress.'[43] But what had provoked the idea of a split and what was luring Paal back to Paris? A year later in an interview, it was made clear that Paal wanted to stay on the stage, but Leif wanted to go into business.[44] This was the beginnings of a change between the twins with both contemplating ending their act as the Rocky Twins and going their separate ways.

Since both their parents had met Mistinguett at the end of her European show in the early summer of 1933, it is not inconceivable that there may have been continued dialogue between Mistinguett via Mrs Roschberg and the twins. Mistinguett had ditched her dancing partner Earl Leslie at the end of her tour, and when her new show, entitled *Folies en Folie*, was staged at the Folies Bergere in late 1933, she had Lino Carenzio as her new partner. Although the show ran throughout 1934, perhaps Mistinguett was still trying to acquire Paal after her abortive attempt to lure him both from Leif and Josephine Baker in Budapest in 1929. Mrs Roschberg finally left America on 17th February from New York via Halifax to Goteborg en route back to Oslo[45] but Paal was not onboard nor did he appear to make a trip back to Europe and nor did the Twins separate.

By June 1934 they signed a contract for the RKO vaudeville circuit in an act with Nitza Vernille, with whom they had danced on the West coast.[46] Vernille had appeared at the Airport Gardens Club, in Los Angeles in late 1933 but then showed up in New York in early 1934 and had been one of the acts appearing in the cabaret show at the Palais Royale, which starred Ethel Waters. So their paths crossed again, and they decided to dance together once more. They first appeared at the RKO Albee Theatre, Brooklyn, in a presentation show before a film along with the comic dancing of Hal Sherman and the eccentric dancing of Inez King[47] They then moved to the Palace Theatre, in New York, the most prestigious vaudeville house in the country[48] where they were described as a 'splendid new combo that ought to get attention in both vaudeville and picture houses.' The twins were thought to be 'two good-looking youngsters who know how to dance' and Vernille was decorative, a good dancer but also knew how to wear clothes to keep all the male eyes riveted on the stage.[49] Along with the Four Gyrals (roller skaters), Grace Barrie (singer), Jack Pepper and his 5 stooges, their act was the finale and was 'the surprise turn and a peach', and they danced together and individually 'equally impressively.'[50]

From New York, they headed to Point Pleasant Beach, New Jersey for a pleasant summer engagement billed as 'dancers deluxe' on the floating nightclub-restaurant called the SS Club Royale. Once the houseboat of the famous millionaire Sir Thomas Lipton, they headed a cast in a floor-show that commenced 27th July with two shows nightly at 9.30 and 12.30 and also featuring the comedian and radio and screen star George Givot, the dancer Barbara Blane, the singer Una Vilon and the Four Admirals.[51]

But it was not all plain sailing. The Club Royale was, in fact, an illicit gambling venue operated by an organised crime gang. On 20th July 1934, after a newspaper campaign exposed the activity on the boat, there was police raid, but it amounted to little. The extent of the corruption was evident when the newspaper and editor were harassed and intimidated most likely under the auspices of Thomas A. Mathis, the so-called governor of Ocean County, who was comparable to Enoch Johnson (Nucky) in Atlantic City made famous in the TV show *Broadwalk Empire*.[52]

Without Nitza Vernille, their dancing partner, the Rocky Twins stepped into the winter cabaret season at the Hotel St Moritz.[53] It was noted at the time that there had been a significant expansion in the number of hotels bidding for popular patronage with newly decorated dinner and supper rooms with elaborate floor entertainments.[54] These included the Cocoanut Grove atop the Park Central Hotel, the Starlight Roof of the Waldorf Astoria, the supper room of the Hotel Biltmore, Chez Folies (formerly Parody Club), Club El Morocco, Del Monico's Club, The Hollywood Restaurant and Peppy De Albrew's Chapeau Rouge, that had an atmosphere reminiscent of Parisian cabarets.[55]

However, the most lavish and the most important cabaret opening of all time took place in December 1933 with another renovated theatre being converted into a theatre-restaurant following in the footsteps of the Casino de Paree. The old Casino Theatre (The Earl Carroll Theatre) at 7th Ave and 50th street became the French Casino and emerged as the flagship for a syndicate with, at one time, branches in Chicago, Miami and London. The new venue could seat 1,500 and had elaborate shows devised by Clifford Fischer, the first being the sparkling *Revue Folies Bergere*.[56]

The newly opened Continental Grill at the Hotel St Moritz, located at 50 Central Park South on 6th Avenue became another much-hyped rendezvous. Built in 1930, it had a magnificent location with over 33 floors and a tea-room and restaurant, café and roof garden. The show commenced at the beginning of September[57] and besides the Rocky Twins, it featured the comedian George Givot (who had appeared with them at the SS Club Royale), the magician Nate Leipzig and the English music hall star Constance Carpenter (who danced with the Rocky Twins).[58]

The Rocky Twins were amusingly described as being 'a little too la-de-da though highly regarded hereabout.' The usage of the term 'la-de-da' was one of many phrases to denote effeminacy, thereby confirming the assumption that they were indeed regarding as being gay.[59]

The Hotel St Moritz illustrates the opulence of New York's nite-life in the mid-1930s

Right Advert for The Hotel St Moritz, New York

Below: The Continental Grill Room of the Hotel St Moritz, New York

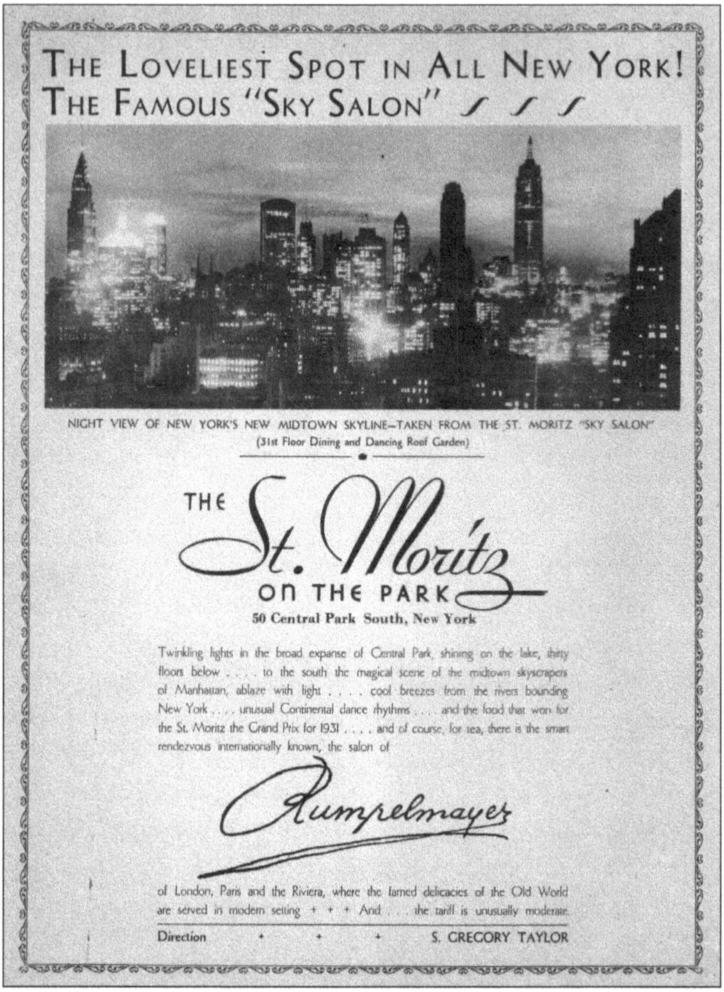

Left: A Portrait of Billy Milton

Later additions to the cabaret show were the singing accordionist Gypsy Nina and the ballroom dancing team of Minor and Root, which might suggest that the Rocky Twins had been replaced.[60]

In late 1934, they must have bumped into an old acquaintance from London and Paris, the entertainer Billy Milton. The suave and good-looking Milton with his sparkling eyes and flashing smile had been doing rather well since he had met the twins in London in 1929 and once again in Paris in late 1931 when he had partnered Mistinguett in *Paris Qui Brille* at the Casino de Paris. After appearing in several British movies, he had spent some time in Australia in three shows including the lead in *Gay Divorce* before sailing for America and trying his luck in Hollywood in the autumn of 1934.

He had not been there long when he, and his young Australian travelling companion Jimmy, were invited to an intimate Sunday lunch of about 20 guests, with the addition of a shapely topless waitress. Lunch was abandoned in favour of a 'blinds drawn' romp on the sofas. Milton lost Jimmy but suddenly 'his face appeared from between a pair of shapely legs', and he said 'Hollywood hospitality is terrific!'

Milton added that he made some good connections both heterosexual and homosexual, so it must have been an interesting mix of very liberal and gender fluid people. This may have been exactly the kind of party the Rocky Twins both staged and participated in during their Hollywood sojourn. Sadly, Milton's Hollywood adventure was short lived. His networking and parties were to no avail, and he also failed his screen tests and so fled to New York.[61]

He fared slightly better on Broadway and was signed by Leonard Sillman for his new show *Fools Rush In*. Rehearsals took place in late November with Betzi Beaton, Imogene Coca and Charlie Walters from *Low and Behold* and *New Faces* and the show was staged at the Playhouse in late December but only lasted a few days. Given the connections it is likely the Rocky Twins went to see the abortive show since they would have known Sillman and the key members of the cast.

In January 1935, the Rocky Twins joined Billy Milton in the Barbizon Plaza Hotel cabaret termed *Sunday Nights at Nine*. The Barbizon, like the Hotel St Moritz, was also built in 1930 and so a new edition to New York at 106 Central Park South. It was the first hotel to devote space to music and the arts with three concert halls and studios for exhibitions. The cabaret was held in one of the concert halls and commenced in November 1933 with a show called *The New Yorker* featuring Shirley Booth who performed sketches by Dorothy Parker with Sam Wren, along with the singing of Nina Tarasova, the tune detective Sigmund Spaeth and the dancing of Felicia Sorel and Demetrios Vilan.[62] Along the way, some of the original acts left the cast making way for Billy Milton and the Rocky Twins.[63] They also did not last long, and Milton soon joined the Normandie club in the Navarro Hotel on Central Park South as a piano act, then went into the El Morocco. The Rocky Twins also re-surfaced in a new night-club called Le Boeuf sur le Toit, where they must have felt very much at home given they were once regular visitors to the Parisian equivalent in the late 1930s.

Le Boeuf in New York was the idea of Charles Brazelle and was located in the basement of the Medical Arts Building at 57 West 57th street with Brazelle's Café Basque upstairs. It was thought to be 'authentic French in every respect'.[64] Brazelle had a Mr Chalomes create the interior décor as a replica of the Boeuf Sur Le Toit in Paris and Alina De Silva, director of entertainment at the Paris Boeuf, was the star of the show that opened on 15th December 1934.

However, Louis Moyses the owner of the original Parisian Boeuf Sur Le Toit was not amused. He was in New York at the time to begin negotiations to install a branch in the Ritz-Carlton hotel. He went to court and won the injunction for unlawful use of the name.[65] Undeterred, Brazelle opened an office in Paris to book talent and appointed the American entertainer Harry Pilcer as his Paris representative.[66]

Brazelle also took on the legendary Joe Zelli, often called the King of Parisian cabaret, as manager, following the closure of his club Chez Zelli.[67] Italian by nationality, French by persuasion and American by adoption, Zelli was happy, congenial and good-natured but some described him as a sleazy and dubious racketeer. He had made his name running several clubs in Paris including the famous Royal Box. Zelli's warm personality and skill in running his club were the chief reasons for its success, and he greeted everyone who entered with a warm handshake and smile. On returning to New York, it was these qualities, and all his valuable contacts, that made Zelli an essential asset to Brazelle.

Despite the law-suit, Brazelle launched a new show at the beginning of February 1935 that starred the Rocky Twins along with the Billy Arnold Orchestra. The twins were described as 'apolloesque' who gave a 'Parisian touch' and danced with a new partner – Helen Gray.

An American dancer, Gray appears to have commenced her career in the late 1920s on the East coast[68] and in early 1930 secured a 3-month tour of Europe in Italy, France and Germany.[69] Back in the USA, she stepped into an intimate revue on Broadway at the Royale Theatre called the *Second Little Show* and then toured in vaudeville.[70]

Gray went back to Europe in early 1932 for a year and was described as 'a fascinating brunette with an arresting personality and a style of dancing which is her own, as well as a gift for amazing contortion.'[71] Starting in Paris, she appeared at the Empire Theatre, visited Monte Carlo and Nice and then spent some time in London dancing at the Palladium, in cabaret at the Savoy and Berkeley Hotels, and a show called *Tell The Truth* at the Saville Theatre.[72] Back in New York in late 1933 and through 1934, she appeared in cabaret at the Paradise Restaurant and in the show *Roberta* at the New Amsterdam Theatre.[73]

It was thought that the twins had changed the way they were dancing and now danced in a modern manner. Their 'Proximity' number was a novelty and very smart, tracing the terpsichorean nearness between partners from the antebellum minuet up until the 1933 Westchester bunny hug. Supporting the trio was the singer Ann Courtney, the French duo Pils and Tabet (two personable young men, one at the piano the other singing fast and racy) and the impressions of Murray and Allan.[74]

By mid-March, the venue had closed but in July 1935 Charlie Journal – previously the front-man of Café Montmartre - expressed interest in re-opening with a different name, but nothing happened.[75] The Rocky Twins announced that they would be making a picture with Paramount before returning to France.[76]

Joe Zelli emerged as Master-of-Ceremonies for the smartly decorated Normandie Club in the Navarro Hotel on Central Park South, where Billy Milton had played earlier in the year. The Normandie was dignified, spacious, high roofed and airy and drew a youngish, well-behaved crowd in a perfect location. A new floor-show commenced in mid-May starring the Rocky Twins and Helen Gray, along with Grace and Charlie Herbert doing politely naughty ditties, a Cuban dancer and singer Dolores Del Viso and Eddie Elkins and his orchestra.

The twins said 'hello' to their admirers from Paris and introduced some patter into their routines. Their 'neat' act benefitted by the fact that Gray matched their slimness and height admirably.[77] A little later there were new additions to the cast, including the singer Ann Courtney and the comic singing of the Yacht Club Boys and the show ran through to the end of April 1935.[78]

At the beginning of May, the twins along with Helen Gray journeyed to Milwaukee, Wisconsin, to take part in Robert Henderson's five-week Ann Arbor Dramatic Festival.[79] Henderson had conceived the idea of staging a dramatic season in 1930. It became the first of its kind in America and its importance grew yearly. He staged a variety of shows and the 1935 season was headed by the highly-acclaimed actress Nazimova and Romney Brent in *The Simpleton of the Unexpected Isles* and *Ghosts* that began in Milwaukee on 13th May. Both plays were also seen in Ann Arbor and Madison in subsequent weeks. Many years later Leif claimed that he appeared in the production of *Ghosts* for a while playing Oswald. But his performance did not go down well, and he was booed and pelted with eggs and rotten oranges.[80] However, Leif fared batter with his brother Paal in Henderson's specially staged revue called *Up to the Stars* that opened the Pabst theatre, Milwaukee on 19th May. Their old colleague, Leonard Sillman was the producer, and although a significant portion of the show contained songs and sketches by Noel Coward (taken from his London success *Words and Music*), other scenes were provided by Sillman from his *New Faces* and *Fool Rush*.[81]

The cast were described as 'International Stars' and featured the Rocky Twins (as the Continental Stars), Walter Slezak (the Viennese Star), Ilka Chase (the American Star), Jessie Royce Landis (the Dramatic Star), Nina Tarasova (the Russian Star), Imogene Coca (the Comic Star), Felicia Sorel and Demetrios Vilan (the Dancing Stars), Patricia Calvert (the English Star) and Helen Gray (the Youngest Star).[82]

The Rocky Twins appeared in at least six scenes: Au Revoir Paris, American Rhythm (with Helen Gray), A Park in Vienna (with the entire company), The Rules of Three (the French Farce version with Imogene Coca, Walter Slezak and Helen Gray), Waltz with Dignity (with Helen Gray) and I want to Dance with Coca (with Imogene Coca).[83]

According to press reports the Rocky Twins also appeared in a Dorian Grey ballet, originally staged by Max Reinhardt[84] and they were also part of an elaborate scene with French Watteau figures wearing costumes of cellophane and the twins as shepherds, Nina Tarasova as their shepherdess and Walter Slezak as an old French peasant. But it is not clear which scenes these formed in the programme.[85]

Up to the Stars toured and in late May was staged for about a week at the Wilson Theatre, Detroit, Michigan. On the 27th May, all the cast including the Rocky Twins took part in a special evening of entertainment with dinner and dancing at the Detroit Athletic Club.[86] The show then went on a nationwide tour from June to September 1935,[87] and they ended up at the Town Casino in Buffalo, New York at the beginning of October. Run by the well-known society band-leader Howard Lanin, it was often described as the largest nightclub between Chicago and New York City and the Twins, and Helen Gray offered several interpretations from *Up to the Stars*.[88]

Left: A Portrait of Lucienne Boyer

With Helen Gray once again, the Rocky Twins joined a company headed by the French singer Lucienne Boyer in November 1935. *Continental Varieties* was conceived as a 'new tangent in show business' and was a variety or vaudeville show posing as a legitimate stage show, finely constructed, arty, and intended for the smart, sophisticated crowd. It had initially been launched in October 1934 at the Little Theatre in New York with no scenery or high production costs, just the talent of the actors. It was a good idea and only suffered from not enough acts.[89]

Boyer had a reputation for being a successful night-club entertainer in the Paris music hall and cabaret, had numerous records to her credit and was best known for her song 'Parlez-Moi d'amour.' She had originally been brought to America by the Shubert Brothers in 1926 and continued to be popular in both Europe and America. She was beautiful, with an exceptionally magnetic personality, a radiant control of her facial muscles and a throaty, sweet voice.[90] Boyer's singing was 'most alluring', and she performed with a delicacy and finesse uncommon on the American stage.[91]

The second edition of *Continental Varieties* opened at the Shubert Theatre Boston on 19th November 1935 and then transferred to the Stella Theatre, in Montreal, Canada. The Stella was the only permanent French language playhouse in Quebec and had become a showcase for well-known Canadian and international actors. Eventually, *Continental Varieties* was staged at the Masque Theatre in New York from 26th December.

Once again, Lucienne Boyer was the lead, along with Georges Andre Martin, a noted French puppeteer, Pills and Tabet, the singers with a piano, (Boyer would later marry Jacques Pills), Raphael (a concertina player), the singer King Lan Chew and Iza Volpin's Continental Quartet.[92] The Rocky Twins and Helen Gray were seen in 'American Rhythm,' 'Proximity' and an impression of musical comedy.[93]

At first, in Boston, Variety thought the Rocky Twins and Helen Gray to 'be winners on anybody's stage. One of the smoothest precision mixed teams in a long time, they unfold routines that raise their very good dancing to the superb division'[94] but on arrival in New York the tune had changed, and they were viewed as 'nice dancers but fail to impress here. It's just flat.'[95]

Generally, the reviews for the Rocky Twins were all favourable and very few expressed any criticism. However, one unidentified review in America from this time upset Leif. It said that the twins could not dance nor sing but they could wake up an audience like an open window bringing in fresh air.[96]

The reaction to the *Continental Varieties* was lukewarm: 'there are a number of pleasant and a few hilarious moments, but the program tends toward monotony'[97] and 'strung together, one turn following the next, gives a general impression that is somewhat languid'[98] Variety thought that it was better than the first edition in 1934[99] and that it was 'pretty good but no more than that.'[100] Slightly more positively, one reviewer admired the 'persuasively night-club like atmosphere' that brought a delightful touch of Paris to New York.[101] The show closed after 9 performances at the end of December 1935.

As the Rocky Twins finished their tour with *Up to the Stars* and as they turned their attention to *Continental Varieties*, another delightful touch of Paris descended on New York in the form of their old friend Josephine Baker. She arrived aboard Normandie on 7th October 1935 to appear in the new *Ziegfeld Follies*, once again produced by the Shubert Brothers. Before attending rehearsals, in late 1935, Baker enjoyed New York and one evening was invited to a dinner party given by Larry Hart. One can only assume that the Rocky Twins were instrumental in providing the introduction and were also guests.[102]

The *Ziegfeld Follies*, had an out-of-town run, opening in Boston in late December 1935 before the New York premiere at the Winter Garden Theatre at the end of January 1936. But it was not good for Baker. Fanny Brice and Bob Hope were given the best scenes, and Baker was effectively eclipsed and sidelined. She was not presented well and was forced to abandon her own costuming, and as a result, the critics were savage. Facing racist comments and attitudes, she was hugely discouraged and eventually got out of her contract with the Shuberts'.[103]

In the meantime, Baker decided to open a night-club in New York on 25th February 1936. The location was Barbara Hutton's former residence at 125 East 54th Street, where during the day it was a smart restaurant called Le Mirage, but at 10.30pm it re-opened as Chez Josephine for the after the theatre clientele with the added bonus of the Ray Benson orchestra.

It was an intimate environment where she could sing what she liked and wear her own unrestrained costumes. Baker thrived, and the club became an instant hit for the cosmopolitan, sophisticated crowd, eager for a new diversion.[104]

The slightly sharp comments continued and although she was described as being 'glamorous as the legend implies' it was noted that she was 'not a sensational singer or dancer, either – though her talents seem more adaptable to a nightclub than to the stage' although it was conceded that 'there is something about her extraordinary appearance and enthusiasm.'[105]

Variety, on the other hand, had decided that the press had given Baker a dirty deal after the opening of the *Ziegfeld Follies*[106] and observed that she had a new manner of being a hostess by being genuine and warm and working in a modest and deferential manner.[107]

Above: A view of the exterior of the Edgewater Beach hotel in Chicago
Below: A view of the the beach walk area at Edgewater Beach hotel in Chicago, where the Rocky Twins performed in the summer cabaret show Moonlight Follies, 1936

At first, the floor-show included the Rocky Twins and Helen Gray and later, when the twins had returned to Paris, one of them stated that they had just appeared in Baker's cabaret.[108] There can also be no doubt that Baker danced with the Rocky Twins in one or more numbers.[109] It has been noted in other publications[110] that Baker danced with two men. For example, the New York Times mentioned that she danced with two fancy Moroccan lads, which was 'a bit on the startling side.'[111] However, the Rocky Twins were only dancing at Chez Josephine for a short while because of a pre-existing engagement and another group of male dancers took their place, and various other acts were added including Willem van Loon and Jean Ashley doing a daring adagio act.[112]

The Rocky Twins and Helen Gray had been booked for Club Versailles, that had opened on 7th February 1935, and was another cabaret-theatre on the site of Little Picture House at 151 East 50th Street. It sought a French flavour and had a very smart, exclusive atmosphere because of limited space[113] and was described as 'New York's distinguished continental rendezvous.'[114] At first the star of the floor-show was the dapper Harry Richman, followed by Lucienne Boyer and the dancers Manya and Drigo and then sometime in late February or early March the Rocky Twins and their partner arrived.[115]

The Rocky twins, seemingly without Helen Gray, accepted a summer engagement at the salubrious Edgewater Beach hotel in Chicago. A resort complex situated in the far north of Chicago with a private beach adjacent to Lake Michigan, this was a Chicago landmark and one of the summer playgrounds of the rich and famous that attracted a wide range of celebrities. Built by two Chicago businessmen in 1916 with 400 rooms, it was in Spanish-style stucco in the form of a Maltese Cross, and most rooms faced the lake. It was so popular that a second 600 room unit was opened to the south of the original in 1922. It became the place to be seen. The marine dining room was the hub of the hotel's nightlife with a strict formal dress code, and it was here that bands played, guests danced, and the entertainment was staged. The cabaret at the hotel was called *Moonlight Follies*, and it was brought outdoors to the beach walk in July. The twins were part of a line up that included the Novelle Brothers and Sally, the dance team of James and Evelyn Vernon and Cecile Blair, with music provided by Bernie Cummins and his orchestra.[116] This was their last known appearance in America. Josephine Baker returned to Paris in June 1936, and the Rocky Twins followed a few months later.

Above: A portrait of the Rocky Twins in their sailor outfits from the late 1920s

CHAPTER NINE
EUROPE AND SEPARATION 1936 = 1941

The Rocky Twins were back in Paris in the autumn of 1936. Why they decided to leave New York is not clear. Were they made an offer to appear in something substantial in Paris? They had been made offers before since they had considered returning to Paris in early 1934 and again in late 1935. However, we have to bear in mind that they had also been thinking of going their separate ways with Leif wanting to go into business and Paal wishing to continue to perform on the stage or in film. Perhaps their meeting with Josephine Baker in New York might have convinced them to return to Paris.

When Paul Derval visited New York in May 1936, he had signed Baker to appear in *En Super Folies*, his next big production at the Folies Bergere staged on 1st October 1936. It is not beyond the realms of probability that Derval may have offered the twins parts in the new Folies Bergere show, but for whatever reason, this did not materialise.

Leif was spotted in mid-October in a Montmartre cabaret and was recognised by a newspaper reporter.[1] He related that they had arrived at the train station in the evening of 16th October just as sirens sounded and as a result they thought war had broken out. In fact, it was an air-raid drill orchestrated by the authorities across Paris for that evening.[2]

Leif also related that they had brought with them a new dancing partner called Nayan Pearce and that they were exploring new opportunities to appear once more in Paris.[3] A few days later one of the twins was spotted by another journalist in the Palermo cabaret located at 6 Rue Fontaine, Montmartre. In conversation, it was announced that the twins were about to appear in a variety programme.[4]

The American Nayan Pearce was of average height and had brilliant red hair and lustrous eyes. Born as Phyllis Pearce in San Francisco she was about the same age as the twins and had the stage in her blood, as her grandfather was a British playwright and grandmother an operatic star. At a young age, she appeared in the Henry Miller play *La Tendresse*,[5] followed by *Bye Bye Barbara* (1924) and John Murray Anderson's *Music Box Revue* (1924) and then joined Miller's stock company in 1925. In 1926 she was seen in Fred Stone's *Criss Cross* (1926/27) before she changed her Christian name to Nayan for John Murray's Anderson's *Music Box Revue* (1927/28). Her family relocated to the New York area, and she supported her mother and brother Roxor, who also took to the stage and became a boy tennis star, but he was tragically killed in 1928 in a car accident aged 16.[6]

Right: Front cover of the Josephine Baker show *En Super Folies* at the Folies Bergere, Paris, 1936-1937

Left: Josephine Baker in *En Super Folies* at the Folies Bergere, Paris, 1936-1937

In 1928, Pearce joined Arthur Knorr's stage presentation unit *Crystals* staged first at the Capitol New York before touring on the publix circuit, and here she was noted for leading the Chester Hale Girls with a high kick waltz and acrobatics.[7] By 1931 she was in a vaudeville act with a singer and dancer called Jay Valie that toured for several years, and at one point it was stated that she was the first person to dance on top of a piano on stage.[8] Pearce was considered for the role in MGM's *Red-Headed Woman* (1932), but Jean Harlow got the role.[9] Greater stardom on the stage occurred when she caught the eye of Max Gordon and offered the leading role in his hit *Roberta* (1933/34). Following this, she appeared in *Keep Moving* (1934) and then joined Don Carthay as ballroom dancing team in cabaret. They were seen in the short film *Here's the Gang* for Universal[10] and at the Cocoanut Grove in New York.[11]

Above: Jacques Haik's Rex Theatre, Paris

The twins had met Pearce during their stay in New York, perhaps via their contact with Max Gordon, or out and about visiting specific nightclubs like the Cocoanut Grove or she went to see them in one of their cabaret shows. Wherever they met they decided to dance together and relocate to Paris. They made a striking trio with their first performance at a dinner dance in the Ritz Hotel on the evening of Thursday 19th November 1936.[12]

However, their debut on the stage was at Jacques Haik's magnificently opulent Rex Theatre in a stage presentation accompanying the movie *Le Grand Refrain* with two other acts: Les Pias and Joe Laurin. Of course, the twins knew Haik, who was also a successful French film producer and had appeared in some of his earlier films in 1929.[13] Since 1929, Haik had expanded his activities and had bought and renovated the Olympia Theatre and built the extravagant art deco cinema, the Rex that opened in December 1932. It was at that time one of the largest cinemas in Europe with 3,000 seats.[14]

The twins and Pearce had developed something a little different to the usual dancing act by introducing comic parodies and imitations. Impeccably dressed, the twins charmed the audience with their 'distinguished humour' and what was termed their 'seductive fantasy'. Pearce was thought to have a remarkably flexible body and attractive feline mannerisms. Together they were described as being 'three mimes' and were particularly entertaining when they played beginners in an imitation of a music hall scene.[15]

After little more than two weeks at the Rex, the team switched to the Gaumont Palace in early December 1936. The Gaumont was a Parisian institution and had been completely modernised in 1931 and could seat 6,000. Once again they were admired for their impeccable taste in their costumes and enthralled the audience with their comedy, charm and attractive stylized movements.[16]

No doubt the twins and Pearce were expecting that their debut would entice the big music hall producers to book them, but this was not the case. Perhaps they went on tour in Europe for a few weeks, but by early 1937 they were in Oslo. Of course, they may have just returned to Oslo for a family Christmas in late 1936. Whatever, the trio became part of a new show staged at the Chat Noir in Oslo in early February 1937.

The Chat Noir (Black Cat) was an Oslo institution and modelled after the Parisian venue of the same name. The singer Bokkon Lasson visited Paris in the late 19th century and had been inspired by the Parisian cabarets of the time and enthralled by singers such as Yvette Guilbert. She transplanted her version of Parisian gaiety to Oslo and established her Chat Noir in 1912 in the Tivoli building, Stortingsgata. Like its Paris counterpart, it was a cultural meeting place for artists, writers and intellectuals with singing, recitals and performances. But when Victor Bernaus ran the venue from 1920 to 1928, it became the home of modern revue and this continued through the 1930s.[17]

The new show was made up of two acts and 36 different numbers and featured a large array of local talent in addition to the Rocky Twins and Nayan Pearce. It was abounding with sketches, singing, parodies, humour and dance and featured the twins Nanna and Vesla Stenersen, the singer Randi Braenne, the popular Lalla Carlsen (in one turn she did a parody of Mrs Simpson), the singer Einar Rose, Arvid Nilssen singing about Norwegian film and the muscle act of the Gets Brothers.[18] It was thought that the dancing part of the show was the best to have been seen in Oslo in years and in particular, an Indian dance that the Rocky Twins did with Nayan Pearce and Monrad Misje was particularly admired.[19]

After the Chat Noir in Oslo, the trio left for Copenhagen to appear in the famous *Cirkusrevyen of 1937*. This was Denmark's largest revue, located in a large tent on the Dyrehavsbakken, an amusement park, north of Copenhagen and was founded in 1935 by the restaurateur Carl Pehrsson, actor Osvald Helmuth, Oscar Holst and musician Herman Gellin.[20]

The *Cirkusrevyen of 1937* must have run for a few months from June 1937, but this was the last show that the Rocky Twins appeared in as an act. Effectively at the ages of 28, they decided to call it a day and separate.

Immediately after completing their contract in Copenhagen the twins must have returned home to Oslo for a short while and then they both went their separate ways with Paal going to Germany and Leif to Sicily. In a later interview, Leif said that they had agreed to part as a preliminary arrangement to see how they both fared.[21]

Explaining this decision, Paal emphasised that the Rocky Twins were successful, but they were smart enough not to overestimate their success and recognise its limits. He added that a 'twin' act was so easily in danger, always having to be careful not to repeat things and to create something new to keep the audience entertained constantly. Finally, he thought that the artistic individuality of each of them perhaps was inhibited and restricted their further development. Because they both saw these issues clearly, they made the rational decision to separate.[22]

But Paal wasn't exactly open and honest and what he didn't say was that there were also other important considerations at work. It was wryly observed later that the sad truth was that the twins together could accomplish anything but individually they were constrained and alone they became lost in the mass of other talented dancers.[23]

From the summer of 1937 through to late 1939, Leif took up residence in the glorious coastal town of Taormina in Sicily.[24] The reason for this relocation to a warmer and sunnier climate – and no work – must have been due to health issues. Although official reports before 1937 suggested that the twins were to separate because Leif was interested in moving into business, it is more likely that Leif had to consider a less strenuous lifestyle. It was revealed in later interviews that Leif had developed a nerve disease that had undermined his health. It was something personal and something he did not want to admit at the time. Symptoms presumably began during his stay in New York, and the diagnosis must have occurred sometime during the period 1936-37.[25]

His condition must have been a degenerative nerve disease, also referred to as neurodegenerative disease, which involves the deterioration of the nerves that impaired balance, movement, heart function, talking and breathing. neurodegenerative disease is an umbrella term for a range of conditions such as Parkinson's, Alzheimer's, and Huntington's disease. Presumably, Leif's symptoms initially were not too severe, and so he was advised to rest in a warm climate.

Taormina had been occupied at one time or another by the Greeks, Romans, Byzantines, Arabs, Normans, the French and the Spanish, all of whom left their mark in one way or another. Built 200 metres above the sea on a rocky outcrop, the town is renowned for one of the greatest views in the world looking onto the deep blue Mediterranean and the volcano of Mount Etna.

Above: Two sketches of the landscape at Taormina, Sicily
Left: The beach Lido at Taormina.
Right: The ruins of the Greek theatre and a view of the coast and Mount Etna

Taormina also had beautifully restored mediaeval buildings, an elaborate network of winding streets with shops, bars and restaurants and a magnificent central square and gardens. There were also the spectacular ruins of a Greek theatre and on the coast, delightful beach areas. Everywhere there were enchanting views.[26]

An integral part of the 'Grand Tour' of European aristocrats and artists in the 18th century, Taormina evolved into one of the most popular tourist destinations in Sicily attracting royalty, artists, writers, photographers, heads of state and later film stars. The classical German writer Johann Wolfgang von Goethe was the first to write about Taormina's charms in the 1780s.

By the late 19th century the French writer Guy De Maupassant visited, the English artist Robert H. Kitson built a villa there, while the eccentric German aristocrat Baron, Wilhelm Von Gloeden, became known for his homoerotic photography of young Sicilian men. Over the years it attracted people like Pablo Picasso, Ezra Pound, Bertrand Russell and Tennessee Williams, Oscar Wilde, Rudyard Kipling and D.H. Lawrence. It became a bohemian and arty place and a magnet for the more affluent and sexually liberated.

Visitors usually stayed in a variety of hotels and guest-houses that littered the hills because it provided vine framed views of the town below. One of the most salubrious venues was the Grand Hotel San Domenico constructed from the original structures of a former Dominican monastery dating back to 1430, and another well-known resort was the Grand Hotel Timeo.

The excellent Mediterranean light, the unique landscape with plants and flowers of every description and all the brilliant colours were all ideal for artists as was the relaxed lifestyle. Leif would have found it an exhilarating and stimulating place to be, and undoubtedly it was here that he became interested in painting himself. Over the years Taormina had become world famous as a health resort 'because nature is here seen at its best under clear and bright skies.'[27] It was the ideal location for Leif given his circumstances.

A reminder of times past in Hollywood surfaced during Leif's stay in Taormina when the MGM movie star Greta Garbo arrived in the Spring of 1938 on a tour with the musician Leopold Stokowski. 20 years her senior, there were rumours of marriage, but they were just that - rumours - and no marriage happened.[28]

While Leif was in Sicily, Paal, on the other hand, continued in show business and was signed by the Tobis film company in Berlin and must have arrived there in August or September 1937.[29] He said that going solo without Leif was not an easy thing to do given that they had performed together for so long. He also had doubts about his own abilities without this twin and so felt that despite all his successes he had to start out from scratch.

Without explaining why he went to Berlin, he said that once there he had to learn German fast and was lucky that Tobis gave him a screen test and luckier still that one of the Tobis director's - Hans H. Zerlett - signed him for an upcoming movie in pre-production.[30]

However, Paal may once again not have told the whole story, and I think it highly likely that he may have made enquiries before going to Berlin and may have been made an offer to become a German film star at some point in 1936 or 1937, perhaps while in Paris.[31] Paal's aspiration to become a singing and dancing movie star with a substantial role finally came to fruition.

Given the political status of Germany and the growing power and ambitions of Hitler and the Nazi party, this move was indeed curious, but the offer of a big part in a major European movie was what he wanted, and so outweighed any thought of the consequences. Once in Berlin, he took German lessons and immediately began 'proper, thorough, acting lessons.' We are also told that he was not dazzled by vain illusions and knew he had to work tirelessly to succeed.[32]

From 1933 when the National Socialists came to power, measures were being taken to assist, but eventually control, the German film industry. Everything was conducted behind the scenes so that the growth of state control and interference was not entirely visible.

Jews were forbidden to work in the industry and this as well as a general distaste for the Nazi regime, resulted in over 1,500 personnel emigrating, among them such luminaries as Erich Pommer, head of UFA, the director Fritz Lang and the actress Marlene Dietrich. By 1937 Joseph Goebbels was taking steps to run the industry as a state propaganda machine, and film content was being censored to ensure that it reflected socialist aims and beliefs. The intervention was aided by spiralling production costs that caused financial difficulties for the big studios. For example, at the end of the fiscal year, 1936-37 Tobis had losses of 5 million marks and was on the verge of bankruptcy. From 1935, the German Government had been buying Tobis stock from its Dutch owners, and it was secret, state loans that saved it. By the end of 1937, Tobis was re-organised with the Nazi party in total control.[33]

It was into this environment that Paal emerged when he was cast in the all-star Tobis production entitled *Es Leuchten Die Sterne* (*The Stars Shine*) that was released in March 1938 and so filmed in late 1937. The plot revolved around a young secretary who travelled to Berlin to seek work as an actress. In a comedy of errors, she was mistaken for a famous dancer, resulting in her heading the cast of a star-studded show.

The trite story-line acted as a backdrop for a Busby Berkeley-style musical revue and featured appearances by numerous stage personalities and Tobis film stars. But in comparison to comparable Hollywood musicals like MGM's *Rosalie* (1938), it simply lacked the glitz and sparkle.

Paal was seen in at least four numbers, and although he was billed as the dancer, he also sang twice. He was first seen wearing cowboy gear and surrounded by chorus girls in similar garb and sang 'Hände Hoch' (Hands Up) and then tap danced on a raised dais. For his other appearances, he was paired with the 'exotic' Viennese dancer La Jana (Henny Heibel). The tall, dark, olive-skinned La Jana, was beautiful and Spanish looking and had appeared in revues in Berlin, Stockholm and London before she made her mark in Zerlett's film *Truxa* (1937).

La Jana became the talk of Berlin and was courted by many including Crown Prince Wilhelm, and Charlie Chaplin allegedly had an affair with her during his visit to Berlin in 1931. Significantly, both Goebbels and Hitler were mesmerised by her. According to London theatre impresario Charles B. Cochran, Hitler was seldom seen in public without her.[34]

Chapter Nine: Europe and Separation 1936-1941

Left: The cover of the Film Kurier magazine for *Es Leuchten Die Sterne* (1937)

Below: Paal Rocky and La Jana in a dancing sequence from *Es Leuchten Die Sterne* (1937)

Above: Paal Rocky in one of dancing sequences in *Es Leuchten Die Sterne* (1937)

The dancing pair were seen in a Spanish number called Tarragona and in two scenes with Paal dressed impeccably in evening suits, one black and one white, and La Jana in suitably glamorous, dancing evening gowns. In another bizarre scene, Paal sang 'Liebe, hochverehrte Großmama' (Love, Great Grandmother) at the piano when La Jana came to life out of a wall painting and both danced separately with Paal bouncing off the furniture and the piano before performing an acrobatic act on a wall shelf.

Paal observed that his dances were not one-sided or traditional but more artistically constructed like a symphony of different elements and incorporated the step, the rhythm, line and form and elements of ballet, acrobatics and humour.[35]

Not surprisingly Variety was scathing of *Es Leuchten Die Sterne* and said 'it's a revue type which connives to play hide and seek with continuity and sense until the bewildered onlooker gives up in annoyed despair.' It was thought that the so-called 'Stars' that were supposed to shine were in fact 'a lot of tired tinsel that barely glitters.' The dancing was thought to be unimaginative, La Jana's 'solo-squirming' was 'old fashioned' and Paal's dancing was 'merely competent.' However, the director Zerlett was praised because 'he can really do things.'[36]

Right: Paal Rocky in his cowboy gear for the number Hände Hoch' (Hands Up) in *Es Leuchten Die Sterne* (1937)

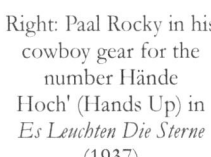

Left: A Portrait of Paal Rocky taken at the time of the making of *Es Leuchten Die Sterne* (1937)

An interesting perspective of the German film industry at the time came from the American producer Anthony Nelle who had spent two years in Germany and produced musicals for UFA and Tobis and returned to the USA in early 1939. He made it clear that living conditions in Germany were unbearable with improper food supplies and as a result, the tense situation demanded light musicals and comedies. He said 'the German studios have the finest mechanical equipment obtainable, but they don't know how to use it properly. The industry lost many of its best directors and technicians because of the racial laws, and the new crop is untrained. No new ideas are being developed. Camera work and lighting are particularly deficient, and the writers and cutters lack knowledge of their trade.' He added that the men in charge of the studios knew little about making pictures and were rigid in adhering to fiscal constraints.[37]

In 1937 Berlin was still a vibrant European capital but underneath the veneer of normality flowed disturbing currents with economic hardships and cultural manipulation by the National Socialists. Paal would have noticed or been aware of the change in Berlin's nightlife and entertainment as a direct result of the government's policies. The restaurants, cafes and coffee houses still thrived, and for example, the incomparable Kempinski Haus Vaterland complex with 12 themed restaurants, was still hugely popular, and variety acts could be seen in the Palm room. The smart hotels like the Eden, Adlon, Esplanade and Excelsior still had dinner and dancing, and the type of place was vividly re-created in *Es Leuchten Die Sterne*. Knowing Paal's fondness for being at the centre of things with an appreciative, well-heeled audience the Eden Hotel would have been a perfect choice.

However, the extensive cabaret scene had been decimated because the Nazi's perceived them to be part of the savoury 'decadence' of the Weimer Republic. All the more alternative venues, like the famous gay haunt the Eldorado, had been closed. Even the once renowned Kakadu bar closed its doors after 1936. Difference, dissent and satire were deplored, and entertainment had to be merely acceptable variety and dancing acts.

Gradually the Nazi party gained control of the Berlin theatres as it had done with the film studios. Goebbels was then able to showcase what the Nazi's considered to be appropriate theatre – mainly drama, operetta and opera.[38]

Interestingly, the two major centres of variety in Berlin – the Scala and the Wintergarten – carried on with little interference although they both adhered to Goebbels's principles. In October 1937 there was a variety-revue staged at the Scala called *Piccadilly* with top billing given to La Jana. Given the fact that *Es Leuchten Die Sterne* was in production at the time it must have been highly likely that Paal went to see the show.

La Jana's performance was not viewed favourably by Variety who observed that her applause was painfully milked and that she had nothing new to offer except the same old routine. Other acts included the comedienne and old-time cabaret star Trude Hesterberg who imitated Mae West, the acrobatics of Ben Dova, the acrobatic dancing of the American Marie Hollis and the dancing of the Scala girls and Gloria, Juanita and Garito.[39]

However, Paal's stay in Berlin was not without criticism or comment. A year or so later the gossip columnist Walter Winchell announced that Paal was now a German film idol, and had become 'a devoted chum of Adolf' and that he was 'a Joosh boy and Hitler knows it…' Strange comments indeed given that all Jews had been forbidden to appear in the film industry from 1933 and Winchell had made an assumption that his surname 'Roschberg' was Jewish. Since La Jana was apparently a favourite of Hitler, perhaps the story was that Paal had been seen in the company of La Jana and Hitler, but that is all.[40]

How long Paal stayed in Germany or if he appeared in other Tobis film productions is not known. However, he must have been uncomfortable in Berlin and did not stay long but returned to Paris, most likely in 1938. In Paris, he continued his film career by transferring to the French branch of Tobis that had been called Films Sonores Tobis but changed to Filmsonor in mid-1938.[41]

According to a later report, during his stay in Paris at this time, he appeared in 7 films[42] but sadly no actual credits can be found. A press advertisement for Tobis Films Sonores in early 1937 announced a programme of 10 films for 1937-38 many of which were made at the Tobis film studio at Epinay. Presumably, a similar programme for the period 1938-39 was also implemented.[43] One such film was *Les Gens du Voyage*, directed by Jacques Feyder who filmed his story of circus life in the Tobis Bavaria Film studios near Munich in early 1938.[44] From 1937 Filmsonor also co-operated closely with Regina Films and various projects were produced and released by them in 1938 and 1939 including a crime trilogy comprising *Cafe de Paris*, *Paris-New York* and *Derriere la Façade*. There was also Marc Allegret's *Entree des Artistes* (The Curtain Rises) that starred Louis Jouvet.

While in Paris, Paal studied with Louis Jouvet, a renowned French actor, director, and theatre director who was also a teacher of acting technique and theatrical history at the Conservatoire de Paris.[45] Since Jouvet appeared in two films made by Filmsonor and Regina, *Entree des Artistes* (1938) and *La Fin de Jour* (1939), this perhaps might suggest a connection.

Between 1938-1939 the situation in Europe deteriorated considerably with Hitler's intent to dominate Europe. The Nazi's occupied Austria in March 1938, the German army was mobilised in August 1938, Czechoslovakia was invaded in March 1939, Poland was invaded at the beginning of September 1939, and as a result, Britain and France declared war on Germany.

Leif and Paal must have returned home to Oslo in the summer of 1939 as events unfolded at an alarming rate. Given the circumstances, it must have been decided that it was safer for both of them to return to America and so they left Oslo aboard the liner Stavangerfjord on the 16th September 1939 for New York, arriving 7 days later on the 26th and stayed in an apartment at 162 West 56th Street.[46] Perhaps both tried to resuscitate their careers in New York, either together as the Rocky Twins or individually. Paal took voice studies with Albert Jeanotte of the Metropolitan Opera and intended to try his luck in film work again.[47]

It is not clear what Leif's objectives were or what he planned to do given his health issues, and conflicting accounts suggested that he either became a businessman or went back to the stage, or perhaps both.[48] Oddly, there must have been rumours about one or both of them being in Hollywood and attempting to revive their film career because in October 1939 the gossip columnist Louella Parsons said she had heard that they were working at RKO. After careful checking, she did not find either Paal or Leif on the lot.[49]

But what Parsons didn't know was that they had just arrived in New York a month before, and Paal must have been in dialogue with RKO hence the rumours. After a short time in New York, Paal headed back to Hollywood. Here he took acting lessons and did voice coaching with Josephine Dillon Gable (a drama teacher who became Clark Gable's first wife), Malvina Fox Dunn (at Warner Brothers), the Max Fleischmann's studio of diction and Drama and Max Reinhardt's dramatic school (the Reinhardt School of the Theatre) on Sunset Boulevard. He also claimed that he did work for RKO, although there are no confirmed credits or indications of what he was doing.[50]

What is more significant is that he was listed in the 1940 American census, taken in April 1940, which also reveals a fascinating relationship. Paal, aged 31, was living at 1330 Schuyler Road, Beverly Hills, in a rather magnificent house that had once been the home of Constance Bennett in the 1930s and was rented for $350 per month. The head of the household was listed as Hans Henkel aged 45, who was of German extraction and had previously lived in France. Paal was described as his partner, along with one male servant.[51]

Henkel had in fact been an important and influential figure in the German film industry in the late 1920s and 1930s. Born in Hermannsburg in Lower Saxony, north of Hanover in about 1895, his name was spelt variously. Herrkel, Haenkel, Henckel or Hinkel. He also had the honorific of Dr attached to his surname, but it may have been for something other than a medical attribute. How he began in film, and in what capacity, is not known but he did begin working for UFA, the most prominent German company at the time, presumably in the mid-1920s.[52]

At some point in the late 1920s, Henkel became associated with the film company Tobis – an umbrella name for an array of different companies. The origins and development of Tobis is complex but stemmed from a concerted move by European film-makers to protect their patents for film sound recording against American dominance and to break the American monopoly in Europe.

Following a conference in Berlin in July 1928, the Tonbild-Syndikat-A.G (meaning Sound Film Syndicate or Tobis for short) was founded in August 1928 as a subsidiary of the record and patent holding company Tri-Ergon-Musik-AG. Later, in early 1929, they merged with the other major German patent company Klangfilm, with the new combine splitting the European market. Klangfilm would engage in the logistics of sound reproduction and projection while Tobis would focus on the recording of sound and film production. The company was based in Holland with Dutch and Swiss financial backing, but there was definite German dominance in the arrangement and Henkel was one of the three managing directors.[53]

Very swiftly Tobis began sound film production, through the formation of a new company Tobis Industrie, of which Henkel was a part and most likely a director. It was after all somewhat important to have sound film product to show. In late 1928, the first German feature film using the Tobis synchronised sound technology went into production entitled *I Kiss Your Hand Madame*. It was released in January 1929. This was a silent film with one sound scene and starred Marlene Dietrich, with Harry Liedkte singing the theme song. Further Tobis films - shorts, features and documentaries followed and eventually studios were established in Johannisthal and Grunewald.[54]

Not content with just German film production, Tobis was intent on branching out throughout Europe.[55] In March 1929, Films Sonores Tobis was formed in Paris under the direction of Hans Henkel, who had decided to move to Paris from Berlin. In interviews, he stressed the co-operative nature of the company and how it would benefit the development of the sound film industry in France. By the end of 1929, the capital was raised from 100,000 Francs to 10 million Francs, and the old Éclair studios at Epinay had been bought and equipped for sound. Two of the initial productions were Henri Chomette's *Le Requin* (1930) and Rene Clair's *Sous Les Toits de Paris* (1930).[56]

Next, Tobis opened in London, and operations also began in other European countries. Henkel once again was a director of the London company and perhaps the other European concerns.[57] By 1932 Henkel was in charge of both the Paris and Berlin offices and had also set up a company in New York called Tobis Forenfilms, headed by the American lawyer Milton Diamond, mainly as a distributor for Tobis films in the USA.[58]

In mid-1935, Henkel was appointed General Manager of the Tobis holding company in the Hague[59] and made a trip to New York in March 1936 to finally conclude an agreement with the big American film studios regarding fees and royalties for usage of the Tobis sound system in Europe.[60] Of interest, it was clear that Henkel was undoubtedly well-connected because, on his journey to New York, the ship manifest listed his friends as the French industrial perfumier Jacques Geurin and the American inventor John Hays Hammond Jr, who was a pioneer in the development of electronic remote control.[61]

However, in mid-1937 things changed considerably. As we have seen earlier, Tobis was on the verge of bankruptcy and the German Government bought up the company. Henkel (along with others) resigned from his various positions in Tobis, including the holding company in Holland in May 1937. But it would appear he carried on as a producer for Films Sonores in Paris and was associated with *Le Joueur*, *Le Tigre du Bengale* and *Nuits de Princes*, all released in 1938.[62]

Whatever his reasons for leaving Tobis, he was apparently not at ease with the Nazi party. It is unlikely that he was Jewish since Jews had been banned from working in the film industry in 1933 but it does look like he was homosexual, and perhaps this may have been an issue. Given his status and employment history, he must have been a very wealthy man and had the good fortune to transfer his assets via his colleague Milton Diamond to America.

Henkel left Cherbourg, France aboard the Queen Mary arriving 8th May 1939 and once again the extent of his contacts were evident when he listed another friend as the French socialite Jacques Coppens de Fontenay.

Of course, the connection between Paal, Hans Henkel and the Tobis film company in Berlin and Paris is of significance. But where and when did they meet? Did they meet in Paris when the Rocky Twins returned from New York in 1936? Did Henkel have anything to with Paal's screen appearance in the Tobis film *Es Leuchten Die Sterne*? Or did they meet when Paal went to Paris in 1938 and appeared in several films for Tobis Film Sonores?

Whatever, the true story of their relationship and how they met, they were together as a couple, and although Henkel arrived in New York in May 1939, Paal followed in September. Henkel must have been another reason for Paal's decision to leave Oslo and travel back to America.

Paal's association with Henkel fits a neat pattern that had started when the Rocky Twins arrived in Paris in 1927, and the mysterious Von Neuman took them under his wing.[63] The allure of older, well-connected and wealthy men was a magnet to the twins, concisely revealed by the Norwegian artist Ferdinand

Finne[64] and also exemplified by their relationship with Arturo Lopez[65] and Larry Hart.[66] Henkel was only 14 years senior to Paal, so the age difference was not too significant. Henkel's financial and moral backing was a huge benefit to Paal, especially in their decision to move from New York to Hollywood.

It looks like Henkel was pandering to Paal's determination to once again break into American movies. Besides taking acting lessons and voice coaching, perhaps Henkel's undoubted network may have been used to Paal's advantage. Paal's possible links with RKO were based on Henkel's friendship with another German exile, Eric Pommer, the ex-UFA executive, who was working for RKO at the time and in fact produced the musical *Dance Girl Dance* (1940).[67]

While Paal was attempting to revive his acting career in Hollywood, Leif was still in New York and met and married a young woman called Maria Vogt (also Maria Vitoria Vogt). Of medium height and blonde with blue eyes, she had been born in Berlin in 1914, and so aged 26. She had been living in Rome but had made her way to Lisbon and managed to escape Europe aboard the liner Saturnia arriving in New York 9th February 1940.[68] Lisbon had become the great escape route for many attempting to avoid the clutches of Nazi Germany, and she was one of the fortunate ones to reach America.

Oddly on her arrival, she claimed that she was married and yet no details were given of her married name or husband, and furthermore she said she was in transit to Havana in Cuba. Leif and Maria married rather quickly in Manhattan on 20th February 1940.[69] A few months later it was made clear that Leif had married her so she could stay in the USA.[70] The swiftness of this marriage brings into question whether or not Leif had met Maria in Italy before he returned to Oslo and then New York in 1939. It was claimed many years later that in fact, he married Maria in Vienna in 1939 – a mystery in itself.[71]

At some point in late March or early April, Maria, dressed for some reason in East Indian garb swathed in veils, was a guest at Milton Diamond's party for Greta Keller in Manhattan. Of course, Milton Diamond was the American lawyer who was a friend and previous work colleague of Hans Henkel. This was an interesting connection, to say the least, as it does suggest that when Leif and Paal arrived in New York, they became part of the social circle that involved Henkel and Diamond. Greta Keller, on the other hand, was a cabaret singer and actress from Vienna who was singing at the Algonquin Supper Club at the time.[72] Apparently, the invitations for the Keller party numbered 65, but more than 200 managed to crash it.[73]

As she indicated on her arrival in New York, Maria inexplicably went to Havana but was only there for a short while since she arrived in Miami on 19th April 1940 by aeroplane from Havana, en-route back to New York and listed her address as East 56th Street.[74]

It may well be that Leif was already in Havana and Maria had gone to join him. Leif did, in fact, arrive in Miami by boat from Havana on 21st June 1940 and listed his occupation as an author and his last permanent residence as 162 E 56th Street, New York but was going to return to the Shelton Hotel at Lexington Avenue and East 48th and 49th Streets.[75]

The marriage to Maria didn't last long. According to Leif only a week, and they were finally divorced in September 1940.[76] However, Maria at some point had a son called Claude and Leif believed the boy to be his, but oddly there is no record of his birth.[77] Leif recalled that although they did not live together Claude and he became 'nice friends' and Claude called him 'little daddy' unlike Maria's other husbands who eventually came to his home - the other Daddys.[78] Maria married again in May 1942 to a Charles B. Moses in California, but there are no indications of further marriages.[79]

Leif was back in Havana during the rest of 1940 and the first half of 1941. So what was he doing in Havana? In a later interview, he did reveal that he became involved in the film industry in Cuba and had some career as an actor there appearing in, he claimed 28 movies, which sounds a little far fetched. He said that all the movies were the same and he always played a young man who was going to die. His only talent was a crying technique that no-one had seen before.[80]

With the advent of sound, Cuban Cinema-makers were able to film in their language. One pioneer was Ramon Peòn, who, after returning from Hollywood in the late 1930s, established a studio in 1938 and created the film company Pecusa and made 6 films, including *The Romance of Palmar*, but production ceased in 1939. Jose Tabio, a cameraman, also set up a small production company called Cuba-Sono at the beginning of the 1940s and in collaboration with Alejo Carpentier made several films. Apparently, in the 1940s, Cuban efforts were dominated by the Mexican film industry. Perhaps it was through Tobis that Leif gained his new, albeit brief, film career.[81]

It would appear that Leif left Havana for good in the Spring of 1941, arriving in Miami by boat on 25th March and returned to an address at 7 Park Avenue, New York. Life changed considerably after that for both Leif and Paal.[82]

Chapter Ten: The War Years and Later Life

A portrait of the Rocky Twins in their heyday at Paris, late 1920s
Courtesy of the Shubert Archive, New York

CHAPTER TEN
THE WAR YEARS AND LATER LIFE

Years later, in an interview, it was rather eloquently suggested that before either Paal or Leif had any chance to see how they would fare individually, the war changed everything and Leif and Paal signed up for active war service.[1]

According to Leif, his military career was little to write home about, and he did not exactly carry on the family's proud traditions. He enlisted in the American Navy, but after a few weeks was dismissed. Leif did not say why, but it is likely that his illness (degenerative nerve disease) was discovered and he was released on medical grounds. Why else would he have been removed and prevented from continuing?[2]

It is known that about this time, his illness did become so severe and that he was forced to stay in a hospital for two years. This must have been in New York sometime from 1941-1944 since there is a huge gap in any activity or press accounts about him during this period.[3] In 1944 it was claimed he married again to a Jenny Voigt (born in Canada), but again the marriage was dissolved. But there are no records for this marriage or a Jenny Voigt.[4]

However, by 1945 Leif's personal ambition of going into business was realised because he was the manager of what was called 'a swanky men's shop' in Manhattan.[5] Leif had also bought an apartment at 131 East 57th Street, which he would retain for many years to come.

Paal's war years were far more eventful. Allegedly, in 1941, he married a Lillian Turner in San Francisco, but she died in 1946. No records exist to verify this marriage or death, and oddly, many years later it was claimed by Leif that Paal had never married.[6] It was also in 1941 that Paal decided to join the war effort but one can only wonder what happened to his relationship with Hans Henkel. He tried to enlist, first in the American army, and then the navy but his application was rejected because of foreign citizenship. One reporter in 1945 said that because of talk about Paal's stay in Germany as a film star, to prove he was no Nazi partisan he enlisted.[7] Finally, in 1941 or 1942 the Royal Norwegian Air Force accepted him in Canada, and he went to what was called 'Little Norway'.[8] This was a Norwegian training centre established next to Toronto Island Airport, in the autumn of 1940 in agreement with the Norwegian Government-in-exile in London. Officially known as Flyvåpnenes Treningsleir (Air Force Training Camp) it was set up to train expatriate Norwegian airmen and soldiers in Canada. One of the first squadrons departed for active duty, becoming 330 Norwegian Squadron of the British RAF.

In May 1942, the base relocated to a more spacious site at Muskoka Airport, 79 miles north of Toronto. The base stayed there until February 1945, when it was relocated again to the Winkleigh Air Base near Devon, England.[9]

Whatever his length of stay in Little Norway, he was trained as a pilot but at some point, another usefulness was soon discovered. Since he spoke English, French and German, besides his native tongue, he was sent to England as an interpreter and propagandist.[10] What he did for the next three years is not known with certainty, as there are conflicting reports of his activities. What is strange is that he surfaced on 29th September 1943 crossing the border from Mexico to Nogales, Arizona. He was listed as being part of the Royal Norwegian Air Force and gave his address as 131 East 57th street, New York (Leif's apartment) and claimed the purpose of his visit was to reside permanently.[11] In all likelihood, he was making his way to the largest fighter-training base in the world - Luke Field – that was used mainly for advanced flight training.

Finally, after 3 years of action in Europe and elsewhere, he returned to America in early 1945 and was then transferred to the American army. Despite the allied victory against Germany in May 1945, he received his draft notice on V-J day. (15th August 1945).[12]

He was relocated to Sheppard Field Airforce base near Wichita Falls, Texas. This large training base had opened in October 1941 as the US Army Air Corps training, but during the period September to November 1945 it served as a central point for troops being discharged. In an interview in October 1945, he was described as one of the 'best-dressed twins in America' and said that he would like to join the occupation forces. 'I'd be good at occupying Germany, having close accounts of the five years they occupied my country.' He claimed that his brother (presumably Gunnar) spent four years in a German prisoner of war camp and that his 73-year-old father, a cavalry colonel, actively fought the German invasion. He also said that he planned to do a Broadway show when he was de-mobbed and added 'acting . . . is a disease, not a profession.'[13] During his stay at Sheppard Field, he entertained the troops and directed and appeared in, what was described as a 'hilarious musical comedy with an army hospital setting with all GI cast' called appropriately *Pills and Needles*.[14]

Before he was effectively de-mobbed and after October 1945, Paal was sent through basic training in San Francisco, but he was then allowed to return to New York.[15] It was reported that when he stepped off the train in New York in January 1946, he fell and broke a leg. Paal claimed he was to return to Paris to star in a revue but because he would be incapacitated for 6-8 weeks, urged his brother Leif to substitute for him. This did not happen.[16] Staying in his brother's apartment at 131 East 57th Street he also filed his naturalisation papers in April 1946.[17]

An enigmatic story about Paal came from Leif in 1948 when he revealed that Paal had once been engaged to Maria Belita Jepson-Turner, a British ballerina, figure skater and film actress.[18] At the age of 12, she was selected to represent Britain in the 1936 Olympic Games as a skater. In 1938 she arrived in America with her mother where she stayed throughout the war and eventually ended up in Hollywood and married the Hollywood actor Joel McGinnis in 1946.[19] There are no clues as to when Paal met her and got engaged or if this story is accurate. Due to her age it surely cannot have been until the 1940s and also it must have been before she married in 1946 and before 1948 when the account was published.

Once he was mobile again, Paal must have spent at least six months with the American occupational troops in the American zone of Germany based in Frankfurt, leaving New York on 14th June 1946.[20] One can only assume that during this period he was given leave to return home to Oslo and be reunited with his family. He also went to Paris in October 1946 since his passport was renewed or issued there. However, Paal returned to New York aboard Admiral R.E. Coontz from Bremerhaven, Germany on 3rd January 1947.[21]

Above: A portrait of Paal Rocky in the late 1930s or early 1940s

Oddly, in January 1946, when he broke his leg, it was stated that he had been in active service for 4 years 'without suffering a scratch.'[22] However, later reports claimed that he was wounded in a transport aircraft over the Pacific Ocean[23] and Leif also said that he crashed twice and survived but was badly injured. During an operation as a result of one crash, one of Paal's feet had to be shortened thus definitely terminating any thoughts of a future career as a dancer.[24] One can only assume therefore that the crash where he was injured must have taken place after the spring of 1946.

Despite his injury, Paal was still healthy (unlike his brother Leif) and full of enthusiasm, although it was later reported that he had lost the majority of his wealth through property speculation in California.[25] For his war service, Paal was awarded several medals including the Haakon VII 70th Anniversary Medal, which was given to military personnel who served in the Norwegian armed forces in Britain on the King's 70th birthday on 27th October 1942. He also received the Defence Medal 1940–1945 (Deltagermedaljen) rewarded to those military and civilian personnel who participated in the fight against the German invasion and occupation of Norway between 1940 and 1945.

During the late 1940s and into the 1950s, there are few accounts of what Paal was doing or where he was. But Leif later said that he was in fact stationed in Germany, and once again was in the military, but visited France, Switzerland and the Netherlands. Leif added that it was rumoured that Paal worked in the secret service.[26] However, during this period he spent some time in London and attended The Royal Academy of Dramatic Arts gaining an acting diploma in 1950.[27]

Paal also began writing, and in September 1950, his novel, *Skuddarsbarn* (Leap Year Children), was published in Norway by Johan Grundt Tanum. His novel was based on his childhood and adolescence in Oslo with his twin brother when it was called Kristiania.

Seemingly the stories that made up the book had previously been published in a weekly magazine. The two central characters were wild and wanton little boys who played many pranks, but always had their hearts in the right place.

Above: The cover of Paal Rocky's book *Skuddarsbarn* (Leap Year Children)

It was innocent fun, laced with satirical humour, which had no hidden depth or meaning but was merely meant to be entertaining. One reviewer thought that it was best enjoyed in small portions, taking one or two stories a day.[28]

Although the war ended in May 1945, it was not until early 1947 that Leif returned home to Oslo, and he must have also taken a trip back to Paris. He stayed in Europe for several months and returned to New York by plane from Stockholm on 15th June 1947. Interestingly on the manifest, he noted his occupation as artist.[29]

It is strange that it took Leif so long to return home to see his family in Oslo, especially since he had not seen them all for over 6 years and the family must have endured considerable hardship under Nazi occupation. It would be easy to read into this some kind of rift in the family but although there may well have been a general disapproval of Paal and Leif's lifestyle and a big generational chasm with their father, it was probably just due to circumstances, and perhaps Leif's illness prevented travel.

In Paris, the lawyer who had looked after Leif's business interests had been shot by the Germans at an early stage in the occupation. Thus, deductions and interest in connection with his French property had not been paid and allegedly his investment, which was worth a lot of money (it was reputed to be millions), had vanished.[30] Oddly, in 1948 he did claim to have an apartment in Paris so he may have reclaimed the existing apartment that he bought in the 1930s or acquired a new one.[31] Although he declared he had nothing, he still had his apartment in New York and presumably some other investments in America. He was limited in what he could do since his illness was still an issue and it was clear that he would never get well again, but on the contrary, the consensus was that he would get worse.[32]

After the war, he travelled regularly each year between Oslo, New York and Paris.[33] For example, he arrived back in New York after one trip at the end of May 1948 direct from Oslo via Scandinavian airlines.[34] Before leaving Oslo, he gave an interview announcing the 'new look' for men and showing off an outfit that he claimed to be 'revolutionary' by having a utilitarian jacket that extended over the waistline as a large pocket for valuables. It indicates that certainly in the late 1940s Leif was still running a menswear store.[35] Leif also arrived back in New York at the end of January 1949 aboard Queen Mary from Cherbourg.[36] Almost immediately afterwards there was a story that he was to marry a Carmelita Eduards of Argentina, but there are no records for this marriage or a Carmelita Eduards.[37] Leif made another trip home to Oslo in 1949 because again he returned to the USA via Baltimore aboard S.S. Arna on 7th August 1949 and received a fine of $40 for an improper manifest.[38]

Left and below:
Two paintings by Leif Rocky.
Courtesy Doyle New York & invaluable.com

Painting must have become a therapeutic activity for Leif, and this may have started when he visited Taormina in the late 1930s, and he continued throughout the 1940s. In the early 1950s, he had two exhibitions in New York,[39] the first of which was held at the Sutton Galleries on 11th October 1952.[40] Leif worked in oils, using lavish colour and broad brushstrokes and unlike the prevailing fashion for abstract expressionism, his style had a primitive touch with almost fauvist tendencies and reminiscent of the emerging style of contemporary realism.

Despite good sales, for whatever reason, it did not quite work out, and Leif began to take on any job that came along but we are told 'divorces, partying and drinking, and bad nerves limited his opportunities.'

One day in December, Macy's department store in New York advertised that they needed guys to perform as Father Christmas in the exhibition areas. Leif applied and got one of the jobs, and in the following days, he stood wearing a Father Christmas costume as a mannequin.[41] Leif made another trip to Europe in 1953 and arrived back in New York from Oslo on Scandinavian Airlines in June, but this may have been one of his last trips. [42]

At some point in early 1950, Paal had also returned to Oslo and began working in the Norwegian film industry. His first screen appearance was in the romantic comedy entitled *Vi vil Skilles* (or *We Want to be Separated*). Released in September 1952, it was directed by Nils R. Müller and was about the marriage of a young couple and the problems they encounter.[43] He also had a small part in *Det Kunne Vaert Deg* (*It Would Be Yours*) released November 1952 and directed by Kare Bergstrom and Henki Kolstad.

A more significant project was the comedy *Brudebuketten* (*Bridal Bouquets*) where Paal had written the screenplay based on one of his short stories. Released in December 1953 and directed by Bjorn Breigutu it had been in production since mid-1953 and starred Ragna Wettergreen, Per Abel and Lalla Carlsen with Paal also in a small role.[44]

In the spring of 1954, Paal announced plans for a play but no details emerged.[45] For his next project, he adapted a manuscript by Eiliv Odde Hauge (who had headed the Norwegian Government Film Unit during the war) along with Jon Lennart Mjoen for the comedy film *Troll i ord* (The Magic of Words) released in September 1954. It was a Danish and Norwegian co-production with skiing activities for background and glorious landscapes filmed in Tretten near the Gudbrandsdalen river and the Eidsbugarden Hotel located beside Lake Bygdin. Although admired technically, the story was criticised and was thought to be the weakest part of what was otherwise an interesting production.[46] Paal's last film appearance was in the comedy *Portrettet* (*The Portrait*) released in December 1954, which was directed by Per Aabel and Borgwall Skaugen and starred the twins Nanna and Vesla Stenersen along with Per Abel.

On the 15th February 1955 Paal arrived in New York aboard Westerdam from Rotterdam and went to stay in Leif's apartment,[47] but the purpose of his trip is not known, although he did have an operation to remove his appendix and perhaps had chosen to have this done in New York.[48] One of Leif's ex-wives lived downstairs with a maid, but there was a private entrance to his own set of rooms.[49]

While he was recovering from his operation, Paal was found dead in the apartment on the evening of 18th March 1955. The circumstances of his death are confused, and although official reports at the time suggest there was nothing suspicious, it was indeed suspicious.

Miss Eleanor Bentley, who ran a restaurant nearby and had an apartment in the same building as Leif's told the pressman that she had known both of them for many years. She recalled that Paal called her every day and when he didn't she would visit. That day he hadn't called, so she went to see him. She found Paal on the floor and thought he had been there for some hours. She called the police and an ambulance.

According to press reports, Paal was found unconscious with injuries to his head and burn marks on his arm. At first, the police were suspicious because of the marks on his body, but they were later convinced that he fallen and injured himself. Bentley denied reports that there were signs that someone had re-arranged traces of a struggle.

Paal was taken to Bellevue-Hospital, and two days later he died on 20th March. An autopsy and chemical analysis was done as part of the investigation and although the details of this investigation were not revealed it was speculated that Paal was unwell due to his operation and that he collapsed due to this and because of pneumonia [50]

Despite the official version of Paal's injuries and the circumstances in which he was found, there was confusion about exactly what had happened and indifference by the authorities to investigate the incident as a possible crime. Two immediate relatives were clear that Paal was indeed murdered and one of them suggested that in fact, the murderer was a male lover who had become enraged because Paal was saying a final farewell having got engaged to an actress[51] Leif himself said that Paal was murdered and was found 'on the floor with a lamp wire around his throat and was stifled. Who had done it - and why? Nobody knows.'[52]

Certainly, during questioning, Eleanor Bentley and other neighbours and friends would have commented on Paal's lifestyle. As a result, the indifference of the police and authorities could be explained by the prevailing trend of extreme homophobia at the time. By the early 1950s homosexuality was widely viewed as being evil and a sickness, a crime and a perversion. Homosexuality was a focus of social anxiety, and moral panic and known homosexuals were the targets of intense media attention and government crackdowns and arrests.[53]

Paal's death at the young age of 46, would have been devastating not just for his twin brother Leif, but also for the rest of the family. It must have also been deeply perplexing and upsetting for Paal's untimely demise not to be treated with respect with no further investigation into his murder, the motive and the identity of the culprit.

Paal'd body was cremated, and the Norwegian Consulate sent his ashes and a formal report to Oslo. He was finally buried in Oslo on 14th June. Sadly, there was another death that year when Adolf Roschberg, the father of the Rocky Twins died in November 1955.

In the late 1950s following Paal's death, it would appear that Leif did not make any trips back to New York. In the following years, he spent more time at home in Oslo, but he did become a language teacher in Rome for a while. He also settled into a job as a tourist guide in Oslo.[54]

There was another blow when Leif's only son Claude died in about 1962 in New York. It was a deeply sad and tragic tale. Claude had been brought up by his mother Maria, and her second husband, Charles Moses. Claude had grown up with sensitive nature, and he was frugal and kind, but also bad-tempered and crazy when things went wrong. Leif believed that his erratic behaviour was the result of his parent's actions. In his teens, Claude became unsettled 'and a haunted soul' and began to drink too much. A broken engagement knocked him off his feet and then something happened. It appears as if he was involved in a car crash that killed three people and the blame for the accident pointed at Claude. In a desperate attempt to save his son, Leif invested his last capital in New York, but in vain. One week after Claude's 21st birthday, Leif received a telegram to say he was dead.[55]

By the early 1960s, Leif had sold his apartment in New York and was looking after his mother in his parents' home at 22 Nobelsgate, in a pre-war apartment block that was described as being 'marked by confident, cultured family tradition.' It was stated that his health had failed partly, due his nerve illness and that now he mainly worked by teaching English to some private students.[56]

According to the interviewer from Alle Kvinner magazine in mid-1963, there was not much left of the fame, or the millions and all he had was the memories and simply looked back to the good old days.[57] One of the rooms in the apartment was covered by some of his paintings and inscribed photographs from many great stars of the stage and screen from the 1930s. Souvenirs were everywhere. Leif related his life story and many of his adventures with his brother Paal and often sought photographs, postcards, posters and other ephemera from suitcases to punctuate the conversation.

Throughout the interview Leif was restless and while he talked he was in ceaseless motion. He strolled back and forth, stopping often at large wall mirrors and stroking a hand through the rich, black hair, or throwing himself down on a couch, getting up and lighting a cigarette or pouring a glass of wine. At one point Leif played a record and briefly forgot the time and place. His gaze was distant, and his body looked for the rhythm and rocked gently. Leif also played Hände Hoch, the song that Paal recorded in Germany for the film *Es Leuchte Die Sterne* in 1938.[58]

Leif rarely went outdoors and spent most of the day with the curtains half-drawn, and even on hot days, the windows would be closed because he didn't like the noise of the traffic outside. It appeared as if his only connection with the outside world was the telephone, which stood on the floor. When he had a call, he sat up on the couch, stacked with pillows and had long conversations about everything and nothing.

The journalist thought that you would expect to find a bitter and disillusioned man, broken down by illness, disappointments and tragedy. If he was, Leif kept it to himself. He talked with an America accent about his career with his brother Paal without sadness, and the impression was given that he rather regarded it all like a good joke He smiled when he talked and was ironic and did not take himself seriously

According to the interviewer, Leif's age was hard to determine. At first sight, you would think he was in his early 40s, but he was in reality in his early 50s. He was slim, with long dancer legs and a narrow waist, and his body still reflected the relentless hard training that he used to endure. He still looked like a dancer. Leif was asked about his appearance and whether it had been a burden to go through life being regarded as one of the most beautiful men in the world. He looked up, smiled and said 'Yes, I'll admit that I would rather look like you....' This was a good example, the journalist thought, of his humility and humour.

After the interview in 1963, Leif carried on as before in his private world. His mother, Gudrun, died in April 1964 and then his brother Gunnar, died in March 1965. Leif Rocky died aged only 58 on 10th May 1967 in Oslo, Norway.

In the interview for the magazine Alle Kvinner, in 1963,[59] Leif was asked: 'You have been at the peak of success.... you had the world at your feet, are you not bitter at your fate?' He shrugged his shoulders and said 'I have a talent, which is greater than everything put together. Adaptability. Goodbye.'

ACKNOWLEDGMENTS

I would like to thank the following individuals and institutions for all their help: Marethe Turner, Mike Everson, Runar Jordaen, Thore Elton, Henning Roschberg, Mark Swartz (Shubert Archive, New York), Haakon Howard. Fleming Hagensen (Royal Danish Library), Tyler Alpern, Victoria Kastner, (Hearst Archive), Molly Haigh (UCLA Archives), Mary Huelsback (Wisconsin Center for Film and Theater Research / Wisconsin Historical Society), Roberto Joly (Oslo Public Library), J.D. Doyle, Robert Brooks, Roald Rynning, Mirko Stopar, ancestry.com, lantern.mediahist.org, gallica.com, British Newspaper Library Archive, Mary Evans Picture Library and Archive, Herman Berthelsen (Det Glade Arkiv) and Oslo Kommune Deichmanske Bibliotek.

PICTURE CREDITS

All images in this book are from the author's private collection with the exception of those referenced in the captions. I would like to thank the following for providing these particular images: Mike Everson, Shubert Archive New York, J.D. Doyle Archives, Bison Archives and Hollywood HistoricPhotos.com, Mary Evans Picture Library, Doyle New York & invaluable.com, Lincoln Center Theatre Collection New York, Library of Congress Prints and Photographs Division and Wisconsin Center for Film and Theater Research / Wisconsin Historical Society

ABOUT THE AUTHOR

Gary Chapman has always been fascinated by the 1920s and the Jazz Age, and his degree in archaeology left him with a passion for uncovering the truth about his subjects.

After living and working for many years in London working in book publishing, he now lives in Stroud, Gloucestershire. He is fortunate in being able to pursue his various passions – publishing, marketing books, writing, the Jazz Age and cake decorating.

CHRONOLOGY

1909 (27 Feb)	Born, Oslo
1920	Debut in Amor Sommer Theatre, Oslo
1923	Their book Til Eventyrland is published
1927 (Aug)	Visit London
1927 (Oct)	Appearance at Chez Victor's, London
1927 (Late)	Visit Paris
1927 (Dec)	Casino de Paris - *Les Ailes de Paris* launched 15/12/27 continued to appear through 1928
1927 (Dec)	Chiquito Club with Alanova (the basque bar Biarritz in Paris)
1928 (June)	Appearance at the first dance of the Paris Season for the Henri Van Heukelom's
1928 (Summer)	Concert Mayol, Paris. *La Volupte de Paris*
1928 (Oct)	Emil Schwarz revue in Vienna *Sie Werden Lachen* 9/10/28- 22/2/29 (Stadt Theater)
1929 (10 Jan)	Appearance in the film *L'Argent* directed by Marcel L'Herbier, released Paris
1929 (March)	Budapest with Josephine Baker
1929 (Apr-May)	Visited London with Mistinguett & appeared in cabaret at the Kit Cat Restaurant, London
1929 (May)	Trip to the Riviera & Venice (spring / April)
1929 (Summer)	The Bernaus revue at the Chat Noir, Oslo
1929 (Aug)	Back in Paris
1929 (Sept)	Andre Charlot's cabaret in the Grosvenor House, Park Lane, London,
1929 (Nov)	Launch of *Paris Miss*, Casino De Paris with Mistinguett, continued through Aug 1930
1930 (Feb)	Film *Dix Minutes au Music-Hall*
1930 (Mar)	Le Bal de la Pharmacie, Paris
1930 (Apr)	Trip to the Riviera (spring / April)
1930 (Sept)	Leave France for New York
1930 (Oct)	Party / dancing at the Ritz Carlton Hotel, New York
1931	(Early) Return to Paris
1931 (Mar-June)	Tour of Europe with Mona Lee
1931 (April)	Berlin engagement
1931 (May)	Rode Molle, Oslo
1931 (June)	Apollo Theatre, Copenhagen
1931 (July)	Rode Molle, Oslo
1931 (Aug)	Ernst Rolf's revue, China Theatre, Stockholm
1931 (Aug)	One of twins hurt in Stockholm
1931 (Summer)	Leif may have married first wife in Sweden
1931 (Oct)	Trip to USA and onto Hollywood Travel to Galveston 21/10/31
1932 (spring)	Appearance at The Ship Cafe, Venice Beach
1932 (Mar)	Dancing with Julanne Johnston in the Garden Room of the Biltmore Hotel, Hollywood
1932 (Apr)	Stage show at the Paramount Theatre, Los Angeles

1932 (June-July)	Production of *Blondie of the Follies* at MGM with Marion Davies. Released September
1932 (Sept)	Floor-show at Club New Yorker, Los Angeles with Julanne Johnston and Jean Malin as MOC
1932 (Oct)	Report that Leif divorced Swedish wife
1932 (15 Dec)	The Los Angeles Examiner Christmas Show
1932 (23 Dec)	*Tattle Tales*, Los Angeles
1933 (Mar)	RKO vaudeville show Tip Top with Nitza Vernille (in San Francisco)
1933 (April)	Club New Yorker, Hollywood with Julanne Johnston, hosted by Jean Malin
1933 (May)	Filming of *Midnight Club* (released July)
1933 (May)	*Low & Behold*, musical revue at Pasadena Community Playhouse
1933 (Autumn)	Signed by the Shuberts for the *Ziegfeld Follies*. Returned to New York and began rehearsals for two weeks but dropped from the show because of Equity regulations.
1933 (Nov)	Club Montmartre, New York
1933 (Dec)	Gudrun Roschberg (their mother) arrived New York
1934 (June)	Act with Nitza Vernille, RKO vaudeville, New York
1934 (July)	SS Club Royale, New Jersey
1934 (Oct)	Continental Grill, Hotel St Moritz
1935 (Jan)	New York Brabazon Plaza Hotel Revue *Sunday Nights at Nine* with Billy Milton and Shirley Booth
1935 (Feb)	Le Boeuf sur le Toit, New York
1935 (Mar)	Joe Zelli's Normandie Club, New York
1935 (May)	Robert Henderson's revue *Up to the Stars* (Milwaukee & tour June-Sept)
1935 (Oct)	Howard Lanin's Town Casino, Philadelphia (with Helen Gray)
1935 (Nov)	*Continental Varieties*, vaudeville-revue (first at the Stella Theatre, Montreal, Canada, then Shubert Theatre Boston & the Theatre Masque, New York)
1936 (Feb)	Appeared with Josephine Baker in her nightclub, New York
1936 (Mar)	Versailles restaurant, New York (with Helen Gray)
1936 (Summer)	Edgewater Beach Hotel, Chicago
1936 (Oct)	Returned to Paris
1936 (Nov)	One of the attractions at the Ritz Hotel, Paris (with Nayan Pearce)
1936 (Nov)	Part of stage show at Jacques Haik's Rex Theatre, Paris with Nayan Pearce
1936 (Dec)	Part of stage show at Gaumont Palace, Paris with Nayan Pearce
1937 (Feb)	Chat Noir, Oslo
1937 (Summer)	Cirkusrevyen, Copenhagen
1937 (Autumn)	Rocky Twins effectively split as an act
1937-38	Leif lived for 2 years in Taormina in Sicily
1938	Film career for Paal in Paris and Berlin with Tobis
1938	Paal appeared in the film *Es Leuchte Die Sterne* released 17/3/38
1939 (Sept)	Leif & Paal arrived back in New York (26/9/39) from Oslo Paul lives in Hollywood with ex-Tobis executive Hans Henkel
1940	RKO, Hollywood (Paal)
1940 (Feb)	Leif married Maria Vogt in New York

1940 (June)	Leif arrived Miami from Havana
1940 (Sept)	Leif divorced Maria Vogt but son Claude born
1941 (Mar)	Leif arrived Miami from Havana
1941	Allegedly, Paal married Lilian Turner 1941 in San Francisco. Divorced in 1946
1941	Paal accepted by Royal Norwegian Air Force in Canada
1943 (Sept)	Paal crossed the border from Mexico to Nogales, Arizona possible enroute to Luke Field air base
1944	Allegedly, Leif married Jenny Voigt in Canada but divorced
1945 (late)	Paal - basic training in San Francisco before being de-mobbed
1946 (Jan)	Paal arrives New York
1946	Paal spends 6 months with the American occupational troops in Frankfurt
1947 (Jan)	Paal returned to New York from Bremerhaven, Germany
1947	Leif returns to Oslo. Arrives back in New York June 1947
1948 (May)	Leif arrived back in New York direct from Oslo
1949 (Jan)	Leif arrived back in New York from Cherbourg
1949	Report that Leif was to marry Carmelita Eduards
1949 (Aug)	Leif arrived back in New York
1950 (Sept)	Paal's novel *Skuddarsbarn* published
1952 (Sept)	Exhibition of Leif's paintings in New York
1952 (Sept)	Paal appears in the film *Vi vil Skilles*
1952 (Nov)	Paal appears in the film *Det Kunne Vaert Deg*
1953 (June)	Leif arrived back in New York from Oslo
1953	Paal wrote the screenplay and appeared in the film *Brudebuketten (Bridal Bouquets)*
1954	Paal given credit as writer on the film *Troll i ord*, a comedy filmed in Norway with the director Jon Lennart Mioen
1954	Paal appears in the film *Portrettet (The Portrait)*
1955 (Feb)	Paal arrives in New York from Oslo
1955	Paal died 21 March in New York
1967	Leif died 10 May in Kristiania, Norway

FOOTNOTES

Author's note
1 Alle Kvinner, No34, August 1963.

Introduction
1 Variety, 20/11/29.
2 The Evening News, Harrisburg, 20/4/45.
3 See The Dolly Sisters: Icons of the Jazz Age by Gary Chapman.
4 Alle Kvinner. No34, August 1963.
5 The Evening News, Harrisburg, 20/4/45.
6 Dagbladet, 13/4/67.
7 Email Tyler Alpern and programme online.
8 Kay Thompson: From Funny Face To Eloise by Sam Irvin.
9 Jazz Age Club.com.

Chapter One: The Early Years 1909-1927
1 Family information derived from various online family history sites including My Heritage, Ancestry and Geni. Cyrano,15/7/28, Dagbladet,10/4/48 and Illustrierte Kronru-Zeituas, 14/4/29.
2 Who is Who 1948 / project Runeberg at http://runeberg.org/hvemerhvem/1948/0444.html and Studentene Fra, 1927 / Oslo 1952.
3 Alle Kvinner, No32 / 7 August 1963.
4 Oslo Census 1910 / https://digitalarkivet.no/census
5 Alle Kvinner, No32 / 7 August 1963
6 Paal Rocky / Utisolen, 1951 and Dagbladet, 27/1/31.
7 Sol Gjennem Skyer By Signe Lund.
8 Dagbladet, 10/4/48.
9 Dagbladet, 10/4/48, Arbeiderbladet, 20/11/24 and Alle Kvinner, No32 / 7 August 1963.
10 Alle Kvinner, No32/ 7 August 1963.
11 Alle Kvinner, No32/ 7 August 1963.
12 Cyrano, 15/7/28.
13 Oslo Illustrate, 12-19 September 1928.

Chapter Two: The Heavenlies' or 'The Black Orchids of the North' in London
1 Alle Kvinner, No33, August 1963.
2 Alle Kvinner, No33, August 1963.
3 Music For All Pictorial Supplement.
4 Music For All Pictorial Supplement and Play Pictorial.
5 The Stage, 1/9/27 and programme w/c 12/9/27.
6 The Stage, 16/6/27.
7 Dancing Times, June 1927.
8 The Stage, 1/9/27 and Dancing Times, October 1927.
9 Alle Kvinner, No33, August 1963.
10 Cyrano, 15/7/28.
11 The Stage, 14/4/27.
12 Cyrano, 15/7/28.
13 Cyrano, 15/7/28.
14 Alle Kvinner, No33, August 1963.
15 Alle Kvinner, No33, August 1963.
16 Alle Kvinner, No33, August 1963.
17 Alle Kvinner, No33, August 1963.
18 Brooklyn Daily Eagle, 17/1/26.
19 The Dancing Times, December 1925.
20 The Restaurants of London by Eileen Hooton-Smith.
21 Dancing Times, December 1927 and Eve, 26 May 1926.
22 Alle Kvinner, No33, August 1963.
23 Nights in London by Horace Wydham.
24 Evening News, 18/8/24 and Vogue UK, 5/10/27.
25 Illustrated Police News, 17/11/27 and The Stage, 12/4/28.
26 Nordisk Tidende, 3/11/32.

Chapter Three: Double Rendezvous, Paris 1927-1928

1 All attempts to identify Von Neuman have proved elusive.
2 Alle Kvinner, No33, August 1963.
3 Nordisk Tidende, 3/11/32.
4 Oslo Illustrate, 12-19 September 1928.
5 Basil Woon The Paris That's Not in Guide Books.
6 Chicago Tribune, 26/10/27, 16/11/27, Bricktop by Bricktop and Vogue UK, 30/11/27.
7 Dancing Times, February 1928.
8 The Bugatti Queen by Miranda Seymour.
9 Chicago Tribune, 21/12/27.
10 Le Temps, 31/12/27.
11 Comoedia, 23/2/28.
12 Mistinguett Queen of the Paris Night by Mistinguett.
13 Paris Soir, 28/2/28.
14 I went to Paris (Jag for till Paris) by Thora Dardel.
15 Dagbladet, 28/11/33.
16 Szinhazi Elet, 7 April 1929.
17 Dagbladet, 2/6/26.
18 I went to Paris (Jag for till Paris) by Thora Dardel.

19 Vogue UK, Early May 1927.
20 The Secret Paris of the 1930s by Brassai and detail the blog post Queer Paris at Jazzage.com.
21 The Ox on the Roof by James Harding, The Mistinguett Legend by David Bret and Vogue US, 15/5/25.
22 Alle Kvinner, No32 / 7 August 1963.
23 I went to Paris (Jag for till Paris) by Thora Dardel and Alle Kvinner, No2 / 7 August 1963.
24 I went to Paris (Jag for till Paris) by Thora Dardel.
25 I went to Paris (Jag for till Paris) by Thora Dardel.
26 I went to Paris (Jag for till Paris) by Thora Dardel.
27 Vogue, 1/6/28.
28 Mistinguett Queen of the Paris Night by Mistinguett.
29 The Tatler, 29/8/28.
30 La Rampe, June 1928.
31 The Folies Bergere by Charles Castle.
32 Oslo Illustrate, 12-19 September 1928.
33 Oslo Illustrate, 12-19 September 1928.
34 Paris Soir, 24/6/28.
35 Cyrano, 15/7/28.
36 La Rampe, June 1928.
37 Comoedia, 19/6/28.
38 Oslo Illustrate, 12-19 September 1928.
39 Mistinguett Queen of the Paris Night by Mistinguett.
40 Folies Bergere by Charles Castle.
41 Paradise Mislaid by Billy Milton.
42 Naked at the Feast by Lynn Haney.
43 Cyrano, 15/7/28, Mistinguett Queen of the Paris Night by Mistinguett and photographs seen in one the albums belonging to socialite Richard Colley.
44 http://fabulorum.com/tag/arturo-lopez-willshaw.
45 Secrets by Roger Peyrefitte and A Prince Amongst Stones by Prince Rupert Loewenstein.
46 Mistinguett Queen of the Paris Night by Mistinguett.
47 Bricktop by Bricktop and The Evening News, Harrisburg, 20/4/45. See also Chapter Five.
48 Oslo Illustrate, 12-19 September 1928 and Alle Kvinner, No32 / 7 August 1963.
49 Description from Ancestry.com / passenger lists.
50 Mistinguett Queen of the Paris Night by Mistinguett and Paradise Mislaid by Billy Milton.
51 Paradise Mislaid by Billy Milton.
52 Alle Kvinner, No33 August 1963.
53 Mistinguett Queen of the Paris Night by Mistinguett.
54 Paradise Mislaid by Billy Milton.
55 Alle Kvinner, No33, August 1963.
56 Alle Kvinner, No34, August 1963.
57 Alle Kvinner, No34, August 1963.
58 Oslo Illustrate, 12-19 September 1928.
59 Alle Kvinner, No32 / 7 August 1963.
60 Oslo Illustrate, 12-19 September 1928.

Chapter Four: European Tour 1928-1930
1 Oslo Illustrate, 12-19 September 1928.
2 Die Theatralische Revue in Berlin und Wien by Franz-Peter Kothes.
3 Programme in the Czettel scrapbook Lincoln Centre, New York and Die Theatralische Revue in Berlin und Wien by Franz-Peter Kothes.
4 Freiheit!, 10/11/28.
5 Illustrierte Kronen Zeitung, 12/4/29.
6 Wiener Sonn- und Montags-Zeitung, 15/10/28.
7 Dance Magazine, September 1927, Paris Plaisirs, July 1927.
8 Low and Behold! Programme cited in Kay Thompson: From Funny Face to Eloise by Sam Irvin.
9 Mistinguett Queen of the Paris Night by Mistinguett.
10 Europe after 8:15.
11 Vienna Yesterday and Today by J. Alexander Mahan.
12 Vienna's Musical Sites and Landmarks by Addie Funk.
13 The Vienna that's not in the Baedeker.
14 Vienna Yesterday and Today by J. Alexander Mahan.
15 The Vienna that's not in the Baedeker.
16 The Night Side of Europe by Karl Kitchen, The Vienna that's not in the Baedeker and Vienna's Musical Sites and Landmarks by Addie Funk.
17 The Night Side of Europe by Karl Kitchen and Vienna Yesterday and Today by J. Alexander Mahan.
18 Vienna Yesterday and Today by J. Alexander Mahan.
19 The Night Side of Europe by Karl Kitchen, The Vienna that's not in the Baedeker.
20 The Vienna that's not in the Baedeker, Europe after 8:15 and The Night Side of Europe by Karl Kitchen.
21 Vienna Yesterday and Today by J. Alexander Mahan.
22 Die Buhne, 24/1/29.
23 The Vienna that's not in the Baedeker.
24 Illustrierte Kronen Zeitung, 12/4/29.
25 Los Angeles Times, 21/9/32.

26 Folies Bergere by Charles Castle.
27 Bricktop by Bricktop.
28 The Mistinguett Legend by David Bret.
29 Naked at the Feast by Lynn Haney and Josephine: The Hungary Heart by Jean-Claude Baker and Chris Chase.
30 Variety, 7/4/26, Variety, 28/4/26.
31 Bricktop by Bricktop.
32 Vogue UK, early May 1927.
33 Naked at the Feast by Lynn Haney and Variety, 23/5/28.
34 Variety, 14/11/28 and 5/12/28.
35 Variety, 9/1/29 and 20/2/29.
36 Aris Az Est, 19/12/28 and Esti Kurir, 6/12/28.
37 Budapest Hirlap, 18/1/29.
38 Press adverts Budapest, 28 February 1929.
39 Budapest Hirlap, 2/3/29.
40 Dagbladet, 13/3/48.
41 Dagbladet, 13/3/48.
42 Szinhazi Elet, 7/4/29.
43 Comoedia, 23/3/29.
44 Az Est, 27/3/29.
45 Alle Kvinner, No34, August 1963.
46 Szinhazi Elet, 7 April 1929.
47 Pesti Hirlap, 27/3/29.
48 Szinhazi Elet, 7 April 1929.
49 Dagbladet, 13/5/29.
50 Alle Kvinner, No34, August 1963.
51 Illustrated Graphic, 23/3/29.
52 Az Est, 10/4/29 and Magyarorszag, 10/4/29 and Magyarorszag, 10/10/29.
53 Illustrierte Kronru-Zeituas, 12 and 14/4/29.
54 Alle Kvinner, No34, August 1963.
55 Comoedia, 4/4/29.
56 Theatre World, May 1929 and programme.
57 The Sketch, 22/5/29.
58 Nottingham Evening Post, 20/4/29.
59 Comoedia, 12/4/29 and 22/4/29 and Nottingham Evening Post, 20/4/29.
60 Mistinguett Legend by David Bret.
61 The Stage, 11/4/29 and The Times, 7/4/29.
62 The Winnipeg Tribune, 25/5/29.
63 The Stage, 11/4/29 and 18/4/29.
64 Variety, 17/4/29.
65 The Stage, 2/5/29.
66 The Mistinguett Legend by David Bret.
67 Comoedia, 1/5/29.
68 Alle Kvinner, No34, August 1963.
69 Variety, 17/7/29.
70 Alle Kvinner, No34, August 1963.
71 Alle Kvinner, No33, August 1963.
72 Dagbladet, 13/5/29.
73 Oslo Illustrate, 19-26 June 1929.
74 Dagbladet, 13/5/29, 11/7/29, 6/8/29, 17/8/29 and 20/8/29 and Ardeiderbladet, 02/07/29.
75 Ardeiderbladet, 02/07/29.
76 Arkivverket Digitalarkivet, 25/8/29.
77 The Paris That's Not in the Guide Books by Basil Woon.
78 The Film Daily, 1/10/29.
79 The Stage, 10/10/29.
80 Variety, 30/10/29.
81 The Stage, 5/9/29.
82 The Bystander, 4/9/29.
83 The Stage, 5/9/29 and The Mistinguett Legend by David Bret.
84 Paradise Mislaid by Billy Milton and http://www.jazzageclub.com/personalities/frank-leveson.
85 Variety, 16/10/29.
86 Variety, 20/11/29.
87 Shubert Archive, 31/1/30
88 Mistinguett: Queen of the Paris Night by Mistinguett.
89 Variety, 11/12/29.
90 Variety, 20/11/29.
91 Variety, 11/12/29.
92 Chicago Tribune, 22/11/29.
93 Variety, 11/12/29.
94 Variety, 22/1/30.
95 Variety, 5/3/30.
96 Mistinguett: Queen of the Paris Night by Mistinguett.
97 The Mistinguett Legend by David Brett.
98 Arbeiderbladet, 25/1/30.
99 Oslo Illustrerte, 26 Feb – 5 March 1930.
100 Chicago Tribune, 24/2/30 and L'Intransigeant, 6/3/30.
101 Alle Kvinner, No34, August 1963, Oslo Illustrerte 26 Feb – 5 March 1930, Nordisk Tidende 3/11/32 and Low and Behold! Programme cited in Kay Thompson: From Funny Face to Eloise by Sam Irvin.
102 Variety, 15/5/29.
103 Motion Picture News, 14/12/29.
104 Variety, 23/10/29.
105 Variety, 5/2/30.
106 Variety, 12/2/30.
107 Listing 27/1/31 La Semaine à Paris : Paris-guide.
108 Oslo Illustrerte, 26 Feb – 5 March 1930.
109 Ferdinand Finne by Thore J. Elton.
110 Chicago Tribune, 11/1/29 and Variety, 22/9/31.
111 Ferdinand Finne by Thore J. Elton.
112 Private email with Thore J. Elton.
113 The Tatler, 2/4/30.
114 Variety, 23/4/30.
115 Variety, 7/5/30.
116 Dagbladet, 17/6/31.

117 Variety, 2/7/30.
118 Variety, 6/8/30.

Chapter Five: First Trip to New York and back to Europe 1930-1931

1 Variety, 20/8/30.
2 Variety, 3/9/30 and Ancestry.com.
3 Picture Play Magazine, September 1930.
4 Alle Kvinner, No34, August 1963
5 Chicago Tribune, 7/5/30.
6 Alle Kvinner, No34, August 1963 and Nordisk Tidende 3/11/32. Note: Myrna Loy never visited NYC until 1935.
7 The Evening News, Harrisburg, 20/4/45.
8 http://www.newyorker.com/magazine/2004/09/27/a-life-in-good-taste.
9 The Evening New Harrisburg 20/4/45.
10 Variety 25/6/30.
11 Gay New York by George Chauncey.
12 Gay New York by George Chauncey.
13 Variety, 4/1/28.
14 Variety, 10/9/30.
15 Radio Digest, February 1931.
16 Variety, 16/10/29 and The Night Club Era by Stanley Walker.
17 Gay New York by George Chauncey.
18 Variety, 20/4/30, 7/5/30, 21/5/30 and Gay New York by George Chauncey.
19 Strange Brother by Blair Niles.
20 Gay New York by George Chauncey.
21 Feature on www.outtraveler.com.
22 Gay Rebel of the Harlem Renaissance by Richard Bruce Nugent and Bulldoggers, Pansies and Chocolate Babies by James F. Wilson.
23 Variety, 9/4/30.
24 Variety, 9/4/30 and 10/9/30.
25 Radio Digest, February 1931.
26 Variety, 10/9/30.
27 Variety, 17/9/30 and 22/10/30.
28 Variety, 17/12/30.
29 Variety, 15/10/30.
30 Variety, 11/2/31.
31 Variety, 25/2/31.
32 Comoedia, 24/3/31.
33 Dagbladet, 17/6/31 and Naked at the Feast by Lynn Haney.
34 Josephine: The Hungary Heart by Jean-Claude Baker and Chris Chase.
35 Variety, 11/10/23.
36 Variety, 10/6/25.
37 Variety, 15/7/25 and 21/10/25.
38 Variety, 17/3/26.
39 Variety, 26/10/27.
40 Variety, 11/1/28.
41 Exhibitors Herald & Moving Picture World, 5/5/28 and Variety, 2/5/28.
42 Variety, 26/12/28.
43 Variety, 29/5/29.
44 Nordisk Tidende, 3/11/32.
45 Variety, 13/5/31.
46 Arbeiderbladet, 25/1/30 and Variety, 4/2/31.
47 Los Angeles Times, 21/9/32, The Michigan Daily, 19/5/35 and Milwaukee Journal, 14/5/35.
48 Dagbladet, 16/5/31 and Arbeiderbladet, 16/5/31.
49 Dagbladet, 17/6/31, Nordisk Tidende, 3/11/32, Variety 14/7/31 and 18/8/31.
50 Variety, 8/1/30.
51 Variety, 2/7/32, 30/4/30 and 23/4/30.
52 Brochure from http://runeberg.org/rolf1931 and in author's collection.
53 Variety, 18/8/31.
54 Harlem in Montmartre by William A. Shack and Variety, 1/12/31.
55 Variety, 27/10/31.
56 Variety, 13/10/31 and 1/12/31.
57 Paradise Mislaid by Billy Milton and The Folies Bergere by Charles Castle.
58 Paradise Mislaid by Billy Milton.

Chapter Six: Hollywood, MGM and the Pansy Craze 1931-1932

1 Dagbladet, 17/6/31.
2 http://www.danskefilm.dk/skuespiller/10428.html.
3 Variety, 13/10/31.
4 Variety, 18/8/31.
5 Max Gordon Presents by Max Gordon, Variety 20/10/31, 10/11/31 and 24/11/31. In fact, Gordon left for Hollywood with the Marx Brothers in January 1932 and spent some time as a consultant for Paramount.
6 The Brooklyn Daily Eagle, 28/10/32.
7 Variety, 21/10/31.
8 Variety, 3/11/31.
9 Variety, 17/11/31.
10 Variety, 11/1/28.
11 The Film Daily, 1/10/29.
12 The Film Daily, 16/3/30.
13 Dagbladet, 12/11/32.
14 Motion Picture News, 9/11/29 and Exhibitors Herald World, 16/11/29.
15 Film Daily, 21/3/30.
16 Motion Picture News, 10/5/30.
17 Exhibitors Herald-World, 8/11/30.
18 See http://www.jazzageclub.com/dancing-duos/the-dodge-twins.
19 Hollywood Filmograph, 8/2/30.
20 Alle Kvinner, No34, August 1963.
21 Paris Soir, 14/6/33.
22 Dagbladet, 09/7/32.
23 Variety, 17/5/32.

24 Alle Kvinner, No34, August 1963.
25 Dagbladet, 12/11/32.
26 Alle Kvinner, No34, August 1963, Dagbladet, 09/7/32 and 12/11/32 and Paris Soir, 14/6/33.
27 Variety, 5/4/32, Hollywood Filmograph, 12/3/32 and 19/3/32.
28 Bohemian Los Angeles: and the Making of Modern Politics by Daniel Hurewitz.
29 Variety, 5/4/32 and 12/4/32, Martin turnbull.com and Hughes The Private Dairies Memos and Letters by Richard Hack.
30 Variety, 29/3/32.
31 Modern Screen, March 1932.
32 Picture Show Annual, 1926 and Picturegoer, December 1924
33 Hollywood Filmograph, 22/3/30 and Silver Screen, December 1930.
34 The Film Daily, 25/10/31, Variety, 13/10/31 and 25/10/31 and Los Angeles Times, 21/10/31.
35 Los Angeles Times, 13/3/32.
36 Nordisk Tidende, 3/11/32.
37 Variety, 26/4/32
38 Sin in Soft Focus: Pre-Code Hollywood by Mark A. Vieira.
39 Wisecracker: The Life and Times of William Haines, Hollywood's First Openly Gay Star by William J, Mann
40 Wisecracker: The Life and Times of William Haines, Hollywood's First Openly Gay Star by William J, Mann.
41 Edmund Goulding's Dark Victory: Hollywood's Genius Bad Boy by Matthew Kennedy.
42 Dagbladet, 09/7/32.
43 Sin in Soft Focus: Pre-Code Hollywood by Mark A. Vieira.
44 Detail derived from existing stills from the film.
45 Cine-Comoedia, 17/10/32.
46 Dagbladet, 12/11/32.
47 Cine-Comoedia, 17/10/32.
48 Dagbladet, 12/11/32.
49 Dagbladet article @ Paal Rocky 27/10/51 quoted in American Motion Pictures in Norway by Gilbert Lawrence Geis (1953) via Wisconsin Center for Film and Theater Research, University of Wisconsin-Madison.
50 Captured on Film: The True Story of Marion Davies (Notes to TV movie).
51 Hearst and Marion: The Santa Monica Connection by Taylor Coffman.
52 Dagbladet, 12/11/32.
53 Dagbladet, 12/11/32.
54 Dagbladet, 12/11/32. All detail about San Simeon from Hearst and Marion: The Santa Monica Connection by Taylor Coffman, The Times We Had: Life with William Randolph Hearst by Marion Davies.
55 Dagbladet, 12/11/32.
56 The San Antonio Light, 8/8/32.
57 The San Antonio Light, 30/9/32.
58 Los Angeles Times, 4/10/32.
59 Ave Kvinner, no 34, August 1963.
60 Gay LA: A History of Sexual Outlaws, Power Politics and Lipstick Lesbians by Lilian Faderman & Stuart Timmons.
61 Here Lies the Heart by Mercedes de Acosta
62 Gay LA: A History of Sexual Outlaws, Power Politics and Lipstick Lesbians by Lilian Faderman & Stuart Timmons.
63 Edmund Goulding's Dark Victory: Hollywood's Genius Bad Boy by Matthew Kennedy and Brits in Hollywood: Tales From the Hollywood Raj by Sheridan Morley.
64 The Fixers: Eddie Mannix, Howard Strickling and the MGM Publicity Machine by E.J. Fleming.
65 Edmund Goulding's Dark Victory: Hollywood's Genius Bad Boy by Matthew Kennedy.
66 Wisecracker: The Life and Times of William Haines, Hollywood's First Openly Gay Star by William J. Mann.
67 The Merchant of Dreams by Charles Higham, Wisecracker: The Life and Times of William Haines, Hollywood's First Openly Gay Star by William J. Mann, The Fixers: Eddie Mannix, Howard Strickling and the MGM Publicity Machine by E.J. Fleming and Cecil Beaton: The Authorised Biography by Hugo Vickers.
68 New Movie Magazine, July 1932.
69 The New Movie Magazine, December 1932.
70 George Cukor: A Double Life by Patrick McGilligan and Gay LA: A History of Sexual Outlaws, Power Politics and Lipstick Lesbians by Lilian Faderman & Stuart Timmons.
71 Bohemian Los Angeles: and the Making of Modern Politics by Daniel Hurewitz.
72 Variety, 4/10/32.
73 Hollywood Filmograph, 23/7/32 and 6/8/32 and Variety, 27/9/32.
74 Variety, 27/9/32.
75 Variety, 4/10/32, Montana Butte Standard , 2/10/32 and Los Angeles Times, 21/9/32.
76 Variety, 13/9/32 and Los Angeles Times, 21/9/32.
77 Modesto News Herald, 25/9/32.
78 Variety, 22/11/32.
79 Montana Butte Standard, 2/10/32, Variety 13/9/32 and 4/10/32, Los Angeles Times , 21/9/32 and Modesto News Herald, 25/9/32.
80 Montana Butte Standard, 25/11/32.

81 Hollywood Filmograph, 15/10/32 and 22/10/32.
82 Fresno Bee Republican, 4/11/32, Syracuse New York Journal, 5/11/32, Modesto News-Herald, 4/11/32.
83 Michael Curtiz: A Life in Film By Alan K. Rode.
84 Gay LA: A History of Sexual Outlaws, Power Politics and Lipstick Lesbians by Lilian Faderman & Stuart Timmons.
85 Variety, 4/10/32, Bohemian Los Angeles: and the Making of Modern Politics by Daniel Hurewitz and Gay LA: A History of Sexual Outlaws, Power Politics and Lipstick Lesbians by Lilian Faderman & Stuart Timmons.
86 Variety, 29/11/32.
87 Hollywood Filmograph, 10/12/32 and 24/12/32.
88 Variety, 24/5/32.
89 Dagbladet, 12/11/32.
90 Dagbladet, 12/11/32.
91 Variety, 17/5/32.
92 Motion Picture Herald, 10/8/32.
93 Alle Kvinner, No34, August 1963.
94 Alle Kvinner, No 32, 7 August 1963.
95 The Evening News, Harrisburg, 20/4/45.
96 Alle Kvinner, No34, August 1963.

Chapter Seven: Larry Hart and Low and Behold 1932-1933

1 Hearst and Marion: The Santa Monica Connection by Taylor Coffman.
2 Dagbladet article @ Paal Rocky 27/10/51 American Motion Pictures in Norway by Gilbert Lawrence Geis (1953) via Wisconsin Center for Film and Theater Research, University of Wisconsin-Madison.
3 Max Gordon Presents by Max Gordon.
4 Los Angeles Examiner, 1/12/32.
5 Variety. 23/9/25, 3/2/26, 27/10/1926, 22/8/28 and 26/12/28.
6 Moving Pictures: Memories of a Hollywood Prince by Budd Schulberg.
7 A Life of Barbara Stanwyck: Steel True 1907-1940 by Victoria Wilson.
8 A Life of Barbara Stanwyck: Steel True 1907-1940 by Victoria Wilson.
9 Variety, 3/1/33.
10 Los Angeles Times, 23/12/32, 29/12/32, 31/12/32, Arcadia Tribune, 30/12/32 and Dagbladet, 10/4/48. Grable later married her first husband Jackie Coogan in 1937.
11 Variety, 3/1/33,
12 Los Angeles Times, 31/12/32.
13 Los Angeles Times, 14/1/33, The Hollywood Reporter, 13/1/33, Variety, 3/1/33, 17/1/33 and 7/2/33, and A Life of Barbara Stanwyck: Steel True 1907-1940 by Victoria Wilson.
14 Le Matin, 19/2/33.
15 Exhibitor's Herald, 28/8/20.
16 Variety, 25/3/21.
17 Variety, 22/2/23.
18 Variety, 25/3/25.
19 The Bystander, 17/10/28 and The Stage , 22/11/28.
20 Le Gaulois, 14/2/29.
21 Cine-Comoedia, 23/2/29 and Chicago Tribune, 25/2/29.
22 Columbia Spectator, 15/5/30.
23 Hollywood Filmograph, 19/11/32 and 26/11/32.
24 Variety, 10/7/34.
25 Variety, 14/3/33.
26 Paris Soir, 14/6/33.
27 The New Movie Magazine, December 1932 feature entitled Dancing the Night Away.
28 Hollywood Filmograph, 11/2/33.
29 Hollywood Filmograph, 18/2/33.
30 Hollywood Filmograph, 25/3/33, 15/4/33 and 22/4/33.
31 Hollywood Filmograph, 6/5/33, 20/5/33 and 27/5/33.
32 Hollywood Filmograph, 4/2/33 and 11/2/33.
33 Hollywood Filmograph, 22/4/33.
34 Variety, 18/4/33.
35 Variety, 16/5/33.
36 Variety, 30/5/33.
37 Los Angeles Times, 31/3/33 and Los Angeles Examiner, 8/4/33.
38 The Fresno Bee, 9/4/33.
39 Variety, 23/5/33.
40 Film Daily, 10/6/3.3
41 Hollywood Filmograph, 6/5/33.
42 Rodgers & Hart: Bewitched, Bothered & Bedevilled by Samuel Marx & Jan Clayton and Here Lies Leonard Sillman: Straightened Out at Last by Leonard Sillman.
43 The Film Daily, 5/11/31, Variety, 1/12/31 and Motion Picture Herald, 26/12/31.
44 A Ship Without a Sail: The life of Lorenz Hart by Gary Marmorstein.
45 Film Daily, 2/5/32, Variety, 22/5/32 and Film Daily, 21/6/32.
46 Rodgers & Hart: Bewitched, Bothered & Bedevilled by Samuel Marx & Jan Clayton
47 A Ship Without a Sail: The life of Lorenz Hart by Gary Marmorstein.
48 Rodgers & Hart: Bewitched, Bothered & Bedevilled by Samuel Marx & Jan Clayton.
49 A Ship Without a Sail: The life of Lorenz Hart by Gary Marmorstein.
50 Rodgers & Hart: Bewitched, Bothered & Bedevilled by Samuel Marx & Jan Clayton.

51 Richard Rodgers by Geoffrey Block and We'll Have Manhattan: The Early Work of Rodgers and Hart.
52 Variety, 19/7/32.
53 Rodgers & Hart: Bewitched, Bothered & Bedevilled by Samuel Marx & Jan Clayton.
54 Rodgers & Hart: Bewitched, Bothered & Bedevilled by Samuel Marx & Jan Clayton.
55 Rodgers & Hart: Bewitched, Bothered & Bedevilled by Samuel Marx & Jan Clayton.
56 Rodgers & Hart: Bewitched, Bothered & Bedevilled by Samuel Marx & Jan Clayton.
57 Rodgers & Hart: Bewitched, Bothered & Bedevilled by Samuel Marx & Jan Clayton.
58 Lorenz Hart: A Poet on Broadway by Frederick Nolan.
59 Rodgers & Hart: Bewitched, Bothered & Bedevilled by Samuel Marx & Jan Clayton.
60 Lorenz Hart: A Poet on Broadway by Frederick Nolan.
61 Bender became theatrical manager for a host of other celebrities such as Desi Arnaz. He died in 1964 and had been writing an autobiography titled Always on a Bender, which was never published. New York Times 4/3/64.
62 A Ship Without a Sail: The life of Lorenz Hart by Gary Marmorstein.
63 Kay Thompson: From Funny Face to Eloise by Sam Irvin.
64 Here Lies Leonard Sillman: Straightened Out at Last by Leonard Sillman, Vaudeville Old & New: An Encyclopedia of Variety Performances in America Volume 1 by Frank Cullen and Variety 21/6/32.
65 Here Lies Leonard Sillman: Straightened Out at Last by Leonard Sillman.
66 Screenland, June 1931.
67 Screenland, November 1931.
68 Beyond Paradise: The Life of Ramon Novarro by Andre Soares.
69 Charlie Walters: The Director who made Hollywood Dance.
70 Here Lies Leonard Sillman: Straightened Out at Last by Leonard Sillman.
71 Arcadia Tribune 24/3/33.
72 Charlie Walters: The Director who made Hollywood Dance.
73 A Ship Without a Sail: The life of Lorenz Hart by Gary Marmorstein.
74 Hollywood Filmograph. May 1933.
75 Here Lies Leonard Sillman: Straightened Out at Last by Leonard Sillman.
76 Charlie Walters: The Director who made Hollywood Dance.
77 A Ship Without a Sail: The life of Lorenz Hart by Gary Marmorstein.
78 Kay Thompson: From Funny Face to Eloise by Sam Irvin.
79 Here Lies Leonard Sillman: Straightened Out at Last by Leonard Sillman.
80 Here Lies Leonard Sillman: Straightened Out at Last by Leonard Sillman.
81 Kay Thompson: From Funny Face to Eloise by Sam Irvin.
82 Rodgers & Hart: Bewitched, Bothered & Bedevilled by Samuel Marx & Jan Clayton.
83 Arcadia Tribune, 26/5/33.
84 Hollywood Filmography, May 1933.
85 Variety, 20/6/33, New York Times, 2/7/33 and Variety, 15/8/33.
86 Here Lies Leonard Sillman: Straightened Out at Last by Leonard Sillman.
87 Kay Thompson: From Funny Face to Eloise by Sam Irvin.
88 Charlie Walters: The Director who made Hollywood Dance.
89 Motion Picture Herald, 9/6/34.
90 Silent Stars by Janine Basinger.
91 Edmund Goulding's Dark Victory: Hollywood's Genius Bad Boy by Matthew Kennedy.
92 Rodgers & Hart: Bewitched, Bothered & Bedevilled by Samuel Marx & Jan Clayton.
93 Charlie Walters: The Director who made Hollywood Dance.
94 Rodgers & Hart: Bewitched, Bothered & Bedevilled by Samuel Marx & Jan Clayton
95 Motion Picture Herald, 9/6/34 and Hollywood Reporter, 1/6/34.
96 Alle Kvinner, No34, August 1963.
97 Harrison's Report, 6/8/33.
98 Alle Kvinner, No34, August 1963.
99 Hollywood Filmograph, 15/7/33.
100 Rodgers & Hart: Bewitched, Bothered & Bedevilled by Samuel Marx & Jan Clayton.
101 Hollywood Filmograph, 22/7/33 and 5/8/33.
102 Hollywood Filmograph, 12/8/33.
103 Hollywood Filmograph, 2/9/33.
104 Variety, 5/9/33.
105 Variety, 21/11/33.
106 Variety, 24/10/33.
107 Bruz Fletcher: Camped, Tramped and a Riotous Vamp by Tyler Alphern.
108 Gay L.A. : A History of Sexual Outlaws, Power Politics, And Lipstick Lesbians, Gay New York by George Chauncey.
109 Broadway and Hollywood Movies January - May 1934.
110 Dagbladet, 29/5/33.
111 The Mistinguett Legend by David Brett.

Chapter Eight: New York Cabaret 1933-1936

1 The Ziegfeld Touch by Richard and Paulette Ziegfeld.
2 Variety, 20/6/33.
3 Variety, 15/8/33.
4 Variety, 31/10/33.
5 Reading Times 2/12/33.
6 New York Times, 18/10/33.
7 Variety, 24/10/33.
8 Variety, 19/12/33.
9 New York Times. 7/3/34.
10 St Louis Post-Dispatch, 23/8/33.
11 Tallulah! The Life and Times of a Leading Lady by Joel Lobenthal.
12 Tallulah! The Life and Times of a Leading Lady by Joel Lobenthal.
13 Hollywood Reporter, 6/5/33.
14 Broken Face In The Mirror (Crooks and Fallen Stars That Look Very Much Like Us) by David Hernandez.
15 Hollywood Reporter, 6/5/33.
16 Tallulah! The Life and Times of a Leading Lady by Joel Lobenthal and Film Daily 27/12/33.
17 Alle Kvinner, No34. August 1963 and Dagbladet, 10/4/48.
18 Detroit Free Press. 22/2/34.
19 Hollywood Reporter. 2/2/34.
20 Hearst Newspaper Archive, Los Angeles.
21 New York Post, 22/12/33.
22 Variety, 19/9/33, 24/10/33 and 7/11/33.
23 Variety, 19/12/33.
24 Variety, 7/11/33.
25 Buffalo Evening News, 8/5/35.
26 Buffalo Evening News, 8/5/35 and 19/12/35.
27 The Binghamton Press, 29/7/42.
28 Variety, 7/11/33.
29 Olean Times-Herald, 28/7/32.
30 The Brooklyn Daily Eagle, 6/11/33.
31 Variety, 7/11/33.
32 Variety, 7/11/33.
33 Variety, 7/11/33.
34 Variety, 7/11/33.
35 The Brooklyn Daily Eagle, 6/11/33.
36 Brooklyn Eagle, 11/12/33.
37 Brooklyn Eagle, 17/11/33.
38 New York Times, 10/12/33.
39 Syracuse New York Journal, 19/12/33.
40 San Antonio Express, 17/12/33.
41 Ancestry.com.
42 Hollywood Filmography, 10/2/34.
43 Alle Kvinner, No34, August 1963.
44 Milwaukee Journal, 14/5/35.
45 Ancestry.com.
46 Pittsburgh Post Gazette, 2/7/34.
47 Variety, 19/6/34 and The Brooklyn Daily Eagle, 22/6/34.
48 New York Times, 7/7/34.
49 Variety, 10/7/34.
50 New York Times, 7/7/34 and Variety, 10/7/34.
51 Ashbury Park Press, 27/7/34.
52 http://www.mansfieldnewsjournal.com/story/news/history/erik-larsen/2017/09/03/ocean-county-political-machine-boss-thomas-mathis/620961001/.
53 Variety, 27/9/34.
54 New York Times, 6/10/34.
55 New York Times, 6/10/34.
56 http://www.jazzageclub.com/theatre/the-french-casino-project and http://www.jazzageclub.com/venues/the-french-casino.
57 Variety, 4/9/34 and 11/9/34.
58 New York Times, 6/10/34.
59 The Frederick Post, 20/10/34.
60 New York Times, 13/10/34.
61 Paradise Mislaid by Billy Milton.
62 New York Times, 19/11/34.
63 New York Times, 11/1/35 and Paradise Mislaid by Billy Milton.
64 Variety, 27/2/35.
65 Variety, 22/1/35.
66 Variety, 12/2/35.
67 Variety, 5/2/35 and see http://www.jazzageclub.com/personalities/the-incomparable-joe-zelli.
68 Variety, 19/6/29 and 6/11/29.
69 Variety, 15/1/30.
70 Variety, 30/7/30, 10/9/30 and 15/4/31.
71 The Era, 16/3/32.
72 Variety, 26/4/32.
73 Variety, 17/10/33 and 21/11/33.
74 New York Times, 2/2/35, Variety, 5/2/35 and 27/2/35.
75 Variety, 17/7/35.
76 Variety, 27/2/35.
77 New York Post, 16/3/35.
78 Variety, 27/3/35.
79 New York Times, 4/4/35, Milwaukee Journal, 14/5/35 and Variety, 8/5/35.
80 Dagbladet, 10/4/48.
81 New York Times, 16/4/35.
82 Programme for Up to the Stars.
83 Programme for Up to the Stars.
84 The Michigan Daily, 19/5/35 and Detroit Free Press, 19/5/35.
85 The Michigan Daily, 23/4/35 and Milwaukee Journal, 14/5/35.
86 Detroit Free Press .8/5/35 and Detroit Free Press, 2/6/35.
87 Philadelphia Inquirer, 2/10/35.
88 Philadelphia Inquirer, 2/10/35.

89 Variety, 9/10/34.
90 Variety, 9/10/34.
91 Variety, 27/11/35.
92 The Montreal Gazette, 27/11/35.
93 Programme Continental Varieties.
94 Variety, 27/11/35.
95 Variety, 1/1/36.
96 Dagbladet ,10/4/48.
97 Daily Eagle New York, 27/12/35.
98 New York Times, 27/12/35.
99 Variety, 27/11/35.
100 Variety, 1/1/36.
101 Daily Eagle New York, 27/12/35.
102 Naked at the Feast by Lynn Haney.
103 Josephine Baker: Entertainer by Alan Schroeder and Heather Lehr Wagner.
104 Variety, 4/3/36, Josephine Baker by Patrick O'Connor and Bryan Hammond and Naked at the Feast by Lynn Haney.
105 New York Times, 7/3/36.
106 Variety, 4/3/36.
107 Variety, 11/3/36.
108 Le Journal, 29/10/36.
109 Variety, 4/3/36 and The Brooklyn Daily Eagle, 6/3/36.
110 Naked at the Feast by Lynn Haney.
111 New York Times, 7/3/36.
112 Variety, 11/3/36.
113 Variety, 29/1/35.
114 New York Times, 7/3/36.
115 New York Times. 7/3/36, Variety , 18/3/36 and 25/3/36.
116 Chicago Daily Tribune. 12/7/36 and Dagbladet. 29/09/36.

Chapter Nine: Europe and Separation 1936 - 1941

1 Paris Soir, 23/10/36.
2 Le Matin, 16/10/36.
3 Paris Soir, 23/10/36.
4 Le Journal, 29/10/36.
5 Pittsburgh Post-Gazette, 23/8/34.
6 New York Times, 22//8/28 and The Courier News, 29/4/33.
7 The Film Daily, 21/4/29 and Variety, 17/4/29.
8 Variety, 22/9/31 and 27/9/32.
9 Syracuse Herald, 21/3/32.
10 The Film Daily, 17/5/35.
11 Variety, 4/12/35.
12 Le Figaro, 17/1/36.
13 See Chapter 4.
14 Paris Soir, 21/11/36.
15 Paris Soir, 23/10/36, 28/11/36 and Comoedia, 23/11/36.
16 Comoedia, 1/12/36 and Paris Soir, 8/12/36.
17 The venue is still in Oslo but at a different location http://chatnoir.no.
18 Dagbladet. 16/02/37, Dagbladet. 16/02/37 and Dagbladet. 20/2/37 and Dagbladet. 5/4/37.
19 Ardeiderbladet, 20/2/37.
20 Dagbladet, 10/7/37.
21 Alle Kvinner ,No34, August 1963.
22 Filmwelt, 6/5/38.
23 Alle Kvinner, No34, August 1963.
24 Studentene Fra 1927 / Oslo 1952.
25 Alle Kvinner, No34, August 1963 and Studentene Fra 1927 / Oslo 1952.
26 Taormina Guide book, 1937.
27 Taormina Guide book, 1937.
28 Modern Screen June 1938 and New York Times 2 March 1938.
29 Studentene Fra 1927 / Oslo 1952.
30 Filmwelt, 6/5/38.
31 See Chapter 10 about Hans Henkel.
32 Filmwelt, 6/5/38.
33 The Ufa Story: A History of Germany's Greatest Film Company, 1918-1945 by Klaus Kreimeier, Variety 22/12/37 and https://kenneallykaren.wordpress.com/2013/05/14/the-german-film-industry-in-the-early-stages-of-nazi-rule-consolidation-and-co-ordination.
34 http://www.luise-berlin.de/bms/bmstxt01/01072porg.htm and The Adelaide Advertiser, 5/10/42.
35 Filmwelt, 6/5/38.
36 Variety. 13/4/38.
37 Motion Picture Daily, 24/4/39.
38 Goebbels by Peter Longerich
39 Variety, 27/10/37.
40 Nevada State Journal, 10.2.39.
41 Motion Picture Daily, 29/6/38 and Studentene Fra 1927 / Oslo 1952.
42 Sheppard Field Texas (Newspaper) 27/10/45.
43 Le Cinematographie Francais 26/3/37
44 Motion Picture Herald 8/1/38
45 Studentene Fra 1927 / Oslo 1952.
46 Ancestry.com.
47 Studentene Fra 1927 / Oslo 1952.
48 Studentene Fra 1927 / Oslo 1952
49 Endnotes for Kay Thompson: From Funny Face To Eloise by Sam Irvin and Fresno Bee, 31/10/39.
50 Studentene Fra 1927 / Oslo 1952.
51 Ancestry.com.
52 Der Spiegel, 20/12/50.
53 Exhibitors Daily Review, 2/8/28, Der Spiegel, 20/12/50 and City of Darkness, City of Light: Emigre Filmmakers in Paris 1929-1939 by Alastair Phillips, The UFA Story by Klaus Kreimeier and Journal of the Society of Motion Pictures April 1941.

54 Film Daily, 10/2/29 and 18/3/29.
55 Film Daily, 18/3/29.
56 Les Spectacles, 29/3/29, City of Darkness, City of Light: Emigre Filmmakers in Paris 1929-1939 by Alastair Phillips and Comoedia, 21/12/29.
57 Film Daily, 25/8/29.
58 Variety, 9/8/32.
59 Variety, 10/7/35.
60 Film Daily 12/3/36 and The Coming of Sound by Douglas Gomery.
61 Ancestry.com.
62 Variety 5/5/37.
63 See Chapter 3.
64 See Chapter 4.
65 See Chapter 3 and 4.
66 See Chapter 7. It is also important to note that these are the men that we know about, there were clearly others.
67 Ancestry.com. In 1942 Henkel was living in New York and was registered as unemployed and still listing Milton Diamond as a friend. After the war he stayed in New York and was naturalized in 1947. He made frequent trips back to Europe.
68 Ancestry.com.
69 Ancestry.com.
70 The Tampa Tribune 5/4/40.
71 Studentene Fra 1927 / Oslo 1952.
72 Variety 24/4/40.
73 The Tampa Tribune 5/4/40.
74 Ancestry.com.
75 Ancestry.com.
76 Alle Kvinner No34 August 1963 and Reno Evening Gazette 23/9/40.
77 Alle Kvinner No34 August 1963.
78 Alle Kvinner No34 August 1963.
79 In 1948 Maria was naturalised in August 1949 returned to Europe to visit Genoa listing her address as 135 East 56th Street, New York. She died in June 1997 as Maria Vogt in East Hampton. Ancestry.com.
80 Alle Kvinner No34 August 1963.
81 Cuban Cinema by Michael Chanan and The Cuban Filmography: 1897 through 2001 by Alfonso J. García Osuna.
82 Ancestry.com.

Chapter Ten: The War years and Later Life

1 Alle Kvinner, No34, August 1963.
2 Alle Kvinner, No34, August 1963.
3 Studentene Fra 1927 / Oslo 1952.
4 Studentene Fra 1927 / Oslo 1952.
5 The Evening News, Harrisburg, 20/4/45.
6 Studentene Fra 1927 / Oslo 1952 and Alle Kvinner, No34, August 1963.
7 The Evening News, Harrisburg, 20/4/45.
8 Sheppard Field Texacts (Newspaper) 27/10/45 and The Evening News, Harrisburg, 20/4/45. The issue of foreign citizenship is perplexing. There are listings for both Paal and Leif in the US Naturalisation Records dated March 1934 on ancestry.com. This may have been an intent to apply for US citizenship but not fulfilled because in all future passenger lists their nationality is listed as Norwegian. So their status is unclear. When they arrived in the USA in 1939 the passenger manifest details that they had resident permits. In April 1946 Paal petitioned for naturalisation.
9 Paul Roschberg was listed in the unofficial list of personnel associated with Little Norway in http://www.profero.no/littlenorway/Personell_Little_Norway_1940-1945.pdf.
10 Sheppard Field Texacts (Newspaper) 27/10/45 and The Evening News, Harrisburg , 20/4/45.
11 Ancestry.com.
12 The Evening News, Harrisburg, 20/4/45 and Sheppard Field Texacts (Newspaper) 27/10/45.
13 Sheppard Field Texacts (Newspaper) 27/10/45.
14 Sheppard Field Texacts 27/10/45.
15 Sheppard Field Texacts (Newspaper) 19/1/46.
16 The Evening News, Harrisburg, 28/1/46.
17 Ancestry.com.
18 Dagbladet, 10/4/48.
19 Daily Telegraph Obituary, 22/12/05.
20 Studentene Fra 1927 / Oslo 1952.
21 Ancestry.com.
22 The Evening News, Harrisburg, 28/1/46.
23 Studentene Fra 1927 / Oslo 1952 and Arbeiderbladet, 7/9/50.
24 Alle Kvinner, No34, August 1963.
25 Alle Kvinner, No34, August 1963.
26 Alle Kvinner, No34, August 1963.
27 RADA archives and Library.
28 Arbeiderbladet, 7/9/50 and 30/11/50.
29 Ancestry.com.
30 Alle Kvinner, No34, August 1963.
31 Dagbladet,10/4/48.
32 Alle Kvinner, No34, August 1963.
33 Alle Kvinner, No34, August 1963.
34 Ancestry.com.
35 Dagbladet, 2/6/48.
36 Ancestry.com.
37 Nevada State Journal, 15/2/49 & Naugatuck Daily News, 7/2/49.
38 Ancestry.com.
39 Studentene Fra 1927 / Oslo 1952.
40 The Tampa Times, 17/9/52.
41 Alle Kvinner, No34, August 1963
42 Ancestry.com.

43 Firda Folkeblad, 12/5/52.
44 Arbeiderbladet, 23/5/53 and Dagbladet, 4/9/53.
45 Nordisk Tidende, 15/4/54.
46 Arbeiderbladet, 14/9/54, Dagbladet, 11/9/54 and Friheten, 14/9/54.
47 Ancestry.com.
48 Dagbladet, 28/4/55.
49 Alle Kvinner, No34, August 1963.
50 Dagbladet, 28/4/55 and Arbeiderbladet, 22/3/55.
51 Email with a cousin Olwen (Haakon) Howard and Henning Roschberg (grandson of Gunner Roschberg).
52 Alle Kvinner, No34, August 1963.
53 Gay Right and Moral Panic: The Origins of America's Debate on Homosexuality by F. Fejes.
54 Alle Kvinner, No34, August 1963 and Dagbladet, 16/7/60.
55 Alle Kvinner No34 August 1963.
56 Alle Kvinner, No 32 / 7 August 1963.
57 Alle Kvinner, No 32 / 7 August 1963.
58 Alle Kvinner, No34 / 7August 1963.
59 Alle Kvinner, No 32 / 7 August 1963.

OTHER TITLES FROM EDDITT PUBLISHING

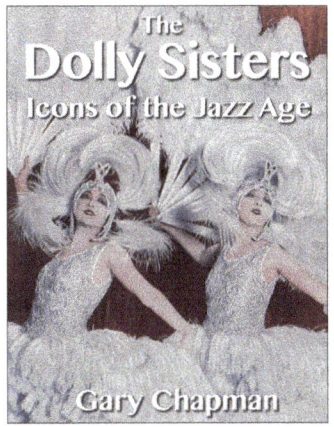
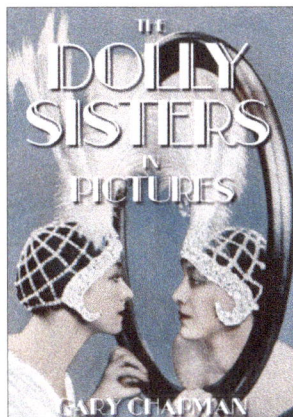
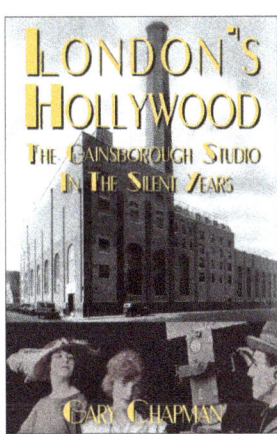

www.eddittpublishing.com

Visit the website for information
about these and other Jazz Age titles.

**Check out www.jazzageclub.com
(Jazz Age Club on Facebook)**
For posts about art, cabaret, dancing, fads, fashion, film,
gossip, people, places, theatre and much more

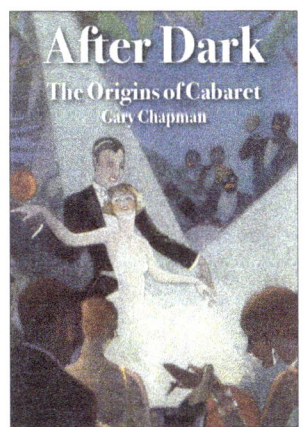

www.ingramcontent.com/pod-product-compliance
Lightning Source LLC
Chambersburg PA
CBHW042114100526
44587CB00025B/4048